Apostles of Bahá'u'lláh

This book is dedicated to Rita Blumenstein (1933–2021), one of the first Yup'ik Bahá'ís in Alaska, whose 61 years of dedicated service to the Faith of Bahá'u'lláh, both as a pioneer and a steadfast servant of the Cause, are worthy of emulation.

From a humble beginning in 1933 on a fishing boat near the village of Tununak on the northwest side of Nelson Island in Alaska's Bering Sea, to sustained significant contributions to the betterment of the world, quite literally on a global stage, Rita Blumenstein was a loving and beloved force of nature . . .

The Bahá'í Writings tell us that every person must be regarded 'as a mine rich in gems of inestimable value. Education can, alone, cause it to reveal its treasures, and enable mankind to benefit therefrom.' What a rich and abundant mine was Rita Blumenstein, and what a blessing to the world that she received an education that revealed so many treasures that would, indeed, benefit humankind.

National Spiritual Assembly of the Bahá'ís of Alaska

Apostles of Bahá'u'lláh

by

Earl Redman

GR

GEORGE RONALD
OXFORD

George Ronald, Publisher
Oxford
www.grbooks.com

A catalogue record for this book is available from the British Library

ISBN 978-0-85398-682-9

Acknowledgement of pictures:
Nos. 1, 2, 3, 7, 12, 13, 14, 17 and 18 © Bahá'í World Centre
Nos. 5, 8, 9, 10, 15, 16 and 19 © US National Bahá'í Archives
Nos. 4, 6 and 11 © Bahá'í International Community

Cover design: Steiner Graphics

TABLE OF CONTENTS

Acknowledgements vii
Introduction 1
Who are the Apostles of Bahá'u'lláh and the Disciples of 'Abdu'l-Bahá? 3
Differences Between Apostles and Disciples 4
The Station of an Apostle 6
The Apostles of Bahá'u'lláh 8
1 Mírzá Músá-i-Núrí – Áqáy-i-Kalím 13
2 Mírzá Buzurg-Khurásání – Badí' 24
3 Siyyid Ḥasan-i-Nahrí – Mírzá Muḥammad-Ḥasan – King of the Martyrs 33
4 Mullá Abu'l-Ḥasan-i-Ardikání – Ḥájí Amín 41
5 Mírzá Abu'l-Faḍl 49
6 Mírzá 'Alí-Muḥammad – Varqá 66
7 Mírzá Maḥmúd-i-Furúghí 76
8 Mullá 'Alí-Akbar-i-Shahmírzádí – Ḥájí Ákhund 86
9 Mullá Muḥammad – Nabíl-i-Akbar – Faḍl-i-Qá'iní 94
10 Ḥájí Mírzá Muḥammad-Taqí-i-Afnán – Vakílu'd-Dawlih – Vakílu'd-Haqq 103
11 Ḥájí Mírzá Muḥammad-Taqí-i-Abhar – Ibn-i-Abhar 110
12 Mullá Muḥammad-i-Zarandí – Nabíl-i-A'ẓam 118
13 Shaykh Muḥammad Káẓim-i-Qazvíní – Samandar 127
14 Muḥammad Muṣṭafáy-i-Baghdádí 136
15 Mírzá Ḥusayn-i-Iṣfahání – Mishkín-Qalam 142
16 Mírzá Ḥasan-i-Adíb – Adíbu'l-'Ulamáy-i-Ṭáliqání – Adíb 151
17 Shaykh Muḥammad-'Alí-Qá'iní 161
18 Mullá Zaynu'l-'Ábidín Najafábádí – Zaynu'l-Muqarrabín 174
19 Mírzá 'Alí-Muḥammad – Ibn-i-Aṣdaq 185
Bibliography 193
References 197
Index 211

ACKNOWLEDGEMENTS

As in every other book, this one has a number of people who contributed to its creation and the attempt to eliminate typos, grammatical stumbles and confused writing. First I have to thank Hooper Dunbar, who suggested that I 'look into' the Apostles of Bahá'u'lláh and the Disciples of 'Abdu'l-Bahá. I'd never given them much thought before, but I considered a suggestion from Mr Dunbar valuable, so I 'looked into' them. And found them fascinating. It is because of him that this book was written.

Then I have to thank my wife, Sharon O'Toole. She gave me abundant encouragement and reviewed every chapter to make sure it said what it was supposed to say, not what my fingers occasionally typed. She also permitted me to spend those long hours in front of the computer that are required to find all the sources and merge them all into hopefully coherent stories. She says that my writing keeps me out of trouble, but I think it more probable that it keeps me out of her hair.

The Bahá'í World Centre Research Department helped me to understand what Apostles and Disciples were and provided a list of Arabic and Persian resources for some of the lesser known Apostles. They also contributed photographs of some of the Apostles.

I have to particularly thank Kamran Mesbah and Rowshan Mustafa who very generously provided me with their translation skills. Kamran translated long portions of Azizu'llah Sulaymani's epic biographies of 99 early Bahá'ís, *Lamps of Guidance (Masabih-i-Hidayat)*, from Persian to English. He also translated parts of *Dhuká'íy-i-Bayḍá'í, Dar Sharh-i-Ahvál va Áthár-i-Jináb-i-Áqá Mírzá Haṣan-i-Adíbu'l-'Ulamáy-i-Táliqání* by Mírzá Ni'matu'lláh and *Tarikhi Zuhur'u'l-Haqq* by Asad'u'llah Fáḍil-i-Mazandarani. Not only did he translate the text, he researched and explained things that were probably not familiar to Western readers, such as names, places and events. His work enabled the shortest stories in the book to be greatly expanded.

Rowshan Mustafa, who has helped me on several of my books, translated parts about most of the Apostles from 'Abdu'l-Hussayn Fikri's *Hawáríyyú Haḍrat-i-Bahá'u'lláh (Apostles of Bahá'u'lláh)* from Arabic, considerably improving a number of the stories.

Several others made contributions. Adib Masumian very graciously allowed me to use his provisional translation of Bahá'u'lláh's *Tablet of Visitation* for Mírzá Músá. Mitra Rahmani very generously translated from Persian the story of Mírzá Maḥmúd-i-Furúghí's meeting with Muzaffaru'd-Dín Sháh. Duane Troxel shared publication quality photos of some of the Apostles he had from the U.S. Bahá'í National Archives. Nesreen Akhtarhavari shared her translation of a poem written by Badí' and given to 'Abdu'l-Bahá when Badí' first arrived in 'Akká.

Edward Sevcik, at the U.S. National Bahá'í Archives, was always helpful. He courteously responded to my all too common queries as I was looking for some extra detail or, in a few cases such as Chester Thacher, anything at all. He constantly came up with appreciated additions.

Violetta Zein and Tahir Taherzadeh reviewed all or parts of the manuscript and made valuable contributions or suggestions. Violetta's specialty is improving introductions, which she did here. Moojan Momen, Tahir and Rowshan Mustafa were particularly helpful with all the Persian and Arabic names and stories.

After 13 years with the same editor, May Hofman, at George Ronald, I have a new editor: Genevieve Seri. This has led to a 'tense' situation – she is a stickler for having correct grammatical tenses while I am notably lazy in that area. This 'tense situation', however, is a good thing because it improves both the flow and readability of the text. She is also very good at catching contradictions and confusing bits, which distinctly improves the writing. She has been a great help in preparing this book so that you, the reader, will hopefully enjoy it.

INTRODUCTION

In August 2018, my wife, Sharon O'Toole, and I attended the Irish Bahá'í summer school in Kilkenny. Hooper Dunbar, former member of the Universal House of Justice, was also there as one of the primary speakers. We had met Mr Dunbar at the two New Zealand Bahá'í summer schools a few years before when he gave the morning sessions, and Sharon and I had told our stories of 'Abdu'l-Bahá, Shoghi Effendi and the Knights of Bahá'u'lláh in the afternoons. When we encountered each other in Kilkenny, we had a few brief chats and in one of our moments together, Hooper asked what I was writing. At that time, *Visiting 'Abdu'l-Bahá, Vol. 1* was awaiting approval from the review committee of the National Spiritual Assembly of the United Kingdom, *Agnes Alexander, Hand of the Cause* was being edited and *A Day for Very Great Things*, a book about Howard Colby and Mabel Rice-Wray Ives, was sitting quietly in George Ronald's publication queue. In other words, I was doing no writing at all.

Finding that I was basically just twiddling my literary thumbs, Hooper suggested that I 'look into' writing a book about the Apostles of Bahá'u'lláh and the Disciples of 'Abdu'l-Bahá. I'd heard of them, but other than having noted that a few of the people appearing in my earlier books had been Apostles or Disciples, I had little knowledge of why they had been given what seemed to be a high station in the Faith of Bahá'u'lláh. But a suggestion coming from Hooper was a good reason to look into the idea.

Initial digging revealed that the Guardian of the Cause, Shoghi Effendi, had designated the Apostles of Bahá'u'lláh and the Disciples of 'Abdu'l-Bahá in *The Bahá'í World*, Vol. III, in 1930, but little else was known about why they were named. Shoghi Effendi had placed a montage of small photographs of the 19 Apostles of Bahá'u'lláh on one page with the adjacent page containing the names and very brief explanations of who each was.[1] A few pages later, there was another montage of photos of the 19 Disciples of 'Abdu'l-Bahá facing a similar page with names and very short descriptions.[2] The same photo montages were included in *The Bahá'í World*, vol IV, with minor spelling changes for three of the Apostles and with Dr Arthur Brauns' name being replaced by that of Consul A. Schwarz, at whose hotel 'Abdu'l-Bahá stayed in Germany, and Mrs Harriet Thornburgh replaced by Miss Ethel Rosenberg.[3] It all seemed quite mysterious, so I began digging deeper.

Confusion was the first thing I found as I looked into those named by the Guardian. Of the 19 Apostles of Bahá'u'lláh, there were two Apostles named Ḥájí Mírzá Muḥammad Taqí, two named Mullá Muḥammad (one of which is Nabíl-i-Akbar and the other Nabíl-i-A'ẓam, both of whom are commonly referred to simply as 'Nabíl', undifferentiated, in some Bahá'í literature) and two named Mírzá 'Alí-Muḥammad. Then there was Mírzá Maḥmúd, who was described in the *Bahá'í World* volume as 'an indomitable spirit and jealous defender of the Faith'. That was all the description given, and it quickly became apparent that there were several Mírzá Maḥmúds who might fit that description: Mírzá Maḥmúd-i-Zarqání ('Abdu'l-Bahá's secretary in America who wrote *Maḥmúd's Diary*); Mírzá Maḥmúd-i-Káshání (a companion of Bahá'u'lláh); Mírzá Maḥmúd-i-al-Álúsí (a famous teacher); Mírzá Maḥmúd-i-Qazvíní (a martyr); as well as Mírzá Maḥmúd-i-Furúghi. Luckily, Hand of the Cause Hasan Balyuzi identified Mírzá Maḥmúd-i-Furúghi as the named Apostle.

I didn't recognise a lot of the names until I discovered that many, if not most, of the Apostles are better known by their titles instead of their real names. For example, Mírzá Buzurg is the young Badí' who delivered Bahá'u'lláh's Tablet to the Sháh, Mírzá Ḥusayn is actually the famous calligrapher Mishkín-Qalam and Mullá 'Alí-Akbar was the well-known Ḥájí Ákhund.

Much of the material about the Apostles in this book came from H. M. Balyuzi's *Eminent Bahá'ís in the Time of Bahá'u'lláh* and the four volumes of Adib Taherzadeh's *The Revelation of Bahá'u'lláh,* with significant contributions from Shoghi Effendi's *God Passes By* and 'Abdu'l-Bahá's *Memorials of the Faithful.* Balyuzi included the stories of six of the Apostles and, after his passing, Moojan Momen added short biographical sketches of eleven more. Taherzadeh's books included longer stories for a number of the Apostles and shorter stories for others. Much of the material from both Balyuzi and Taherzadeh came from a single source, the *Masabih-i-Hidayat* (Lamps of Guidance) written by 'Azizu'llah Sulaymani. Unfortunately for me, his stories about 99 early Bahá'ís were written in Persian — more than 4,600 pages. Luckily, I encountered Kamran Mesbah who solved the language problem.

I recognised most of the 19 Disciples of 'Abdu'l-Bahá, since they are all Western Bahá'ís from America, Germany, France and the United Kingdom, and have all appeared in my various books, with two exceptions: Mr C.I. Thacher and Dr Arthur Brauns. A bit of research found that C.I. Thacher was a Bahá'í involved with the administrative order at the time of Ibráhím Kheiralla's Covenant-breaking activities, but I could find very little on Brauns. For many of the Disciples, with the exception of C.I. Thacher, there was a fair amount of information, including published books on five of them.

A search of the works of 'Abdu'l-Bahá, Shoghi Effendi, and the Universal House of Justice revealed no specific information about how the Apostles of Bahá'u'lláh and Disciples of 'Abdu'l-Bahá were designated or what their station was. It was all quite mysterious, and that made it an intriguing challenge. I wanted to find out more about these thirty-eight people (or forty, including the two replacements) and how they lived their lives that attracted Shoghi Effendi's attention enough to be given special titles.

The book about the Disciples of 'Abdu'l-Bahá will be published separately.

Who are the Apostles of Bahá'u'lláh and the Disciples of 'Abdu'l-Bahá?

Four groups of people have earned titles over the history of the Bahá'í Faith, from the Declaration of the Báb to the election of the Universal House of Justice. These groups are the Letters of the Living, the Apostles of Bahá'u'lláh, the Disciples of 'Abdu'l-Bahá and the Knights of Bahá'u'lláh. Unlike the Hands of the Cause who were designated as such for their loyalty, dedication and knowledge and were part of an Institution given distinct duties, those named in the four groups earned their titles by arising on their own initiative to do what had to be done at four different times of the Faith's development.

The Letters of the Living earned their title by independently discovering and accepting the Báb and His Revelation. All they knew was that the Báb had declared His Mission, but they had to unveil His identity all on their own using their spiritual perception. Twelve sacrificed their lives after accepting the Báb's message and teaching His Cause.

The Apostles of Bahá'u'lláh didn't have to discover the Bábí/Bahá'í Faith without help. The Writings of the Báb were circulating throughout Persia and could be read by all, plus there were those who had already accepted His station to learn from. The Apostles earned their title by remaining steadfast in the face of persecution, imprisonment and death. Thirteen sacrificed their freedom and were imprisoned for their faith and four of these were martyred.

The Disciples of 'Abdu'l-Bahá earned their title by their steadfastness in the face of disunity and Covenant-breaking as the Bahá'í Faith arrived and spread across Europe and North America.

The Knights of Bahá'u'lláh arose during the Ten Year Crusade and opened new territories to the Faith of Bahá'u'lláh all across the world. They sacrificed their homes and friends to spread the Message to the far corners of the earth.

In summary:

18 Letters of the Living – acceptance of the Báb
19 Apostles of Bahá'u'lláh – persecution
19 Disciples of 'Abdu'l-Bahá – steadfastness
255 Knights of Bahá'u'lláh – proclamation

The stories of the 255 Knights of Bahá'u'lláh can be found in *The Knights of Bahá'u'lláh* by this author and published by George Ronald in 2017.

Differences Between Apostles and Disciples

What are the differences between Apostles and Disciples? According to a dictionary, an apostle is one sent on a mission or dedicated to a mission, while a disciple is a follower of someone. About the Apostles of Christ, 'Abdu'l-Bahá wrote: 'Consider how at the beginning of the Christian era the Apostles were afflicted, and what torments they endured in the pathway of Christ. Every day of their lives they were targets for the Pharisees' darts of mockery, vilification and abuse. They bore great hardship; they saw prison; and most of them carried to their lips the sweet cup of martyrdom'.[4] In writing to the North American Bahá'í community, Shoghi Effendi uses the word 'apostle' in the sense that the Bahá'ís of that community had been given a mission:

> The God-given mission, constituting the birthright, and proclaiming the primacy of a community whose members the Founder of that community, the Center of the Covenant Himself, has addressed as the 'Apostles of Baha'u'llah,' can only be fulfilled if they befittingly obey the specific Mandate issued by 'Abdu'l-Bahá in His Tablets of the Divine Plan. The execution of this Mandate is, in its turn, dependent upon the triumphant conclusion of the Second Seven Year Plan, the second stage in the series of specific plans formulated to insure the successful termination of the opening phase in the execution of that Mandate.[5]

The word 'disciple' in the Bahá'í Writings is almost universally used to mean a follower.

Beyond the definitions of the words, an obvious difference between Apostles and Disciples is that the Apostles are all Persian and Iraqi men from one generation while the Disciples are all North Americans and Europeans and were both men and women from the next generation. Their backgrounds and experiences were dramatically different.

The Apostles faced external challenges for the most part, though after the passing of Bahá'u'lláh, they also had to deal with Covenant-breaking. But they had the Writings of the Báb and Bahá'u'lláh in languages they could read and understand. The Apostles came from Islamic backgrounds and lived during a time of intense physical suffering when thousands of Bábís and Bahá'ís in Persia were imprisoned, tortured and martyred. Their stories are packed with drama, intrigue, violence, prisons and, too commonly, death. The Apostles of Bahá'u'lláh sacrificed their lives in a very literal sense since most suffered imprisonment and some death. But overriding all the physical and mental suffering was their detachment from the things of this world, their tranquillity in the face of persecution and imprisonment, their willingness to give up anything except their faith in the Revelation of Bahá'u'lláh, and their insistence on teaching the Faith in the face of it all. Two of the Apostles met the Báb, 16 had the bounty of attaining the presence of Bahá'u'lláh and

11 visited 'Abdu'l-Bahá. None of the Apostles were alive when Shoghi Effendi designated them as Apostles of Bahá'u'lláh, but three of them, Mírzá 'Alí-Muḥammad, Mírzá Maḥmúd-i-Furúghí and Mullá Abu'l-Ḥasan, lived until 1928.

The biggest challenges that the Disciples faced were internal, coming from the Bahá'í community itself. Many of their challenges were due to the lack of authoritative Writings about the Faith and Covent-breaking. There wasn't much translated into English, French or German at that time and what had been translated was commonly not translated well. This led to many misinterpretations, misunderstandings and misguided attempts to do what they thought was the right thing, but in reality was not. The Western Disciples, especially the Americans, were faced with the task of implementing Bahá'í principles, and the conflicts they faced came, in part, from flawed understandings of what the Writings were saying.

None of the Disciples, obviously, had the chance to meet Bahá'u'lláh since the first Westerners to become Bahá'ís didn't discover the Faith until several years after His ascension, but 17 of them were in the presence of 'Abdu'l-Bahá at least once. All came from Christian backgrounds. None suffered imprisonment or death for the Cause, but ten of them lived through the tempestuous time in America when Ibrahim Kheiralla broke away from 'Abdu'l-Bahá and attempted to split the American Bahá'í community in 1900. They remained steadfast in turning to the Centre of the Covenant, 'Abdu'l-Bahá, even if they didn't understand His station, and worked to build unity in the face of disunity.

The commonality between the Apostles of Bahá'u'lláh and the Disciples of 'Abdu'l-Bahá was their deep faith and commitment to the Revelation of Bahá'u'lláh.

The Station of an Apostle

The question of why the Guardian specifically appointed certain believers as Apostles and Disciples is not one that can be clearly answered. In a letter written on behalf of the Guardian on 29 May 1930 to Albert Windust, editorial secretary for publishing *The Bahá'í World* volumes, the photos and captions that appear in Vol. III are mentioned:

> Among these photographs are two collective ones. On each page of these two collective photographs are nineteen reproductions of

> outstanding Baha'is in the East and in the West. The one is entitled, 'Apostles of Baha'u'llah'; the other, 'Disciples of 'Abdu'l-Baha.' He has joined to each a list of the name and title of these Baha'is. He would request the Committee to arrange the two collective photographs in a manner that they would face each other in the book.[6]

No further explanation was included. In a letter to an individual believer, the Universal House of Justice wrote:

> It is obvious that Shoghi Effendi wanted to have in The Bahá'í World some information about outstanding believers of those two periods. Moreover, it cannot be said that he limited the use of the description 'Apostle of Bahá'u'lláh' or 'Disciple of 'Abdu'l-Bahá' strictly to those 19 named in each list. For example, George Latimer is not included in the list of 'Disciples', but when he passed away, Shoghi Effendi referred to him as a 'distinguished disciple of 'Abdu'l-Bahá'.[7]

In response to my question about the stations of the Apostles and Disciples, the Research Department at the Bahá'í World Centre wrote:

> Shoghi Effendi also referred to other distinguished believers, such as Marion Jack, Sayed Mustafa, and Martha Root, as Apostles of Bahá'u'lláh; to others, such as Siegfried Schopflocher, Juliet Thompson, and Valíyu'lláh Varqá, as Disciples of 'Abdu'l-Bahá; and to still other outstanding Bahá'ís, such as May Maxwell, as both.
>
> Regarding the station of the Apostles of Bahá'u'lláh and Disciples of 'Abdu'l-Bahá, the House of Justice has clarified that 'the term "Apostles of Bahá'u'lláh" does not designate an institution of the Faith in the same way as does the term "Hands of the Cause of God".' In fact, Shoghi Effendi did not generally use the terms 'Apostle of Bahá'u'lláh' and 'Disciple of 'Abdu'l-Bahá' in his writings as a title to identify the distinguished believers specifically designated as such in volume III of *The Bahá'í World*, or the other outstanding Bahá'ís elevated to these stations, but rather as a description, such as "Abdu'l-Bahá's beloved handmaid, the distinguished disciple', 'His beloved disciple', 'unique and great-hearted apostle of Bahá'u'lláh', and 'heroic apostle' of Bahá'u'lláh.[8]

Every Apostle of Bahá'u'lláh and Disciple of 'Abdu'l-Bahá the Guardian identified had died prior to his or her being named an Apostle or Disciple. The two Disciples added in the 1933 *Bahá'í World Faith* were still alive when the 1930 book was published, but had passed away by the time the 1933 volume was published. The others, mentioned in the quotations above, were also alive when those two volumes were published.

The Apostles of Bahá'u'lláh

'Abdu'l-Bahá, in the *Tablets of the Divine Plan*, provides the clearest description of the station of the 'Apostles of Bahá'u'lláh', though He wasn't specifically referring to those designated by the Guardian:

> O ye Apostles of Bahá'u'lláh! May my life be sacrificed for you!
>
> The Blessed Person of the Promised One is interpreted in the Holy Book as the Lord of Hosts – the heavenly armies. By heavenly armies those souls are intended who are entirely freed from the human world, transformed into celestial spirits and have become divine angels. Such souls are the rays of the Sun of Reality who will illumine all the continents. Each one is holding in his hand a trumpet, blowing the breath of life over all the regions. They are delivered from human qualities and the defects of the world of nature, are characterized with the characteristics of God, and are attracted with the fragrances of the Merciful. Like unto the apostles of Christ, who were filled with Him, these souls also have become filled with His Holiness Bahá'u'lláh; that is, the love of Bahá'u'lláh has so mastered every organ, part and limb of their bodies, as to leave no effect from the promptings of the human world.
>
> These souls are the armies of God and the conquerors of the East and the West. Should one of them turn his face toward some direction and summon the people to the Kingdom of God, all the ideal forces and lordly confirmations will rush to his support and reinforcement. He will behold all the doors open and all the strong fortifications and impregnable castles razed to the ground. Singly and alone he will attack the armies of the world, defeat the right and left wings of the hosts of all the countries, break through the lines of the legions of all the nations and carry his attack to the very center of the powers of the earth. This is the meaning of the Hosts of God.

> Any soul from among the believers of Bahá'u'lláh who attains to this station will become known as the Apostle of Bahá'u'lláh. Therefore strive ye with heart and soul so that ye may reach this lofty and exalted position, be established on the throne of everlasting glory, and crown your heads with the shining diadem of the Kingdom, whose brilliant jewels may irradiate upon centuries and cycles.[9]

Shoghi Effendi, uses the words 'Apostle' and 'apostle' many times in his letters to North America. In almost every case, however, he is using the word in relation to the North American Bahá'í community and in a generic sense:

> . . . the Plan with which the community of the Apostles of Bahá'u'lláh stands identified is divine in origin, is guided by the explicit and repeated instructions that have flowed from the pen of the Center of the Covenant Himself, is energized by the all-compelling will of its Author, claims as the theater for its operation territories spread over five continents and the islands of the seven seas, and must continue to function, ere its purpose is achieved, throughout successive epochs in the course of the Formative Age of the Bahá'í Dispensation.[10]

> . . . unlike all the Dispensations of the past, the apostles of Bahá'u'lláh in every land, wherever they labor and toil, have before them in clear, in unequivocal and emphatic language, all the laws, the regulations, the principles, the institutions, the guidance, they require for the prosecution and consummation of their task.[11]

And though the Guardian referred directly to Martha Root as an 'apostle' of Bahá'u'lláh[12] and gave Ṭáhirih the 'rank of apostleship'[13], all those named in the *Bahá'í Worlds* as Apostles of Bahá'u'lláh were Eastern men. It is therefore quite interesting that Shoghi Effendi would favour the American Bahá'í community with the appellation 'apostles of Bahá'u'lláh' in giving them a mission, while specifying 19 Eastern Bahá'ís for the title of Apostle of Bahá'u'lláh.

Those specifically given the title of Apostle of Bahá'u'lláh by Shoghi Effendi, in *The Bahá'í World* are (using the names and descriptions from the Bahá'í World volume):

1. Mírzá Músá: the only true brother of Bahá'u'lláh, surnamed Kalím.
2. Mírzá Buzurg: youthful martyr, bearer of Bahá'u'lláh's Tablet to Náṣiri'd-Dín Sháh, surnamed Badí'.
3. Siyyid Ḥasan: one of the martyred brothers of Iṣfahán, surnamed 'Sulṭánush-Shuhadá'.
4. Mullá Abu'l-Ḥasan: faithful steward of Bahá'u'lláh and 'Abdu'l-Bahá, surnamed 'Amín'.
5. Mírzá Abu'l-Faḍl: foremost and authoritative expounder of the Bahá'í Revelation.
6. Mírzá 'Alí-Muḥammad: poet, teacher, and martyr of the Faith, surnamed 'Varqá'.
7. Mírzá Maḥmúd: an indomitable spirit and jealous defender of the Faith.
8. Mullá 'Alí-Akbar: a flame of zeal and devotion.
9. Mullá Muḥammad: learned and steadfast exponent of the Bahá'í Revelation, surnamed 'Nabíl-i-Akbar'.
10. Ḥájí Mírzá Muḥammad-Taqí: cousin of the Báb and chief builder of the Mashriqul-Adhkár of 'Ishqábád, surnamed 'Kabír-i-Afnán'.
11. Mullá Muḥammad-Taqí: prominent teacher.
12. Mullá Muḥammad, poet, historian, and teacher of the Faith, surnamed 'Nabíl-i-A'ẓam'.
13. Shaykh Káẓim: a flame of the love of God, favoured of Bahá'u'lláh, surnamed 'Samandar'.
14. Muḥammad Muṣṭafá: brave and vigilant custodian and bearer of the remains of the Báb.
15. Mírzá Ḥusayn: distinguished calligraphist, and companion-in-exile of Bahá'u'lláh, surnamed 'Mishkín-Qalam'.
16. Mírzá Ḥasan: devoted teacher of the cause, surnamed Adíb.
17. Shaykh Muḥammad-'Alí: eloquent and learned champion of the Faith in Russian Turkestan.
18. Zaynu'l-'Ábidín: noted scribe, chief figure among the exiles of Mosul, surnamed 'Zaynul-Muqarrabín'.
19. Mírzá 'Alí-Muḥammad: zealous advocate in the early days of the proclamation of the covenant of Bahá'u'lláh, surnamed 'Shahíd-ibn-i-Shahíd'.[14]

Beneath the photo montage in *The Bahá'í World*, the Apostles are also called 'Pillars of the Faith'.[15]

INTRODUCTION

The stories of the lives of the Apostles of Bahá'u'lláh illumine their exalted and lofty position, and their complete dedication to His Revelation. They are all narratives that include intoxicated souls, unrestrained teaching of the Cause, persecution, torture and, in some cases, martyrdom. Except for short periods, none of them enjoyed tranquil lives.

1

MÍRZÁ MÚSÁ-I-NÚRÍ – ÁQÁY-I-KALÍM

(1818 or 1819–1887)

Mírzá Músá-i-Núrí was a younger brother of Bahá'u'lláh who, from the time of their youth, had sacrificially served Him. Bahá'u'lláh Himself wrote that of all the members of His family, there were 'only two persons who were adequately informed of the origins' of His Faith, Mírzá Músá and His half-brother, Mírzá Muḥammad-Qulí.[1] Because of Mírzá Músá's selflessness, Bahá'u'lláh gave him the title of Áqáy-i-Kalím, which means Master of Discourse.[2] Navváb, Bahá'u'lláh's wife, and Mírzá Músá were the 'twin pillars who, all throughout the various stages of Bahá'u'lláh's exile from the Land of His Birth to the final place of His confinement, had demonstrated, unlike most of the members of His Family, the tenacity of their loyalty.'[3]

Of Mírzá Músá's early life, we know very little, not even the year in which he was born, but it is thought to be towards the end of the year 1818 or early 1819.[4] We do know that he was the next son after Bahá'u'lláh, who was born in 1817. 'Abdu'l-Bahá, in *Memorials of the Faithful*, wrote that

> Jináb-i-Mírzá Músá was the true brother of Bahá'u'lláh, and from earliest childhood he was reared in the sheltering embrace of the Most Great Name. He drank in the love of God with his mother's milk; when yet a suckling, he showed an extraordinary attachment to the Blessed Beauty. At all times he was the object of Divine grace, favor and loving-kindness. After their distinguished father died, Mírzá Músá was brought up by Bahá'u'lláh, growing to maturity in the haven of His care. Day by day, the youth's servitude and devotion increased. In all things, he lived according to the commandments, and he was entirely severed from any thoughts of this world.

> Like a bright lamp, he shone out in that Household. He wished neither rank nor office, and had no worldly aims at all. His one supreme desire was to serve Bahá'u'lláh, and for this reason he was never separated from his Brother's presence. No matter what torments the others inflicted, his loyalty equalled the cruelty of the rest, for he had drunk the wine of unadulterated love.[5]

Mírzá Músá put himself completely in Bahá'u'lláh's service and, until 'Abdu'l-Bahá reached his maturity, was Bahá'u'lláh's primary assistant.

In August 1844, Mullá Ḥusayn, the first to believe in the Báb, delivered a Tablet from the Báb by messenger to Bahá'u'lláh. The messenger met Mírzá Músá at the gate of the house and he took him in to Bahá'u'lláh. The messenger gave the Tablet to Mírzá Músá who passed it to Bahá'u'lláh. Reading a few passages aloud, Bahá'u'lláh turned to Mírzá Músá and said: 'Músá, what have you to say? Verily I say, whoso believes in the Qur'án and recognises its Divine origin, and yet hesitates, though it be for a moment, to admit that these soul-stirring words are endowed with the same regenerating power has most assuredly erred in his judgement . . .'[6]

Mírzá Músá also accepted that message and 'Abdu'l-Bahá wrote:

> Then the voice was heard, crying out of Shíráz, and from a single utterance of Bahá'u'lláh, his [Mírzá Músá] heart was filled with light, and from a single gust that blew over the gardens of faith, he caught the fragrance. At once, he began to serve the friends. He had an extraordinary attachment to me, and was at all times concerned for my well-being. In Tihrán he occupied himself day and night with propagating the Faith and gradually became well known to everyone; habitually he spent his time in the company of blessed souls.[7]

At the beginning of 1848, Mullá Ḥusayn passed through Tehran on his way to see the Báb in Mákú. When he arrived, Mírzá Músá and a large number of Bábís went to see him.[8]

In early summer of the same year, Ṭáhirih was in Tehran staying with Bahá'u'lláh and He decided to send her to Khurásán to keep her safe. He gave Mírzá Músá the task of escorting her, warning his brother that the guards were looking for a woman trying to leave the city without a permit. Mírzá Músá said that 'Putting our trust in God, we rode out, Ṭáhirih, her attendant, and I, to a place in the vicinity of the capital. None of the guards who were stationed at the gate of Shimírán raised the slightest objection, nor did they enquire regarding our destination'. About 10 kilometres outside the city, they found an empty house being watched over by a caretaker, who agreed to guard Ṭáhirih. Mírzá Músá returned to Tehran and sent Mullá Baqír, one of the Letters of the Living, and an attendant, to join Ṭáhirih.

With Ṭáhirih in safety, Bahá'u'lláh directed Mírzá Músá to prepare for His own departure for Khurásán. Bahá'u'lláh left His family in Mírzá Músá's care while He was gone.[9] On this journey, the Conference of Badasht was held.

Bahá'u'lláh became well-known as a Bábí and, with the Báb imprisoned, the Bábís naturally turned to Him. He also attracted the attention of the Muslim clergy and the government. In 1849, Mírzá Músá and Mullá 'Abdu'l-Karim Qazvíní together went to Bahá'u'lláh and said: 'Considering the enmity and spitefulness of the ulama and the might of the state and the power of the Prime Minister, you are in great danger. Therefore it would be a wise precaution to turn people's attention towards someone else so that you would be protected from persecution and harm for the time being'. Bahá'u'lláh then wrote to the Báb and soon a message was sent to the teenaged Mírzá Yaḥyá, Bahá'u'lláh's younger half-brother, that suggested that he was the designated future leader of the Bábí community — though the Bab never mentioned having a successor, but emphasised that all should be ready for 'Him Whom God shall make manifest'.[10] According to a letter written on behalf of the Universal House of Justice, Mírzá Yaḥyá's station was as a figurehead:

> The Guardian has made it quite clear in 'God Passes By' that Mírzá Yaḥyá was the Báb's 'nominee' and was the 'recognized chief of the Bábí community' following the martyrdom of the Báb. He has also referred to him as 'titular head' and 'a mere figurehead'. The position occupied by Mírzá Yaḥyá was far different from being an appointed Successor of a Manifestation of God in the sense that St. Peter, the Imám 'Alí or 'Abdu'l-Bahá were appointed Successors with far-reaching authority. Obviously the Báb had no need to appoint such a Successor, for He knew that Bahá'u'lláh was already present

> and ready to be revealed at the appointed time. He seems, therefore, merely to have nominated a titular head for the Bábí community as a focal point of unity until such time as He Whom God will make manifest would decide to unveil Himself.[11]

Though this must have inflated Mírzá Yaḥyá's ego, it seems from his actions during the following years that it also terrified him.

On 15 January 1850, Mírzá Músá was with Bahá'u'lláh in Tehran when Vaḥíd, the distinguished cleric sent by Muḥammad Sh͟áh to establish the truth of the Báb and who had become a devout Bábí, arrived at the house. Bahá'u'lláh's 'loving solicitude' of Vaḥíd greatly surprised Mírzá Músá and he realised that their visitor would one day do heroic deeds for the Faith.[12] These deeds came to pass just six months later when Vaḥíd led the defence of the Bábis in Nayríz and was martyred when they were attacked by the government.

After the martyrdom of the Báb in July 1850 and the clandestine recovery of His body, Bahá'u'lláh directed Mírzá Músá to arrange for the transfer of those Holy Remains to Tehran, since He Himself was departing for Karbilá. Mírzá Músá did so and, when they arrived in Tehran, he and Mírzá Aḥmad, the Báb's amanuensis, collected the Holy Remains from the local shrine where they had initially been hidden, and put them in a place unknown to anyone else. For the next thirteen years, only those two men knew the whereabouts of the sacred treasure.[13]

On 15 August 1852, two misguided Bábís tried to avenge the martyrdom of the Báb by shooting Náṣiri'd-Dín Sh͟áh. The Sh͟áh was only wounded, but the Bábí community was immediately attacked. Bahá'u'lláh Himself was arrested, stripped of His shoes and turban, and taken to prison. Mírzá Músá quickly helped Bahá'u'lláh's wife, Ásíyih K͟hánum (Navváb), and her three children to escape from their home, and found them a house in which to hide while Bahá'u'lláh was in the Síyáh-Chál, the Black Pit.[14]

At some point while Bahá'u'lláh was imprisoned, Mírzá Músá went to the Russian Consulate. As he walked, the enemies chased after him and robbed him of his robe-like 'abá. When the Russian Consul heard of this incident and learned that the Blessed Beauty was being cruelly treated in the Black Pit, he went to the Sh͟áh and successfully insisted that He be released. Later, when Bahá'u'lláh was exiled, the Russians assigned two guards to travel with Him, to ensure His safety.[15]

Bahá'u'lláh left Tehran for Baghdad on 12 January 1853. Mírzá Músá and his half-brother Mírzá Muḥammad Qulí travelled with Him and His immediate family.[16] As the group struggled through the bewintered mountains, they passed through Kirmán<u>sh</u>áh at about the half-way point. Mírzá Yaḥya, during this time of upheaval in Tehran, had been in hiding, but reappeared in Kirmán<u>sh</u>áh. Mírzá Músá searched him out and after considerable effort, convinced him to join the group. Mírzá Yaḥyá said that he wanted to go to Baghdad and set up a business, so Bahá'u'lláh gave him some money and bought him a few bales of cotton. With that, he disappeared again until Bahá'u'lláh was well established in Baghdad. One day, Mírzá Músá opened the door of Bahá'u'lláh's house in Baghdad to a knock and at first did not recognise Mírzá Yaḥyá, because he was dressed as a dervish with a begging bowl. He only stayed a few days and begged not to be identified to anyone. Living in a part of town where there were no Persians, he emerged only at night to meet with Mírzá Músá. He was so paranoid that he threatened to 'excommunicate' anyone who revealed his identity.[17]

On 10 April 1854, because of the ensuing disunity created by Mírzá Yaḥyá in Baghdad, Bahá'u'lláh decided to leave the city without telling anyone what He was doing or where He was going.[18] For two whole years, no one knew His whereabouts. The burden of protecting the Bábís in the face of Mírzá Yaḥyá's nefarious agitations fell on Mírzá Músá. 'Abdu'l-Bahá wrote that 'During the days when Bahá'u'lláh had vanished from sight, that is, when He was on the journey to Kurdistan, Mírzá Músá lived on the edge of an abyss; his life was constantly in danger, and each day that passed was worse than the one before; still, he bore it all, and knew no fear.'[19]

After two years without Bahá'u'lláh, the Bábí community only barely existed. Then Abu'l-Qásim, Bahá'u'lláh's servant in His self-imposed exile, was murdered on his way from Hamadan to Baghdad. He lived just long enough to say that the money the murderers stole belonged to Darvish Muḥammad in Sulaymaniyyih. The murder was reported in an Iranian newspaper that 'Abdu'l-Bahá and Mírzá Músá saw at the Iranian embassy one day. They instantly knew that Darvish Muḥammad was Bahá'u'lláh and sent two Bábís to beg Him to return.[20]

The searchers found Bahá'u'lláh in the town of Sulaymaniyyih and implored Him to come back to Baghdad:

> Witnessing the great love and affection which the people of the town had for Bahá'u'lláh, they dared not openly talk of his return to Baghdad. They merely presented the petitions that they had brought and retired to the caravanserai where they were quartered. Bahá'u'lláh visited them there and was at first unwilling to accede to their request that he return. He pointed to the treachery and back-biting to which he had been subjected in Baghdad and contrasted this with the sincere devotion and high regard with which he was held among the Kurds. The Babis said that they would stay in Sulaymaniyyih and that many other Bábís would undoubtedly migrate there also.

Bahá'u'lláh finally agreed and returned, stating:

> But for My recognition of the fact that the blessed cause of the Primal Point was on the verge of being completely obliterated, and all the sacred blood poured out in the path of God would have been shed in vain, I would in no wise have consented to return to the people of the Bayán, and would have abandoned them to the worship of the idols their imaginations had fashioned.[21]

Sometime after Bahá'u'lláh's return from Sulaymaniyyih, Mírzá Músá married the daughter of Shaykh Sulṭán-i-Karbilá'í.[22]

With Bahá'u'lláh back at home, everything improved. After two years of trying to hold the Bábí community together, Mírzá Músá was probably able to relax a bit. Bahíyyih Khánum noted that 'Mírzá Músá and his wife were always devoted to Bahá'u'lláh. This uncle, Mírzá Músá, who came into exile with us, was a very kind helper in everything. At one time he did almost all the cooking, for which he had a talent, he would also help with the washing'.[23]

Bahá'u'lláh would commonly deputise Mírzá Músá to meet with governmental officials, notables and clerics in His place. In 1860, Bahá'u'lláh sent him to meet with the Persian Consul in Baghdad, Mírzá Buzurg Khán-I-Qazvíní, the Persian consul-general and inveterate enemy of Bahá'u'lláh.

> One day the foolish Consul, in all haughtiness, told Mírzá Músá that he could do whatever he liked about Bahá'u'lláh. Mírzá Músá replied: 'Why is it that I come occasionally to visit you? Do you

> think I come to ask you for a post, an office, an allowance? It is only to show you our friendly intent. By God! Should His favour towards you cease, these very men who are close to you would assuredly destroy you.' Then Mírzá Músá went on to recount all the Consul's intrigues and evil actions, so precisely and effectively that all he could reply was: 'The past is past. Should He [Bahá'u'lláh] consider me with favour in future, I shall be of service to Him.'[24]

In the same year, the prominent Persian cleric Shaykh 'Abdu'l-Ḥusayn Ṭihrání came to Baghdad. He intensely hated Bahá'u'lláh and schemed with the Persian Consul to have Him murdered. Word of the plot got back to Bahá'u'lláh, and He was urged to move to other quarters for a while. This He did not do. One night, an assassin tried to attack Bahá'u'lláh. The culprit later described how he had waited for Bahá'u'lláh with a pistol, but as soon as he saw Bahá'u'lláh coming, a great consternation overtook him and the pistol fell from his hand. Bahá'u'lláh told Mírzá Músá to pick it up and return it, then to escort the shaken assassin back to his house as he looked lost.[25]

Frustrated, Ṭihrání then gathered the clerics to declare jihad on the Bábís. News of this plot also made its way to Bahá'u'lláh:

> The following night, a group of one hundred or more Shi'á Kurds schemed to go past Bahá'u'lláh's house performing the Muharram ritual of beating their chests and lamenting the martyrdom of Imam Ḥusayn. It was planned that as they passed the house of Bahá'u'lláh, they would attack it and kill all the occupants. When hearing about this, some of the Bábís planned to be in the apartment next door fully armed and ready to do battle, but Bahá'u'lláh sent them away. That night, when the Kurds arrived, Bahá'u'lláh sent Mírzá Músá to open the door and let them in and to give them refreshments. Bahá'u'lláh then sat down and spoke to them in such a way that they left amazed at the way their enmity and anger had been transformed into affection and acquiescence.[26]

The situation was tense. Mírzá Músá

> felt certain that soon they would all be arrested and turned over in manacles to the Persian authorities, because he knew only too

> well the motives of the populace of Baghdád and their notables. However, he had not wished to report such matters to Bahá'u'lláh, lest they should cause Him sorrow. 'One night,' he related, 'sleep departed from my eyes. I kept pacing up and down the courtyard, wondering what would happen to our wives and children, once we were apprehended. Then I heard a knock and, going to the door, I was told that a number of people had been detailed to keep watch and patrol outside in the street . . . When I heard that, I knew that all would be well . . . and went to sleep.'[27]

Mírzá Músá had rented a farm on the banks of the Tigris a short distance south of Baghdad in early 1863 and Bahá'u'lláh's family and all of the Bábís would often go there. This area would become known as the Garden of Riḍván. During Naw-Rúz that year, Bahá'u'lláh's newly revealed *Tablet of the Holy Mariner* was read there by Mírzá Áqá Ján: 'Oceans of sorrow surged in the hearts of the listeners when the *Tablet of the Holy Mariner* was read aloud to them . . . It was evident to everyone that the chapter of Baghdad was about to be closed, and a new one opened, in its stead'.[28]

On 24 March 1863, Mírzá Músá and 'Abdu'l-Bahá went to call on the Governor, Namiq Pasha, to offer the customary greetings on the third day after the completion of the Muslim fast of the month of Ramadan. The governor asked that Bahá'u'lláh call upon him. Bahá'u'lláh, however, replied that He never went to the government building but that He would meet the governor in the mosque nearby. Bahá'u'lláh went to the mosque as arranged but at the last minute, Namiq Pasha, in fear and embarrassment, changed his mind and sent a representative. At this meeting, Bahá'u'lláh was shown the communications received from Constantinople (now Istanbul) asking Him to proceed to that city.[29]

After announcing that He was 'Him Whom God shall make manifest' in the Garden of Riḍván, Bahá'u'lláh left Baghdad for Constantinople accompanied by Mírzá Músá, Mírzá Muḥammad Qulí and twenty-six others. The group was joined by Nabíl-i-A'ẓam, the future author of *The Dawn-Breakers*, on the way.[30]

Mírzá Yaḥyá, who had long feared exposure as the purported head of the Bábís after the martyrdom of the Báb, had spent years avoiding the Bábís and hiding using various disguises, such as a dervish, a shoe merchant and a silk merchant, all under assumed names. When

Bahá'u'lláh's group arrived in Mosul, Mírzá Yaḥyá, who had been traveling clandestinely, made tentative contact. Mírzá Músá went in the middle of the night to meet him and invited him to join them, should he so wish. He declined.[31]

Bahá'u'lláh and His companions only stayed in Constantinople for about six months before they were further exiled to Adrianople on 1 December 1863.

For the next four and a half years, Bahá'u'lláh and His followers, plus Mírzá Yaḥyá and his cohorts, lived in Adrianople. It was here that Mírzá Yaḥyá tried everything in his power to destroy Bahá'u'lláh. Several times he tried to murder Him. In 1865, after learning about various herbs and poisons from Mírzá Músá, who was well versed in medicines, he tried to poison Him. The attempt failed, but left Bahá'u'lláh seriously unwell and with residual effects that would last His entire life. He then unsuccessfully tried to get Bahá'u'lláh's barber, Ustád Muḥammad-i-'Alíy, to kill Him in the bath.[32]

Mírzá Músá always defended Bahá'u'lláh and the nascent Faith. One day in 1866, he went with 'Abdu'l-Bahá to the apartment of Siyyid Muḥammad, who Shoghi Effendi later labelled 'the Antichrist of the Bahá'í Dispensation',[33] and smoked his water pipe. At one point, Siyyid Muḥammad saw a cart go by on the street below and said, 'His Holiness the Báb, the Remembrance of God, was like that cart: even as the next man, He came, He went.' Mírzá Músá erupted in rage and called Siyyid Muḥammad 'shameless' for his blasphemous statement.[34] Siyyid Muḥammad was a prime instigator of Mírzá Yaḥyá's rebellion and went on to become one of the leading Covenant-breakers.

> It was during their time in Adrianople that Mírzá Músá detected from Mírzá Yaḥyá the odor of rebellion. Day and night he tried to make him mend his ways, but all to no avail. On the contrary, it was astonishing how, like a deadly poison, the temptings and satanic suggestions of Siyyid Muḥammad worked on Mírzá Yaḥyá, so that Áqáy-i-Kalím finally abandoned hope. Even then he never ceased trying, thinking that somehow, perhaps, he could still the tempest and rescue Mírzá Yaḥyá from the gulf. His heart was worn away with despair and grief. He tried everything he knew . . .
>
> When all hope was gone, he ended the relationship, saying: 'O my brother, if others are in doubt as to this affair, you and I both know

> the truth. Have you forgotten the loving-kindness of Bahá'u'lláh, and how He trained us both? What care He took with your lessons and your penmanship; how constantly He saw to your spelling and your composition, and encouraged you to practice the different calligraphic styles; He even guided your copy with His own blessed fingers. Who does not know how He showered favors on you, how He brought you up in the haven of His embrace. Is this your thanks for all His tenderness—that you plot with Siyyid Muḥammad and desert the shelter of Bahá'u'lláh? Is this your loyalty? Is this the right return for all His love?' The words had no effect whatever; on the contrary, with each passing day, Mírzá Yaḥyá disclosed a greater measure of his concealed intent. Then at the end, the final rupture took place.[35]

In March 1866, Bahá'u'lláh had revealed a Tablet that unmistakably declared His claims. Mírzá Yaḥyá then proclaimed that he, too, had received a divine revelation and that all the Bahá'ís had to turn to him. On 10 March, Bahá'u'lláh abruptly moved His family out of the house in which they and others had been living. He ordered Mírzá Musa to divide up everything in the house, with half going to Mírzá Yaḥyá. He also asked Mírzá Músá to spend several hours each day doing Yaḥyá's shopping. Bahá'u'lláh then withdrew with His immediate family from everyone, leaving Mírzá Músá and 'Abdu'l-Bahá to carry the weight of the community.[36] This act, called the 'Most Great Separation', split the faithful believers from the followers of Mírzá Yaḥyá.

Then on 26 July 1868, Bahá'u'lláh was ordered to the prison city of 'Akká. With Him went His two faithful brothers, Mírzá Músá and Mírzá Muḥammad Qulí, and sixty-four others. When the exiles arrived in the barracks in 'Akká, many of them fell ill and 'Abdu'l-Bahá, Mírzá Músá and Áqá Riḍá nursed them back to health, though two of them died.[37]

In October 1872, Munírih Khánum arrived in 'Akká. She was the daughter of an uncle of the King and Beloved of the Martyrs (see Chapter 3). She arrived by ship in the dark of night and was met by Mírzá Músá, with whom she lived for the next five months. One day, Mírzá Músá went to her and said, 'I have brought you a wonderful gift from the Blessed Perfection. He has given you a new name: Munírih [Luminous]'. She and 'Abdu'l-Bahá were married on 8 March 1873.[38]

For his remaining years, Mírzá Músá continued to serve Bahá'u'lláh. In 1887, he aided Nabíl when he began his greatest work, *The Dawn-Breakers*.[39] Mírzá Músá died later in 1887 before the book was completed. 'Abdu'l-Bahá wrote that 'Mírzá Músá was indeed a true brother to the Blessed Beauty; this is why he remained steadfast, under all conditions, to the very end. Unto him be praise and salutations, and the breath of life, and glory; upon him be mercy and grace'.[40]

Bahá'u'lláh revealed a most poignant Tablet of visitation in honour of His beloved brother in which He considered him to be the beginning of faithfulness amongst the chosen ones and the dawn of acceptance amongst the true ones.[41] Below is a provisional translation by Adib Masumian of a portion of the Tablet:

> O Pen of the Most High! The direst calamity and the most grievous affliction hath come to pass. Make mention of the one who repaired to the Most Exalted Companion and ascended to the All-Glorious Horizon.
>
> Say: Upon thee rest the first splendor that appeared and shone forth from the horizon of the mercy of thy Lord, the King of names and Fashioner of the heavens, and the first fragrance wafted up from the gardens of bounty and immortality, O dayspring of faithfulness amidst the righteous, O dawning-place of contentment among the pure in heart! I bear witness that thou didst hold fast to the Book when the disbelievers cast it behind their backs, and that thou didst cling firmly to the hem of generosity when the transgressors rejected it at the prompting of their own caprices. Blessed art thou, O My brother, for thou wast made a target for the darts of divine decree in the path of God, the Possessor of the Kingdom of Names, and happy indeed art thou, O Kalím, in that thou didst attain to the Light of the Ancient of Days. I testify that thou wast faithful to the Covenant at a time when the people of sedition had broken it, and that thou didst hasten to the Supreme Horizon when the Call was raised between earth and heaven.[42]

2

MÍRZÁ BUZURG-KHURÁSÁNÍ – BADÍ'

(1852–1869)

Mírzá Buzurg-Khurásání, known universally as Badí', was the 17-year-old youth who delivered Bahá'u'lláh's Tablet to Náṣiri'd-Dín Sháh and then joyously gave his life for the Cause of God. Badí' was the son of Ḥájí 'Abdu'l-Majíd, a survivor of the battle at Shaykh Tabarsí. Born in 1852 in Nishábúr, near Mashhad, little else is known of Badí''s life until about 1868.[1] At that point, the life of a petulant teenager was dramatically changed.

Sometime in early 1868, Nabíl-i-A'ẓam (see Chapter 12), came to Nishábúr and visited his old friend Ḥájí 'Abdu'l-Majíd. Nabíl-i-A'ẓam noticed that his friend was attending to all the chores of being a host, something customarily done by a son of the host. Nabíl-i-A'ẓam was quite surprised at this because a normally respectful son would not allow his father to serve guests personally.[2]

When asked about this, 'Abdu'l-Majíd simply said that his son did not obey him. Nabíl-i-A'ẓam asked to see him and Badí' came in, a 'tall, gangling youth'. Nabíl-i-A'ẓam said that the son should carry out the duties of being the host, and proceeded to 'mention matters, very moving, which would melt a heart of stone'. He quoted passages from Bahá'u'lláh's long poem called *Qazídiy-i-'Izz-i-Varqá'íyyih*, composed while He was in Sulaymáníyyih. When he heard these verses, Badí''s colour 'reddened, his eyes welled with tears, and the sound of his lamentation rose high'. The next morning, 'Abdu'l-Majíd said that he had never heard his son cry before. 'I thought that nothing could move him. Now, what is the spell cast on him to make his tears flow and to cause him to cry out, to make him afire with the love of God? This manner of losing one's self is exactly what I desired. If he remains firm in the Cause of God, I myself shall serve him'.[3]

Badí' wanted to leave with Nabíl-i-A'ẓam, who was going to

Mas͟hhad, but his father insisted that he stay and learn to read and write first. After a time, S͟hayk͟h Fání, who would later be martyred in Tabríz, passed through Nis͟hábúr on his way to Adrianople, via Baghdad, where Bahá'u'lláh was at that time. He was allowed to take one person with him. So it was arranged that Badí' would join him in Baghdad and accompany him into the presence of Bahá'u'lláh. Badí''s father gave him a horse and some money for the journey. Badí' travelled with S͟hayk͟h Fání as far as Yazd. At that point, Badí' gave his companion everything that he possessed and began the long trek to Baghdad alone and on foot.

In Baghdad, Áqá 'Abdu'l-Rasúl was serving as the water-carrier for the Bahá'ís there. When the enemies of the Faith killed him, Badí' took over the task. As simple as it appeared to carry a water skin over his shoulder, he was attacked and stabbed with knives by the enemies several times.

In July 1868, 88 Bahá'ís in Baghdad were exiled to Mosul in northern Iraq. Badí' departed ahead of the exiles, but they caught up with him in that city and Badí' again became their water-carrier for a time. When word came that Bahá'u'lláh had been imprisoned in 'Akká, Badí' could no longer delay his desire to be in Bahá'u'lláh's presence. Leaving Mosul, he walked to 'Akká, arriving in early 1869.[4]

When Badí' reached 'Akká, he was still wearing the clothes of a water-carrier, a long cloak of coarse cotton, and consequently he had no difficulty avoiding the guards and entering the city. But once inside, he didn't know how to contact Bahá'u'lláh or the other Bahá'ís. Not sure of what to do, Badí' went to the Al-Jazzar Mosque to pray. While there, a group of Persians entered and Badí' recognised 'Abdu'l-Bahá amongst them. Writing a quick, short poem that read, 'I follow the example of the Son of God. I prostrate myself before the Mystery of God. No truth, but Bahá'u'lláh. No God, but God.'[5], he gave it to 'Abdu'l-Bahá, Who welcomed him and was able to get him inside the barracks where Bahá'u'lláh was incarcerated.[6]

Badí' was twice in Bahá'u'lláh's presence alone. What was said is not known, but Bahá'u'lláh, in one of His Tablets, wrote that 'God was about to create a new creation and Badí' himself was unaware of it'. In another Tablet, Bahá'u'lláh stated that He recreated him 'with the hands of power and might and sent him out as a ball of fire.' It was during one of these meetings that Bahá'u'lláh bestowed upon him the title of 'Badí'', which means 'Wonderful'. Though Badí' never said what happened in his meetings with the Blessed Beauty, Bahá'u'lláh did in a Tablet to Badí''s father. Adib Taherzadeh summarised the Tablet:

> He [Bahá'u'lláh] indicates that when He desired to create a new creation He summoned Badí' to come to His room and uttered 'one word' to him, a word which caused his whole being to tremble. He affirms that had it not been for the divine protection vouchsafed to him at that moment, Badí' would have swooned away. Then the Hand of Omnipotence, according to Bahá'u'lláh's description, began to create him anew and breathed into him the spirit of might and power. So great was the infusion of this might, as attested by Bahá'u'lláh, that single and alone he could have conquered the world through the power of God, had he been ordered to do so.
>
> Bahá'u'lláh states that when this new creation came into being, he smiled in His presence and manifested such steadfastness that the Concourse on High were deeply moved and exhilarated and the voice of God was heard calling aloud: 'Hallowed and glorified be Bahá for having fashioned a new and wonderful creation.' Bahá'u'lláh testifies that He disclosed to the eyes of the 'Kingdom of Revelation', and as a result his whole being was filled with ecstasy that rid him of all attachments to this world and made him arise to assist his Lord and bring victory to His Cause.[7]

Badí' walked into Bahá'u'lláh's room as a Persian youth, but he walked out as a new being.

Many Bahá'ís had wanted to deliver the *Lawḥ-i-Sulṭán*, the Tablet Bahá'u'lláh wrote to Náṣiri'd-Dín Sháh, but none had been offered the opportunity until Badí' was transformed. When Badí' learned of the Tablet, he begged for the chance to deliver it to the arrogant emperor. He did this knowing that it meant his death.[8]

Bahá'u'lláh sent Badí' to Haifa. In 'Akká, He entrusted the Tablet to Ḥájí Sháh-Muḥammad-i-Amín, His Trustee for Ḥuqúqu'lláh, and directed him to take it to Badí'. Ḥájí Amín wrote:

> I was given a small case . . . and was instructed to hand it to Badí' at Haifa together with a small sum of money. I did not know anything about the contents of the case. I met him at Haifa and gave him

> the glad-tidings that he had been honoured with a trust . . . We left the town and walked up Mount Carmel where I handed him the case. He took it into his hands, kissed it and knelt with his forehead to the ground. I also delivered to him a sealed envelope [a Tablet of Baháʼu'lláh for Badíʻ himself]. He took twenty or thirty paces, sat down facing the most Holy Court [ʻAkká], read the Tablet and again prostrated himself to the ground. His face was illumined with the radiance of ecstasy and the tidings of joy. I asked him if I could read the Tablet also. He replied: 'There is no time.' I knew it was all a confidential matter. But what it was, I had no idea. I could not imagine such a mission.
>
> I mentioned that we had better go to the town [Haifa] in order that, as instructed [by Baháʼu'lláh] I might give him some money. He said, 'I will not come to the town; you go and bring it here.' I went; when I returned I could not find him, in spite of much searching. He had gone.[9]

So Badíʻ left. During the following four months, he walked towards Tehran, keeping completely to himself and avoiding towns and people. He did encounter one Baháʼí, Ḥájí ʻAlí, and travelled with him for a distance before they reached Persia. Ḥájí ʻAlí later said that

> He was a very happy person, smiling, patient, thankful, gentle and humble. All that we knew about him was that he had attained the presence of Baháʼu'lláh and was now returning to his home in Khurásán. Many a time he could be seen walking about a hundred feet from the road in either direction, turning his face towards ʻAkká, prostrating himself to the ground saying: 'O God! do not take back through Thy justice what thou hast vouchsafed unto me through Thy bounty and grant me strength for its protection.'[10]

Badíʻ arrived in Tehran in July 1869. When he learned that the Sháh was camping outside the city, he made his way there and sat on top of a rock across from the royal pavilion for three days and nights, during which he fasted. On the fourth day, the Sháh spotted white-clad Badíʻ on the rock through his binoculars.

Muḥammad-Valí Khán was a colonel in the Sháh's army and his father was a general. The two officers arrived at the camp just after a strange event had happened. Upon entering the camp, they went to visit Káẓim Khán-i-Warachih-Daghi, the Farrásh-Bashí (and executioner) for the Sháh and he told them the extraordinary story. In March, 1913, Muḥammad-Valí Khán told the story to 'Abdu'l-Bahá in Paris:

> The Shah had pitched his tents many miles away from Teheran and my father and myself were commissioned to go around the surrounding villages and prepare the commissariat. While we were riding . . ., we heard a great noise and confusion, servants running to and fro in great consternation. My father asked what is the cause of all these noises. An officer . . . said that a few minutes ago His Imperial Majesty was driving in the royal carriage when a youth waved a banner towards him. The Shah sent for him several of his body-guards to find out what he wanted. He told them that he had to see the Shah in person; he had a message to deliver into his hand. At first they searched him, fearing he may attack the Shah with a secret weapon and they tried to make him tell the message to them, but he repeated, 'No, I must see the Shah and give the message to him'. . .
>
> The Shah seeing that his body-guards did not return sent more servants to bring them back. 'What was the reason of your delay?', the Shah asked imperiously. 'This man' they said, 'desires to deliver a message personally to your Majesty. We tried to get it from him but he would not give it.' 'Bring him', then Badi was brought before the carriage of the Shah.
>
> 'What is your wish young man?'
>
> 'I have brought a Firman [a royal mandate or decree issued by a sovereign] from the part of my Lord for thee!' and he took out immediately the Tablet of Baha'Ullah and delivered it into the hand of the Shah. The body-guards realizing what had happened gathered around Badi, and the Shah almost beside himself with anger ordered Kazem Khan to take the young man and force him to give the names of his accomplices . . .
>
> I saw a soldier surrounded by many others was carrying on his back a young man whose hands and feet were strongly tied with ropes. They were making sport of him that this is the man who had brought a 'Firman' for the Shah! 'Just think of his foolhardiness and audacity to say loudly to the King of Kings that he had brought a 'Firman' and not a petition!'

. . . after 8 days we heard that he was killed. One morning my father told me, 'Let us go and call on Kazem Khan' . . . My father asked Kazem Khan; – 'What did happen to that young Bahai who had brought a letter from Baha-Ullah for the Shah. We heard that he is killed. As you had him in your charge, tell us about it'.

'Really!' Kazem Khan answered, 'It was one of the most marvellous things that has ever transpired, a very marvellous event, almost a miracle. It is an astounding story. You remember the day he was caught while handing the 'Firman of his Lord' to the Shah. Well! His Majesty turned him to me with the injunction that I must get out of him the names of his friends. I brought him to my tent and while his hands and feet were tied, I addressed him thus: – 'Thou art a young, comely youth! Tell me where are thy friends and I will give thee freedom'. He answered: 'My dear Sir! I have no friends! I do not know anyone. I have not even seen the Revelator of the Firman. I am not informed with its contents. The Firman was given me to deliver it into the hands of the Shah. I have not seen any one either on my way or in Teheran. Now I am most happy that I have fulfilled my duty. I have nothing else to say'.

I told him: – 'Young man! Art thou mad? Dost thou not know that this is the sacred Command of His Majesty? If thou dost not reveal the names of thy friends and accomplices in Teheran we will be forced to make thee confess by inflicting upon thee severe tortures.'

He said: 'I have already said what I know. Whatever punishment you inflict upon me will be of the essence of happiness; the severer the torture the greater my gratitude to you. I am ready'.

While I was beside myself with rage, I was secretly admiring the calmness and imperturbability of the youth. So I ordered the Farashes to bring the Bastonado [a rod with which to beat the soles of a person's feet] and putting his feet through it they inflicted a severe beating . . . upon the soles of his feet. The more they struck the more marvellous was his calmness and poise. He cried not neither did he plead for mercy. Wonder of wonder! he laughed, he sung. Was it possible? It was as though this punishment had no effect upon him! . . . I jumped out of my seat, got several branches together and continued to beat him as though the demon had possessed me . . . Again he laughed! His face was wreathed with smiles! He chanted the songs of praise and glorification! . . .

Now I was tired . . . I ran out of the tent and with consternation in my eyes I presented myself before the Shah. 'Your Majesty! There is no use. We have almost killed him under Bastonado but he does not reveal anything. On the contrary, he sings!'

'Go' the Shah said 'he must divulge the names of his accomplices or he will be put to death' . . .

I ordered my servants to prepare a great fire . . . and many iron rods and bricks brought in. The rods and bricks were put in the midst of the burning coal till they got as red as fire. Then I addressed Badi: 'If thou dost not reveal the names of thy friends, thy whole body will be branded with these fiery spikes and bricks. Thou may confess that thou hast brought a "petition" for the Shah and not a "Firman"'. I thought that these means of torture will so frighten him that he will confess without any further difficulty. But he astonished me when he said: – 'I have brought a "Firman" for the Shah and not a "petition". All my life I have been hoping for the realization of this day. Whatever torture you heap upon me, you must know of a certainty that it is not torture but it is the greatest of all the divine gifts. I am ready Sir.'

Well we started . . . yet he did not flinch, he did not show any sign of pain . . . His face was peaceful . . . I took out of the fire the red hot spike and branded his back and front and run it through his body . . . He was completely insensible to pains . . . When the executioners would get tired, lo and behold he would take with his own hand one of the red spikes and put in on his body . . . he laughed, he was really happy, he chanted some Arabic prayers. We were simply awe-struck.

At this point the Shah passed by the tent and called for me: 'Kazem Khan . . . has the young man confessed?' 'No' I answered. 'We have inflicted upon him the worst kinds of tortures, but they have made no effect whatsoever upon him . . .' Then the Shah said: – 'He must either tell the names of his friends or he dies.'

Then I returned again to the tent and ordered the Farrashes to bring a big piece of log. I asked him to put his head on the log which he did willingly. Then I put a heavy bludgeon in the hand of one of the Farrashes, told him to raise it in the air and stand over his head. Then I addressed him: – 'young man if thou dost not desire to divulge the names of thy friends . . . at least say you have brought a "petition" for His Majesty and not a Firman. Then thou will be made free.'

'Free!' he cried out. 'Do not talk to me about freedom! I am the freest man in the world . . . Now that this chalice of divine felicity is made ready, is it not unjust that I may heedlessly let it pass by without drinking it? I tell you Sir, for the last time that I have brought the "Firman" of my Lord and not a petition.'

Then I made a sign to the man with his raised mace to do his work and with the first and second strike, his head was splintered and life flew out of his body . . .

This was the wonderful story of the martyrdom of Badi . . .[11]

A year and a half later, Káẓim-Khán died in chains after going mad.[12] Náṣiri'd-Dín Sháh ruled over Persia for another 26 years, something that confused many Bahá'ís at the time. Though branded as the 'Prince of Oppressors' by Bahá'u'lláh, He also explained why the Sháh was given his respite before divine chastisement struck him down in 1896. In one Tablet, Bahá'u'lláh states that the perversity of the Persian divines and their continual attacks on the Faith were cause, if it had not been for His mercy, for the 'entire company of enemies of the Cause of God' to perish. The reasons they, and the Sháh, were spared was divine forgiveness for the misdeeds of those who claimed to be His followers (the two who had tried to assassinate the Sháh). To Badíʻ's father, Bahá'u'lláh said that the delay in the Sháh being called to account was because of the 'ignorant believers who in the early days of the Faith made an attempt on his life'.[13] The Sháh's reckoning came when he was assassinated in 1896 on the eve of his jubilee (50 year anniversary) celebration.[14] A year after Badíʻ's martyrdom, Persia suffered a devastating famine that Bahá'u'lláh affirmed was God's punishment for Badíʻ's death.

In the three years after the martyrdom of Badíʻ, Bahá'u'lláh extolled his deed in almost every Tablet He wrote, giving him the title of 'Pride of the Martyrs'. Adib Taherzadeh explains the significance of Badíʻ's sacrifice and the delivery of the Tablet to the Sháh:

> As attested by Bahá'u'lláh in a Tablet, not until this momentous epistle was delivered to the King had the nature of the Cause of God, or the claims of its Founder, or its principles and teachings,

been clearly enunciated to those who held the reins of power in their hands. He mentions in the same Tablet that before Badí' had delivered that weighty epistle to the King, God's testimony had not been fulfilled and the conclusive proofs of His Faith had not been declared. But after the proclamation of His Message, there was no remaining excuse for anyone to arise against His Cause. And, since the people of Persia did not respond to the Call of God, which was clearly raised in that Message, sufferings and tribulations which had already been prophesied by the Pen of Bahá'u'lláh descended upon them as a punishment from God.[15]

3

SIYYID ḤASAN-I-NAHRÍ – MÍRZÁ MUḤAMMAD-ḤASAN – KING OF THE MARTYRS

(1836–1879)

Siyyid Ḥasan-i-Nahrí, whose full name was Mírzá Muḥammad-Ḥasan, and his brother, Mírzá Muḥammad-Ḥusayn, were called the King of the Martyrs and the Beloved of the Martyrs, respectively, by Bahá'u'lláh, Who wrote of them in over 100 Tablets. Though only Mírzá Ḥasan was named an Apostle of Bahá'u'lláh by Shoghi Effendi, their stories are inseparable and involve the evil machinations of three men: Shaykh Muḥammad-Báqir, Mír Muḥammad-Ḥusayn and Ẓillu's-Sulṭán. Bahá'u'lláh called Shaykh Muḥammad-Báqir the 'Wolf'. Mír Muḥammad-Ḥusayn the Imám-Jum'ih, He labelled the 'She-Serpent'. Ẓillu's-Sulṭán was one of Náṣiri'd-Dín Sháh's sons.[1]

The two brothers were born in Iṣfahán, Mírzá Ḥusayn in 1834 and Mírzá Ḥasan in 1836. They were nine and ten years old when the Báb declared His Mission in 1844. The boys had two uncles: Mírzá Hádí and Mírzá Muḥammad-'Alí, the father of Munírih Khánum — 'Abdu'l-Bahá's future wife. Both uncles had accepted the Faith in its early years and both attended the Conference of Badasht. Their uncles' father, Mírzá Ibráhím, did not become a Bábí until later, but one day hosted the Báb in his home. The two young boys, along with their uncles, met the Báb and quickly became strong believers. Later, Mírzá Ḥasan and Mírzá Ḥusayn went with their uncle Mírzá Muḥammad-'Alí to Baghdad and met Bahá'u'lláh, Whose Station they recognised before His declaration.

The two boys grew up and became very successful and rich merchants. Though wealthy and held in high esteem by the people of

Iṣfahán, they were completely detached from those attributes, giving generously wherever it was needed. They supported Bahá'u'lláh in His exiles, as well as Zaynu'l-Muqarrabín and the exiled Bábís in Mosul (see Chapter 18) and the poor in Iṣfahán. They were well known for their 'trustworthiness, honesty, compassion, loving kindness and generosity'.[2] Dr C.J. Wills visited the men and 'found their house beautifully furnished and their hospitality was great; they discoursed much on the subject of religion, and they were very eloquent on the injustices perpetrated in Persia'.[3]

Bahá'u'lláh obviously knew of their futures. In a Tablet written before their deaths, He wrote that

> believers should act with wisdom and prudence to protect themselves. But if the occasion demands it they should be willing to lay down their lives in the path of God. He affirms that since death is inevitable for everyone, it is much more praiseworthy, if the situation requires it, to die as a martyr than by natural cause. He further explains that a believer who has truly recognized Him will not even become saddened by the terror and persecution of the enemies, much less be frightened by them.[4]

Mírzá Ḥasan and Mírzá Ḥusayn worked for Mír Muḥammad-Ḥusayn, the Imám Jum'ih or leading Imám of Isfahán. Being the most trustworthy people he could find, the Imám Jum'ih put his financial affairs in their hands. As a consequence, Mír Muḥammad-Ḥusayn became very wealthy. Everything went smoothly until one day, the Imám Jum'ih was informed that he owed the two brothers a large sum of money. While conducting the Imám Jum'ih's business, they had settled many debts with their own funds.[5] This resulted in the Imám Jum'ih owing them about 18,000 túmáns (approximately $2.5 million).[6]

When the Imám Jum'ih realised how much he owed the brothers, he immediately began to look at ways to avoid paying them. His actions led to 'Bahá'u'lláh's denunciation of this wicked Imám as "Raqshá" (the She-Serpent), poised to strike mercilessly at the two embodiments of loving-kindness and compassion'. One day in the public bath, Imám Jum'ih met with the arch-enemy of the Faith, Shaykh Muḥammad-Báqir, one of the most renowned Mujtahids of the town, and explained his dilemma. The two then devised a plan to destroy the two brothers and confiscate their wealth and property. Their plan gained Shaykh Muḥammad-Báqir the title of the 'Wolf' by Bahá'u'lláh.[7]

The plan was simple: to ask Ẓillu's-Sulṭán, the Governor of Isfahán, to arrest and execute the two men. To help the Governor make up his mind, they offered him a substantial portion of the brothers' wealth. On 11 March 1879, Mírzá Ḥasan and Mírzá Ḥusayn, along with their younger brother, Mírzá Ismá'íl, went to pay their respects to the Imám Jum'ih. Mírzá Ḥasan was warned of the nefarious deed that was about to happen and escaped to the home of the man who warned him, Áqá Muḥammad-Báqir-i-Mudarrís, Ẓillu's-Sulṭán's fair-minded father-in-law. The other two brothers went to Imám Jum'ih and, as was the custom, asked his permission to leave. Noticing that Mírzá Ḥasan was not with them, he immediately sent men to find him. The men broke into his house and searched everywhere, even the andarúní, the room where the women of the household lived. They finally found Mírzá Ḥasan when a 'mischief maker' directed them to his hiding place.

With Mírzá Ḥusayn and Mírzá Ismá'íl already under arrest, Mírzá Ḥasan was brought before Ẓillu's-Sulṭán, who 'immediately grew violent in his denunciation. Seeing that Mírzá Ḥasan would not yield an inch in renouncing his Faith, he took that noble siyyid's firmness as a personal insult and struck Mírzá Ḥasan's head and face with his cane, drawing blood'. The three brothers were dragged off to prison.[8]

Over the next several days, Ẓillu's-Sulṭán interrogated Mírzá Ḥasan and accused him of being a Bahá'í. Mírzá Ḥasan replied that:

This is true, but the reason that the Imám-Jum'ih is inimical towards me is this:

> I have for several years defrayed all the expenses of his household, what they ate and what they wore. He owes me a sum of money and because I have lately asked him to settle his debt he has turned against me'. Ẓillu's-Sulṭán agreed with what he had said, but insisted that he 'renounce this Faith, and curse its leaders'. Jináb-i-Mírzá remained silent. Ẓillu's-Sulṭán continued to press him, saying: 'I swear by the salt of His Majesty the monarch, and the pure soul of the Commander of the Faithful ['Alí, the First Imam] that should you curse them, I would always give you help and support, get from the Imám-Jum'ih all that he owes you and make your enemies disappointed, make them abandon their hostility.' Again

> that manifestation of constancy said nothing. In the end the Prince said: 'Come, by my life, and curse them.' But his insistence was of no avail. Seeing that, the Prince was infuriated and shouted: 'Why don't you curse them?' Jináb-i-Mírzá, at last, spoke: 'If Your Highness knew what I know, you would not order me to do any cursing.' Hearing this, the Prince became totally a changed man, enraged, bestial, burning with fury, completely beside himself, his face alarmingly darkening, and his hand went several times to his sword, half unsheathing it. Finally he took up his walking-stick and so pounded the head and face of that Rock of Constancy that the blessed visage was covered with wounds.[9]

Following that, Mírzá Ḥusayn and Mírzá Ismá'íl were brought in. Mírzá Ḥusayn stood fast in his faith and was arrested, but his younger brother cursed the Báb and was released.[10]

These interrogations were held in the presence of the city's chief merchants, who looked on helplessly. Mírzá Ḥasan and Mírzá Ḥusayn asked the merchants what they had done that their former friends would ignore what was happening. They received no response.[11] Mírzá Ḥasan and Mírzá Ḥusayn were taken to prison and savagely beaten. While they were in prison, the people ransacked their homes and beat and insulted the women of the families. Being forced from their home, the women tried to go to the homes of friends, but they were refused entry out of fear. Finally, they found refuge in the European-run telegraph office, but had no food or money. A few days later, other members of the family, in order to stop the 'scandal' of them living with Europeans, took them into their own homes.[12]

Worried that the prestige and wealth of Mírzá Ḥusayn might result in his freedom, the trio of conspirators had a message sent to Náṣiri'd-Dín Sh͟áh that the

> 'ulamá of Isfahán had, in their concern for the security of the sovereign, detained and imprisoned two Bábís, and now requested his permission to have them put to death, so that rendering him this service they should be considered as truly well-wishers of the State. Having received the telegram, the Sh͟áh ordered Ẓillu's-Sulṭán to dispatch the two brothers in chains to Tihrán.[13]

Ẓillu's-Sulṭán lost his courage in the face of his father's command, but the Wolf and the She-Serpent came up with a new scheme to destroy the brothers through public rioting. On 17 March, the two divines ordered all tradesmen and shopkeepers in the bazaar to shut their businesses. Then Imám Jum'ih, S͟haykh Muḥammad-Báqir Áqá and about 50 other 'ulamás converged on the residence of the Governor with large crowds of 'rascals and rioters'. The city was suddenly in an uproar and Ẓillu's-Sulṭán, who was in his bath at the time, was greatly alarmed. He was told that the 'ulamás were demanding that Mírzá Ḥasan and Mírzá Ḥusayn be put to death. Meeting with the 'ulamás, the prince told them that the S͟háh had ordered him to send the prisoners to Tehran, so he could not sanction their execution. With this, the 'ulamás declared that 'We will order their execution and shoulder the responsibility'.

At this point, one of the 'ulamás, the son of S͟haykh Muḥammad-Báqir Áqá — the 'Wolf', known as S͟haykh Najafí and named the 'Son of the Wolf' by Bahá'u'lláh, arrogantly stepped forward and declared that 'With our own hands we will slay them'. In order to exculpate his own guilt, Ẓillu's-Sulṭán demanded that they 'Write me an edict and state the necessity of putting them to death. This is a document that I shall require.' With his excuse in hand, signed by 50 'ulamás, Ẓillu's-Sulṭán stepped out of the way and the mob immediately dragged Mírzá Ḥasan and Mírzá Ḥusayn out of their cells.[14] Ẓillu's-Sulṭán made one final effort to get the brothers to recant their faith, and when they refused, left them to their fates.

Even though many of those in the mob, including the executioner, were indebted to them for their charitable and philanthropic assistance, they still dragged Mírzá Ḥasan and Mírzá Ḥusayn into the street. When faced with his victims, he was mortified at what was demanded of him. The two brothers, however, assured him of their forgiveness. Mírzá Ḥasan even took the ring off his finger and gave it to the man as a gift.

So on 17 March 1879, the Wolf and the She-Serpent plus the mob watched as 'these noble brothers, the twin "shining lights", stood with their arms around each other ready to give their lives in the path of God. Their faces portrayed the beauty and the strength of their faith as they communed in spirit with their Lord, invoking him to accept from them the sacrifice of their earthly lives and admit them into the spiritual realms of nearness to Him'. Each brother pleaded with the executioner to be the first to be martyred. Finally, Mírzá Ḥasan, the

King of the Martyrs (Sulṭánu'sh-Shuhadá), was beheaded, followed by Mírzá Ḥusayn, the Beloved of the Martyrs (Mahbúbu'sh-Shuhadá).[15]

Once beheaded, their feet and bodies were tied with rope and dragged through the town for everyone to see. The bodies were then dumped in an abandoned and demolished house. Their younger brother secretly retrieved the bodies and buried them.

Bahá'u'lláh wrote about the two brothers in over 100 Tablets. In one prayer revealed for the King of the Martyrs, Bahá'u'lláh 'bestows such bounties upon his soul and upon that of his brother as no pen can adequately describe. He testifies that he had wholly detached himself from all earthly things, and that he had succeeded in attaching himself with the cord of servitude to the exalted dominion of his Lord.' In another Tablet, Bahá'u'lláh stated that 'the soul of the Prophet Muḥammad in the highest paradise laments the martyrdom of the two brothers and denounces the people of Islám for the wicked crime they had perpetrated'. In other Tablets, He called the brothers 'the great trust of God', 'the spirit which appeared in the form of a human temple to serve God', 'the tree of love', 'the breeze that God wafted over the city', and 'a fruit upon the tree of fidelity'. In still another Tablet, Bahá'u'lláh declared that Mírzá Ḥasan and Mírzá Ḥusayn were already accounted as martyrs while they were alive because they sacrificed themselves completely for the Cause of God. He stated that 'many would be astonished if they knew how glorious was their first martyrdom'.[16]

Soon after the martyrdoms, Bahá'u'lláh revealed the *Lawḥ-i-Burhán*, addressed to Shaykh Muḥammad-Báqir Áqá, the 'Wolf'. This Tablet is a contrast between 'the pretensions of the two clergymen to be exponents of the Law and faith of Islam and cruelty of their killing two descendants of the Prophet himself'. Bahá'u'lláh compares the Wolf to the 'Jewish priests who condemn Christ to death and to the leaders of the cult of idols in Mecca who opposed Muḥammad.'[17] In it, He calls the Wolf 'the heedless one', 'the perverse hater', 'the ignorant' who had 'gone far astray' and was 'engulfed in evident folly', 'wrapped in thick veil', and 'joined partners with God'. He also wrote that the Apostle of God (the Prophet Muḥammad) lamented, 'the hearts of the Concourse on high' were consumed, 'the soul of the Chaste One [Fáṭimih] melted, 'the inmates of Paradise wept', 'Gabriel [the angel who appeared to Muḥammad] groaned', 'all created things' lamented, 'the limbs of the holy ones' quaked, and 'darkness fell upon all regions'.[18] 'In such wise,'

'Abdu'l-Bahá has written, 'was the blood of these two brothers shed that the Christian priest of Julfá cried out, lamented and wept on that day.'[19]

None of the three conspirators in this drama lived long to enjoy their 'victory'. A vicious quarrel broke out between the Imám Jum'ih, the She-Serpent, and Ẓillu's-Sulṭán just days after the martyrdoms over the sharing of the ill-gotten wealth. About 25 days after the martyrdom, Imám Jum'ih gathered a great number of his followers and besieged the Governor's headquarters. As the situation worsened, the government in Tehran secretly dispatched soldiers who arrested Imám Jum'ih, ransacked his home and carried away all his possessions. The She-Serpent was then exiled to Khurásán. Shoghi Effendi wrote that

> Mír Muḥammad-Ḥusayn, surnamed the 'She-Serpent', whom Bahá'u'lláh describes as one 'infinitely more wicked than the oppressor of Karbilá, was . . . expelled from Isfahán, wandered from village to village, contracted a disease that engendered so foul an odor that even his wife and daughter could not bear to approach him, and died in such ill-favor with the local authorities that no one dared to attend his funeral.[20]

During the discussion about murdering Mírzá Ḥasan and Mírzá Ḥusayn, the Imám Jum'ih was reported to have placed his hand on his neck and said, 'If there be any sin in this let it be upon my neck'. His disease may have been cancer of the throat which caused a huge abscess on his neck.

Shaykh Muḥammad-Báqir Áqá, the Wolf, was sent in disgrace by Ẓillu's-Sulṭán to Najaf in Iraq and was never able to return home to enjoy his misbegotten gains. Shoghi Effendi wrote that 'Shaykh Muḥammad-Báqir, surnamed the 'Wolf', who, in the strongly condemnatory *Lawḥ-i-Burhán* addressed to him by Bahá'u'lláh, had been compared to 'the last trace of sunlight upon the mountain-top', witnessed the steady decline of his prestige, and died in a miserable state of acute remorse'.[21]

The third conspirator, Ẓillu's-Sulṭán, who ruled up to two thirds of all of Iran at that time, tried to rule it all, securing the support of the British government to overthrow the Sháh. He even wrote to Bahá'u'lláh asking for the Bahá'ís to support his effort to become king. Ẓillu's-Sulṭán surrounded himself with all of the pomp and majesty of a king. But in the end, he went into a steady decline with his authority drastically reduced and his aspirations frustrated. He was then exiled to Europe where he met 'Abdu'l-Bahá and tried to place the blame for his actions on his father, Náṣiri'd-Dín Sháh. When allowed back to Iran, he died in 'ignominy'.[22]

In a Tablet to Mírzá 'Alí-Muḥammad, Bahá'u'lláh affirmed that God vouchsafed His special favours on the King of the Martyrs and the Beloved of the Martyrs and that they 'appeared among the people as embodiments of honour and glory'. Bahá'u'lláh further stated that 'people would be dumbfounded if the station of even those who worked for them as servants were to be disclosed'.[23]

4

MULLÁ ABU'L-ḤASAN-I-ARDIKÁNÍ – ḤÁJÍ AMÍN

(c1831–1928)

Mullá Abu'l-Ḥasan, more commonly known as Ḥájí Amín, was the Trustee of Ḥuqúqu'lláh for 47 years during the ministries of Bahá'u'lláh, 'Abdu'l-Bahá and Shoghi Effendi. He also travelled with 'Abdu'l-Bahá in Great Britain.

Ḥájí Amín was born in the village of Ardikan, near Yazd, in about 1831. When he was 17, his parents arranged his marriage to the daughter of a local merchant and farmer, Mullá Rajab-'Alí. Ḥájí Amín's new father-in-law, having six sons and only a single daughter who he wished to keep near, insisted that, contrary to custom, Ḥájí Amín move into his house instead of the couple settling into the groom's house. Ḥájí Amín's parents agreed to this and thus their son came into contact with the Bábí Faith when it turned out that his father-in-law and all of his six brothers-in-law were Bábís. Though a dedicated Muslim, as was his new wife, Ḥájí Amín was convinced by the brothers to examine the Faith of the Báb. In 1851, after many long discussions with other Bábís, such as Mullá Muḥammad-Riḍá, Ḥájí Amín became a Bábí himself. He then brought his wife into the Faith.[1]

After hearing the claim of Bahá'u'lláh and reading some of His Writings, Ḥájí Amín was immediately convinced of His station and became a Bahá'í. This transformed him and he completely dedicated his life to Bahá'u'lláh. Because his wife's family were all very respected Bábís, Ḥájí Amín was able to travel around Iran bringing many Bábís into the new Faith of Bahá'u'lláh. He was always warmly welcomed by those he visited, because of the love and encouragement he poured out. Some parents, in this time of arranged marriages, even asked him to suggest suitable partners for their children.

Bahá'u'lláh had appointed Ḥájí Sh͟háh-Muḥammad as His Trustee of Ḥuqúqu'lláh. Sometime during the 1860s, Ḥájí Sh͟háh-Muḥammad took Ḥájí Amín as his assistant and the two initially travelled all around Iran together collecting Ḥuqúqu'lláh contributions for Bahá'u'lláh. After a while, Ḥájí Sh͟háh-Muḥammad came to so completely trust Ḥájí Amín that he would send his assistant on long trips alone. Not wishing to spend any of the funds given for Ḥuqúqu'lláh, Ḥájí Amín supported himself on these lengthy trips by trading and writing letters for people. He also delivered Tablets from Bahá'u'lláh to the Bahá'ís and letters from the Bahá'ís to Bahá'u'lláh.[2]

Ḥájí Amín lived a life of detachment from material things and because of his example, the Bahá'ís were generous with their money. He lived an austere life and did not like extravagance. The Bahá'ís knew this and whenever he was expected for dinner, they would prepare simple dishes. But even that was not enough; he would insist that only a single dish be served and that it be the simplest food. If he arrived at a home where dinner was being prepared, he would tell the cook to just add some water but no extra ingredients. This became known as 'The soup of Ḥájí Amín'.[3] Even Bahá'u'lláh laughingly remarked on his frugality: 'We must impose a fine upon Jináb-i-Amín. We have one treasurer and he is bankrupt! Gracious God, there is one treasury belonging to God and that is empty of funds. Indeed, by virtue of its exalted station, such a treasury ought to be freed and sanctified from earthly things and not be confused with the treasuries of the world'.[4]

Bahá'u'lláh arrived at the Most Great Prison in 'Akká on 31 August 1868. A rigid ban was imposed upon anyone trying to visit Him, but a few managed to sneak into the old city. Nabíl-i-A'ẓam (see Chapter 12) was one of the first Bahá'ís to enter 'Akká in an effort to see Bahá'u'lláh, but he was recognised and expelled. He, like a few others who reached 'Akká in those early days, was only able to catch a glimpse from beyond the moat of His face in the window.[5]

In the earliest part of 1869, Ḥájí Amín went with a group of pilgrims to Mecca and then travelled on to 'Akká. Though he was able to enter the city, he could not get into the Most Great Prison, so he met Mírzá Áqá Ján outside and passed over all the funds and letters he had collected. When he returned to Iran, he was the first to bring news of where Bahá'u'lláh was and the circumstances of His captivity.[6]

Still in early 1869, Ḥájí Amín and Ḥájí Sh͟háh-Muḥammad, the

Trustee of Ḥuqúqu'lláh, conceived a plan to meet Bahá'u'lláh. Knowing the dangers of trying to enter 'Akká, they bought a number of camels, disguised themselves as Arabs and went to the ancient city as merchants. Since camel selling was a common occupation at that time, the ruse worked and they found themselves inside 'Akká.

Their next problem was how to get word to Bahá'u'lláh that they were there. Somehow, they did so, and His response was that they should go to the Al-Jazzár public bath on a Friday, which was the one day a week Bahá'u'lláh was allowed to go there Himself. But He told them that they could only do so if they did 'not approach Him or giving any sign of recognition'. That Friday, the two pilgrims entered the chain of rooms that formed the bath and stationed themselves in the largest. Then they waited for Bahá'u'lláh's arrival. The moment that Bahá'u'lláh arrived, however, Ḥájí Amín became so overwhelmed with emotion at His majestic appearance, that 'his body shook, and he stumbled and fell to the stone floor, striking his head so severely that blood gushed out. He had to be carried out'.[7]

Afterwards, Bahá'u'lláh wrote a Tablet to Ḥájí Amín calling him the first pilgrim:

> Thou art the first one to attain the divine presence in His mighty, His Most Great Prison. Take heed lest what thou hast heard from the tongue of thy Lord, the Potent, the Powerful, be obliterated from thy heart. Make thou mention of Him all the time and call to mind the days when thou didst enter the most desolate of the cities until thou didn't present thyself before the face of thy Lord, the Ruler of the Day of Judgement, and achieved that which is ordained for thee in His preserved Tablet.[8]

In 1873, Ḥájí Amín made his next journey to 'Akká and was again able to be in Bahá'u'lláh's presence. Two years later, after travelling through the province of Azerbaijan along with Ḥájí Sháh-Muḥammad, he continued on to 'Akká to again deliver the funds collected and letters they had been given from the believers. In 1879, the two men trekked a second time to 'Akká, this time via Trabzon and Constantinople in Turkey. Returning from 'Akká, they went back through Azerbaijan either in late 1879 or early 1880 and were ensnared by the Kurdish rebellion of Shaykh 'Ubaydullah against the Ottoman Empire. During violence in the village of Miyanduab, south of Tabríz, Ḥájí Sháh-Muḥammad was killed and Ḥájí Amín shot in the leg. Ḥájí Amín managed to escape to Tabríz, where he spent a good while recovering from his wound.[9]

Following the killing of Ḥájí Sháh-Muḥammad, Bahá'u'lláh appointed Ḥájí Amín to be the Trustee of Ḥuqúqu'lláh and stressed to him that he was not to accept any funds from anyone unless he was completely sure the person was doing so 'with the utmost joy and devotion'. In one Tablet, Bahá'u'lláh wrote:

> O Abu'l-Ḥasan
> May my Glory rest upon thee! Fix thy gaze upon the glory of the Cause. Speak forth that which will attract the hearts and the minds. To demand the Ḥuqúq is in no wise permissible. This command was revealed in the Book of God for various necessary matters ordained by God to be dependent upon material means. Therefore, if someone, with utmost pleasure and gladness, nay with insistence, wisheth to part of this blessing, thou mayest accept. Otherwise, acceptance is not permissible.[10]

In another Tablet, Bahá'u'lláh wrote:

> Everyone must have the utmost regard for the dignity of the Word of God and for the exaltation of His Cause. Were a person to offer all the treasures of the earth at the cost of debasing the honour of the Cause of God, were it even less than a grain of mustard, such an offering would not be permissible. All the world hath belonged and will always belong to God. If one spontaneously offereth Ḥuqúq with the utmost joy and radiance it will be acceptable, and not otherwise.[11]

In 1882/1883, Ḥájí Amín journeyed through the areas of Yazd and Kirman and in September 1886, he made another trip to 'Akká. He returned to Iran through the Caucasus and Azerbaijan. In 1889, he returned to 'Akká again, arriving back in Iran in June.

In the 1880s, two cousins of the Báb established a business in Constantinople that became highly successful because of its honesty and fairness. This made it the focus of attacks by the followers of Mírzá Yaḥyá, Bahá'u'lláh's half-brother and breaker of His Covenant. One of

Mírzá Yaḥyá's followers, Muḥammad-'Alí, was made a partner in the business in order to quiet his attacks on the Bahá'ís, but by 1889, he owed the company a large sum of money and was vigorously attacking the Bahá'ís. Bahá'u'lláh sent Siyyid Aḥmad-i-Afnán, Ḥájí Amín and Abu'l-Qásim-i-Názir to Constantinople to clean up the mess created by Muḥammad-'Alí. Bahá'u'lláh later added Shaykh Muḥammad-'Alí (titled Nabíl-i-Nabíl, by Bahá'u'lláh) to the group. Bahá'u'lláh's emissaries were unable to force Muḥammad-'Alí to pay his debts, and he continued to create trouble for the Bahá'ís.[12]

In April 1891, the political situation in Iran was fraught, so Kámrán Mírzá, the Náyibus-Saltinih or Governor of Tehran, ordered the ringleaders of the agitators to be arrested and thrown into prison. For the Governor's own reasons, two Bahá'ís who had nothing to do with the revolt were also arrested and thrown into prison: Ḥájí Amín and Mullá 'Alí-Akbar (see Chapter 8). They were jailed initially in Tehran and then transferred to Qazvín and what Bahá'u'lláh called the 'mighty Prison' in a Tablet known as *Lawḥ-i-Dunyá*, written upon their arrest:

> Praise and thanksgiving beseem the Lord of manifest dominion Who hath adorned this mighty Prison with the presence of their honours 'Alí-Akbar and Amín, and hath illumined it with the light of certitude, constancy and assurance. The glory of God and the glory of all that are in the heavens and on the earth be upon them.[13]

The Tablet also contains the well-known prayer for the Hands of the Cause (Light and glory, greeting and praise be upon the Hands of His Cause . . .).

At first, on 14 May 1891, the French Minister, M. de Balloy, sent a dispatch that indicated that the two Bahá'ís were to be put to death:

> They announced, for yesterday, the execution of the two Bábís who would each be attached to the mouth of a canon, but it did not take place.
>
> The situation is certainly serious . . . but there is no need to hide the fact that one aspect of the agitation is a sham and the result of different intrigues. Bábism, which is a scapegoat, is a philosophical and religious doctrine much superior to the sensualist dogmas of Islam . . . To consider them responsible would be unjust; to proceed

> against them with bloody or cruel repressions would only result in exasperating them and awakening the heroism of which they have given proof at other times.[14]

Obviously, it was a threat never carried out.

Náṣiri'd-Dín Sháh was impressed by his Bahá'í prisoners and had a photograph taken of Ḥájí Ákhund and Ḥájí Amín, both with chains around their necks and their feet in stocks. The men exude absolute resignation and calm, and appear unperturbed by their afflictions. 'Abdu'l-Bahá was so impressed by the photograph that He placed a copy in the hallway across from His room in 'Akká.[15]

Though 'Alí-Akbar was released after two years, 18 months of which were in Qazvín, Ḥájí Amín was kept imprisoned for an additional year and 'suffered gravely, his legs in fetters and a chain around his neck. His jailers, in order to torment him, would add castor oil to his food. With manifest resignation and submission, he would neither complain nor refuse the food, eating as though nothing were amiss'.[16]

After finally being released from prison in 1894, Ḥájí Amín returned to the work he had been doing before his imprisonment – travelling around the country collecting contributions as the Trustee of Ḥuqúqu'lláh and making periodic trips to 'Akká to give the funds and the many letters to 'Abdu'l-Bahá. But with the passing of Bahá'u'lláh, he had the added task of promoting and explaining the Covenant as he visited the Bahá'ís. His travels took him through Khurásán, Turkistan, Ottoman Turkey, Egypt and Syria.[17]

On 19 December 1912, Ḥájí Amín arrived in London, travelling via Paris. The trip was apparently uneventful, except for the section between Paris and London, which he did twice. Since he spoke neither French nor English, he carried letters with names and addresses to help him reach his destination. Somehow, after leaving Paris and crossing the English Channel, he inexplicably found himself back in Paris. When finally encountering 'Abdu'l-Bahá in London, the Master joked that the Ḥájí 'could not forsake the delights of Paris and had to hurry back there'.[18] Aḥmad Sohrab noted that 'it was most interesting to see dear Haji Ameen this morning coming in with the other Persians in the most reverential and happy frame of mind to ask . . . what they should do'.[19]

The day after his arrival, Ḥájí Amín visited 'Abdu'l-Bahá. Aḥmad

Sohrab described what happened when Ḥájí Amín opened his handkerchief, in which he carried letters from Persian Bahá'ís:

> What caught my eyes at first glance were two small loaves of bread and an apple which were sent from a Baha'i from far off Russia. This was all this poor man could send to the Beloved with his devotion and love. 'Abdu'l-Bahá looked at this love offering with such tenderness, with such joy and kindness in his eyes, that I shall never forget it. He ate a piece of the stale bread and gave the rest to Said Asadullah for him to serve the rest at the table.[20]

Ḥájí Amín went with 'Abdu'l-Bahá to Scotland and back to London, and then on to Paris. While in the French capital, 'Abdu'l-Bahá sent Ḥájí Amín at the head of a delegation to call on the Persian Minister in Paris.[21] On 7 February, Ḥájí Amín and six other Persians left Paris for Persia. 'Abdu'l-Bahá sent all of the other Persians to see them off.[22]

In 1916, with his advancing age, Ḥájí Amín chose Ḥájí Ghulam-Riḍá to be his assistant for Ḥuqúqu'lláh, and 'Abdu'l-Bahá approved his choice.

For the next six years, Ḥájí Amín probably continued his travels around Iran as the Trustee of Ḥuqúqu'lláh, but the details are not known. In 1922, he visited the family of Alí Kuli Khán in Tehran. Florence Khán, who had met him in 1906 when he told her that he had made 19 pilgrimages to the Holy Land, wrote that

> Ḥájí Amín was the old man who lived nowhere, but journeyed here and there on his donkey, staying briefly with the believers in their homes. Loved and revered, the trustee of the Ḥuqúqu'lláh (Right of God), he was the keeper of the purse, his duty being to collect funds for the Faith . . . he was now, in 1922, eighty-six years old. Feeble, but his spirit and presence like the freshest rose, and his eyes as shining as a boy's.
>
> He had now served the Faith some fifty-nine years. When he first came into the presence of Bahá'u'lláh he gave up his entire fortune and all the rest of his life to the Manifestation. Homeless now, he was told by 'Abdu'l-Bahá that his nest was everywhere, and wherever he served and taught he would eat and sleep. All his children and grandchildren had prospered, and they would send him thousands of túmáns for the Faith.[23]

As he grew older and weaker, Ḥájí Amín finally moved into Ghulam-Riḍá's home in Tehran and it was there that he ascended in the spring of 1928 at the age of about 92.

In describing his life, the Universal House of Justice wrote:

> He was a symbol of magnanimity and detachment. He had no worldly possessions, no home or shelter of his own. His habitation was in the hearts and souls of the Bahá'í friends who would receive and entertain him with warmth and love. Each one would impatiently await his arrival, to enjoy the sweet melody of his prayers and chanting of the Tablets, and the glad-tidings and encouragement he would bring. Every day he would bid goodbye to one family to spend the night in another household, illumining another gathering with his presence. He was continually on the move, travelling to most Iranian cities and being the trusted adviser of many Bahá'í friends in their personal affairs.
>
> During his long life he witnessed the last eleven years of the Ministry of Bahá'u'lláh, the twenty-nine years of the Ministry of the Centre of the Covenant, and seven years of the Guardianship of Shoghi Effendi. Towards the end of his life he became ill and frail and was confined to bed, living in the home of his friend and assistant, Ḥájí Ghulam Riḍá, who, at the express desire of 'Abdu'l-Bahá, had been appointed his successor as Trustee of Ḥuqúqu'lláh. Upon his passing in 1928, Jináb-i-Ḥájí Amín was named by the beloved Guardian a Hand of the Cause of God.[24]

5

MÍRZÁ ABU'L-FAḌL

(1844–1914)

Knight of Bahá'u'lláh Amin Banani wrote that Mírzá Abu'l-Faḍl was a 'scholar of towering intellect and prodigious erudition, who by any standard may well be considered the most learned man of the first century of the Bahá'í Era, was also a model of humility, detachment, service to the Cause, and servitude to his fellow-believers'.[1] 'Abdu'l-Bahá told a group in Haifa that 'In all this time I never heard him use the word "I" — "I said this" or "I wrote that."'[2] This is in spite of Mírzá Abu'l-Faḍl having written the powerful *The Brilliant Proof* in answer to an attack on the Faith by an American Christian minister, and *Miracles and Metaphors*, a collection of scholarly essays written in answer to questions put to him by Bahá'ís. But Mírzá Abu'l-Faḍl's humility was brought about by a conversation with an illiterate blacksmith who happened to be a Bahá'í.

Mírzá Abu'l-Faḍl was born in the town of Gulpáygán in central Iran in 1844. Many in his family were religious scholars so he went to Iṣfahán to study religion. When in his 20s, a student who had written a 1,400-page dictionary gave it to Mírzá Abu'l-Faḍl for his comments. The next day, Mírzá Abu'l-Faḍl gave it back saying that it contained two misaccented words. After a long examination by the learned scholars, he was proved correct.

By the time he was 30, Mírzá Abu'l-Faḍl had become the 'master teacher' at a prestigious Tehran seminary and had developed a reputation for being a scholar. As noted by Mr Banani, he had the veil of 'intellectual pride and traditional learning' which caused him to reject and ridicule any Bahá'ís he met.[3] But Mírzá Abu'l-Faḍl was brought back to earth by the simple, illiterate Bahá'í blacksmith, Ustad Ḥusayn-i-Nali-Band:

> One day as he [Mírzá Abu'l-Faḍl] waited at a roadside blacksmith shop for his donkey to be shod, the blacksmith said to him, 'Mulla, I have heard of some holy traditions of the blessed imams which I have difficulty understanding. Can you help me?'
>
> Abu'l-Faḍl assented.
>
> The blacksmith said, 'I have heard the mullas quoting a holy tradition on the subject of God's mercy in sending down the rains: that every drop of rain is entrusted to an angel of God who brings it down to earth. Is this tradition true?'
>
> Abu'l-Faḍl answered, 'Yes'.
>
> 'Again I have heard', the blacksmith went on, 'on the subject of the ritual uncleanliness of dogs: there is a holy tradition that angels do not descend to houses where dogs are kept. Is this true?'
>
> Again Abu'l-Faḍl answered affirmatively.
>
> 'Then', the blacksmith said, 'we should see no rain fall onto houses which have dogs. How is it that the rains, when they come, come down everywhere?'
>
> Abu'l-Faḍl was greatly perturbed by the man's conundrum, but his companions told him, 'Never mind that troublemaker. He is just a misguided Babi'.[4]

Mírzá Abu'l-Faḍl's intellectual pride was crushed by a Bahá'í who could neither read nor write, and that forced him to begin an examination of the Bahá'í Revelation. But his pride was not quickly quenched and it took another unlettered Bahá'í to guide him further.

In 1876, at the height of his career and before he had met the blacksmith, one of his students had asked him for help in rebutting the arguments of some Bahá'ís. When Mírzá Abu'l-Faḍl learned that a draper, 'Abdu'l-Karím, held meetings in his home for Bahá'ís and seekers, he began to visit him. Then the encounter with the blacksmith occurred, which the blacksmith reported to 'Abdu'l-Kárím, suggesting that since Mírzá Abu'l-Faḍl's pride had been hurt, it might be a good time for him to meet a Bahá'í teacher. The teacher 'Abdu'l-Kárím brought to talk with Mírzá Abu'l-Faḍl also had no education, but 'Every abstruse subject that Mirza Abu'l-Faḍl brought up during the discussion and every objection he raised was dealt with in simple terms and in such a manner that he could not question the validity of the arguments put forward by the Bahá'í teacher'.[5]

Mírzá Abu'l-Faḍl was shocked to discover that the unlearned Bahá'í could so easily refute his arguments, though he was a highly educated and intellectual Muslim. He requested a meeting with an educated Bahá'í of his 'own calibre':

> The meeting was arranged, but 'Abdu'l-Kárím did not invite a learned Bahá'í as Mírzá Abu'l-Faḍl had requested. Although uneducated, 'Abdu'l-Kárím in his great wisdom knew that a man who was so proud of his knowledge would be blind to the Message of God. He knew that what Mírzá Abu'l-Faḍl needed most was someone who could expose his real ignorance of true religion. No one would be better suited to carry out this than a simple believer devoid of academic knowledge but possessed of faith and spiritual understanding.
>
> When Mírzá Abu'l-Faḍl arrived for this meeting he found himself again confronted with uneducated people. In the course of discussion he was utterly confounded by the simple yet brilliant proofs which were put forward in support of the Faith and in answer to his questions. He marvelled at these men who were devoid of learning and knowledge yet possessed such a marvellous understanding of the mysteries of the Qur'án and other Holy Books.
>
> In the course of several meetings, discussions between Mírzá Abu'l-Faḍl and his unschooled Bahá'í teachers continued. As anticipated by his host, these discussions had a sobering effect on Mírzá Abu'l-Faḍl. Since his prime motive in coming to Bahá'í meetings was to disclose the absurdity of the claims of the Bahá'ís, he was remarkably humbled by his inability to refute the arguments presented by those few uneducated souls from among the believers, and his pride was badly hurt by the many humiliating defeats he encountered in the course of discussions with them.
>
> However, he requested his host 'Abdu'l-Kárím to arrange a meeting in which one of the learned Bahá'ís would take part, for he desired to have an encounter with a person of his own calibre so that he could establish once and for all his own superiority and demonstrate the falsity of the claims of the Bab and Bahá'u'lláh![6]

When Mírzá Abu'l-Faḍl finally did meet a learned Bahá'í, Mullá Muḥammad (Nabíl-i-Akbar — see Chapter 9), he later declared that 'By God! No one could ever be found capable of withstanding the force of argument of this great man of knowledge'. He also met with Mírzá Ḥaydar 'Alí. Years later, Mírzá Abu'l-Faḍl admitted that at these early meetings, his prime object, writing of himself in the third person,

> was to compel them to surrender and help stifle their growth. For nearly eight months he held many a debate with the learned of this Faith. At the end of this period he found that all his vain imaginings had been broken down and had vanished. He then began to tread the path of search after truth. He exerted all his efforts in investigating the proofs of this Faith . . . made extensive enquiries from both friends and foes concerning the history of the Founder of this Faith, studied the Holy Books attentively . . . and prayed in the dead of night and at dawn supplicating the Almighty in a state of utter helplessness and anguish to bestow upon him guidance and grant him a seeing eye – until at last, through the operation of the will of God, he acquired a penetrating insight into revealed religions, and his distressed heart was filled with calm and certitude.[7]

This was a difficult time for Mírzá Abu'l-Faḍl. Intellectually, he had been unable to refute the Faith, but his heart was still not prepared to accept it. Then the Bahá'ís gave him a copy of the *Kitáb-i-Íqán.* He read it with an 'air of intellectual superiority and was not impressed by it', commenting that he could write a better book. The next day, an important woman asked him to write a letter for her because he was a man of eloquence and a man unsurpassed in the art of composition. But when Mírzá Abu'l-Faḍl picked up his pen, he found himself completely unable to write a single line. The woman left in disgust and the ashamed Mírzá Abu'l-Faḍl remembered what he had said about the *Kitáb-i-Íqán.*[8]

Utterly ashamed and confused, Mírzá Abu'l-Faḍl then decided that he would not accept Bahá'u'lláh until He performed a miracle for him. He wrote a few questions on paper, which he put in a sealed envelope and gave to 'Abdu'l-Karím. He then put a blank sheet of paper in another envelope to be sent to Bahá'u'lláh, saying that he would have no doubts if Bahá'u'lláh could answer his questions. They then went to the home of Ḥájí Muḥammad Ismá'il-i-Dhabíh, who would forward the blank letter to Bahá'u'lláh. Mírzá Abu'l-Faḍl wrote about what happened next:

When we arrived, we learnt that the Ḥájí was not at home, but his wife . . . warmly welcomed us and insisted with such love and hospitality that we went inside . . . We entered a room in which there were books and a case containing Holy Tablets . . . She gave us permission to open the case if we wished and study the Holy Writings. As Abdu'l-Karím was unable to read, he asked me if I would read for him. Through courtesy which was characteristic of me I complied.

There was a Tablet written on blue paper [*Lawḥ-i-Ra'ís*] . . . As I read it, I came upon the story of the 'Show of Sulṭán Salím' [the puppet show] and I was fascinated by it. I found the passages to be of the utmost eloquence, lucidity and sweetness. The more I read it, the more I wanted to read. I had never in all my life come across such wonderful utterances, which captivated my mind and attracted my heart. But I was thinking of everything in my mind except that these were the words of God!

Then I came to these exalted words: 'Soon will We dismiss the one who was like unto him, and will lay hand on their Chief who ruleth the land, and I, verily, am the Almighty, the All-Compelling'.[9]

In this Tablet, Bahá'u'lláh prophesies the fall of the Turkish Grand Vizír 'Alí Pá<u>sh</u>á and the death of the Sulṭán. The passage floored Mírzá Abu'l-Faḍl and he wrote that

I contended that Bahá'u'lláh had made these statements and prophesies in order to mislead ordinary people and keep a hold on His followers. Otherwise it would not be possible for a person who was a prisoner by the order of a King to address him in such strong language and denounce him in such wrathful terms, especially when He was single and alone, without a helper in a foreign land

Anyhow, in order to rescue myself from 'Abdu'l-Kárím, I said to him, 'To possess the power of life over created things is a miracle the like of which has not been manifested by the Prophets of past' . . . Therefore I took back the sealed envelope and my blank letter addressed to Bahá'u'lláh and tore them up and declared that for me the fulfilment of these prophecies would constitute the proof and a criterion for truth. I also got a pledge that no one would talk to me about the Faith any more until these prophecies were fulfilled.

I thought to myself that the incident of going to the house of the

Ḥájí was not only an act of providence which relieved me of further discussion with the Bahá'ís, but also provided a way by which I would be able to guide these souls and rescue them from going the wrong way.

Five or six months passed by. During this period I often thought of Bahá'u'lláh's prophecy concerning the Sulṭán. Until one day I was passing by the Masjid-i-Sháh (the Sháh Mosque) of Tihrán. My eyes fell upon [two Bahá'ís].

These two men were standing in the street and talking together. As I was trying to shun the Bahá'ís and steer clear of them, I pulled my 'abá over my head and began to cross the road away from these two men. But they saw me and called my name, and I had no choice but to respond to their call. They said, 'Now the proof of the Faith of God has been established for you. The news of the dethronement of Sulṭán 'Abdul-'Azíz has reached here by telegram'. This news dealt me an enormously heavy blow. Although I knew what they were aiming at, I flared up with rage and shouted at them angrily, 'It is no concern of mine that the Sulṭán has been deposed. I am not a relative of his'. 'Did you not make your acceptance of the truth of this Faith', they reminded me, 'dependent upon this event?' I was so convulsed with rage that I walked away without saying farewell.

Knowing the immensity of this test, I was overcome with emotion and with tears flowing uncontrollably from my eyes I begged God to assist me so that I might not be misled. While I was in this condition, 'Abdu'l-Kárím and two others arrived. I was in no state of mind to invite them in, so I left the house and did not return home until late at night. These friends knew that I could not face them and that I had run away. They waited two to three days and then came. I apologized for my behaviour on that evening, and said to them that we must now wait until the prophecy of 'We will lay hand on their Chief' be fulfilled. I explained that the term 'lay hand on' did not mean natural death, for everyone dies. It signified that he must be killed.

My zeal in finding the truth had by now reached its climax. I visited all the learned men whom I trusted and discussed the principles of religion with them but found them helpless, while the proofs put forward by the Bahá'ís were, in my view, overwhelming and far superior.

A few days passed and the news of the assassination of the Sulṭán was flashed by telegram. I went out of my mind, and was utterly perplexed . . . At one time I would fight with God, at another I would turn unbeliever, then I would repent and beseech God to assist, guide and protect me. I went through such an ordeal that day and night I could not relieve myself from these thoughts. I could neither eat nor sleep. I could not eat. I only drank tea and smoked and wept.

One night I was roused from my slumber and I began to admonish myself in these words: 'It is about one year that you have been associating and arguing with these Bahá'ís. These men are illiterate and uneducated, yet they have asserted their ascendancy over you every time, they have adduced proofs and demonstrated the validity of their Cause. Although you consider yourself to be a learned man and a researcher in the Holy Books, commentaries and traditions, yet you know that these men are much more resourceful than you are. It is as if they are inspired and assisted by God, and the Holy Spirit speaks through them. You have also been a witness to their exalted character and heavenly virtues. Why then should you interpret their words as the breathings of the evil whisperer? You remember how enchanted you were when you read the story of the 'Show of Sulṭán Salím' in the *Lawḥ-i-Ra'ís*! How you were attracted by the eloquence and sublimity of those words! Now, you ought to read and investigate the writings of the one who claims to be the revealer of the Word of God with the eye of justice and fairness. If this Cause be untrue, the first to contend it is God. Therefore, its survival is impossible.

I arose, performed my ablutions and said prayers. I then took the Tablet of Bahá'u'lláh [*Lawḥ-i-Ra'ís*] which, although it had been in my possession for a long time, I had not been moved to read. I opened it, turned tearfully and with devotion to God, and began to read it. It was then that I heard the voice of God . . . calling me through the mouthpiece of this Manifestation, 'Am I not your Lord?' To that call reaching me from the Beauty of the All-Glorious, I responded with all my heart, 'Thou art, thou art!' I believed.[10]

Mírzá Abu'l-Faḍl was 32 at that time in 1876.

Upon becoming a Bahá'í, Mírzá Abu'l-Faḍl became aflame with the

Faith, which greatly helped the Bahá'ís, but was not good for his career. He was forced from his position at the Tehran Theological College in December 1876, and was then imprisoned for five months.[11] Manikji Sahib, an Indian, offered Mírzá Abu'l-Faḍl work at a Zoroastrian children's school in Tehran and he accepted gladly. Several prominent Zoroastrians who later came into the Bahá'í Faith were his pupils at the school.[12]

For the next ten years, the formerly acclaimed Muslim cleric earned his living by writing letters for those unable to do so. He was able to earn enough to purchase a donkey to ride on. Wealthy Bahá'ís offered to deputise him, but he always said that he relied on God for his needs. Darius Shahrokh wrote that he was continuously in a state of prayer and that 'in refusing any money from the believers, he wrote them that although at times the need necessitated selling of his clothes, but always God provided for him and if people would stop sending money and letters to him necessitating answers, he could spend his time transcribing tablets and thus earning a living'.[13]

In 1882, when large numbers of people were entering the Faith, the clergy and government increased their persecution of the Bahá'ís. Mírzá Abu'l-Faḍl was first confined for a month and then for 22 months. When released, he enjoyed seven months of tranquillity before again being thrown into prison for an additional six months. He was finally released in February 1886. It was at that time that he received a Tablet from Bahá'u'lláh commanding him to arise in His name and invite the people of the world to come to him, so he could tell them of *The Most Great Announcement,* show them *The Most Exalted Horizon* and enable them to hear *The Voice of God.* To Mírzá Abu'l-Faḍl, this meant travelling to teach the Faith, and for the next three years he visited many parts of Iran.

During these years, Mírzá Abu'l-Faḍl was very reluctant to write anything 'because the Supreme Pen was moving'. Then in 1887, he encountered Mírzá 'Alí-Muḥammad, known as Varqá (see Chapter 6). While in the presence of Bahá'u'lláh, Varqá asked if he should employ Mírzá Abu'l-Faḍl as a writer. Bahá'u'lláh commanded it. So, the next year in Hamadán, Mírzá Abu'l-Faḍl wrote answers to questions from a Jewish doctor.[14]

Mírzá Abu'l-Faḍl was a very good debater. At one point, he met Reverend Robert Bruce, a missionary working in Iṣfahán, who was boasting about his political and financial influence. Adopting the approach that the blacksmith had taken years earlier, Mírzá Abu'l-Faḍl asked:

Mírzá Abu'l-Faḍl: Would you please tell me the extent of your contribution?
Rev Bruce: So far I have donated one half million túmáns for famine relief and if necessary I could provide several times more.
Mírzá Abu'l-Faḍl: What is your political influence?
Rev Bruce: Should fanatical Muslims close my church I could direct the governor, who is the son of Ẓillus-Sulṭán, to open it with his own hands.
Mírzá Abu'l-Faḍl: What are your educational qualifications?
Rev Bruce: I am graduate of a university from a foremost country.
Mírzá Abu'l-Faḍl: Being so richly endowed with such influence and knowledge, how many souls have you been able to convert to Christianity since you came to Isfahan?
Rev Bruce: About thirty.
Mírzá Abu'l-Faḍl: Of these, how many are steadfast and do sincerely believe?
Rev Bruce: (After a brief pause) About ten to fifteen.
Mírzá Abu'l-Faḍl: Of these, how many will remain steadfast and are willing to give their lives in the face of persecution?
Rev Bruce: Perhaps two or three.
Mírzá Abu'l-Faḍl: With your permission, I wish to recount my position. I have no assets and at times have nothing to subsist on. My position and political influence is such that for being a Bahá'í I could be put to death, with those killing me receiving honor from the government. As to my knowledge, I received my education in religious schools, but I am the product of an ignorant and dark society. In spite of all these short comings, I have spoken to about one hundred people since my arrival in this city a month ago. Twenty-four souls among them have embraced the Faith and every one of them is willing to lay down his life as many other Bahá'ís have done. Now, in your fair judgment, who in this day is assisted by the Holy Spirit, you or I?

Reverend Bruce had no answer – a simple checkmate made by Mírzá Abu'l-Faḍl.[15]

Bahá'u'lláh sent Mírzá Abu'l-Faḍl to Russian Turkmenistan in 1886, and he remained in that area until 1894. He travelled to 'Is͟hqábád, Buk͟hárá and Samarkand. When in 'Is͟hqábád, he was a witness to the events surrounding the martyrdom of Ḥájí Muḥammad Riḍá and became the main Bahá'í spokesman at the trial of the murders.[16] Bahá'u'lláh had sent Ḥájí Muḥammad Riḍá to 'Is͟hqábád and with his aid, the Bahá'í Faith made remarkable progress. The clergy, highly irate at this success, sent two men to murder Ḥájí Muḥammad Riḍá. The murderers were soon caught and convicted. While the killers were awaiting execution, relatives of the men begged the Bahá'ís to ask the Governor to commute the sentences. Mírzá Abu'l-Faḍl and another Bahá'í went to the Governor and asked that the murderers either be absolved of their crime or to mitigate the sentence of death. Impressed 'by the attitude of the Bahá'ís and their willingness to forgive the assassins', the Governor commuted the sentences.[17]

At one point, Abu'l-Faḍl received a Tablet from Bahá'u'lláh which said that he 'gazes upon the horizons'. He didn't know what that phrase meant at the time, but within two years, he had begun his world travels.[18]

Bahá'u'lláh ascended in 1892 while Mírzá Abu'l-Faḍl was still in Turkmenistan. He was one of the few Apostles of Bahá'u'lláh who did not meet Him. Mírzá Abu'l-Faḍl's reason for why he didn't was because he considered himself to be 'so unworthy, that he felt unable to seek permission to attain His presence'.[19]

In 1894, 'Abdu'l-Bahá told Mírzá Abu'l-Faḍl to come to Haifa.[20] This was the beginning of his 'gazing at horizons'. Mírzá Abu'l-Faḍl was absolutely submissive to the will of 'Abdu'l-Bahá. He would not allow even the smallest deviation from the desires of either Bahá'u'lláh or 'Abdu'l-Bahá. One day, Ḥusayn-i-Rúḥí was in 'Akká and told Mírzá Abu'l-Faḍl about Bahá'u'lláh's disapproval of smoking, as revealed in the *Lawḥ-i-Duk͟hán*. Ḥusayn did not even finish reading before Mírzá Abu'l-Faḍl 'took his cigar case, threw it out in the street and said that this was the end of smoking for him'. Mírzá Abu'l-Faḍl had been a chain-smoker, rolling his own cigarettes by hand and lighting a new one from the old, smoking non-stop from morning till night. He then said: 'O Rúḥí Effendi, I have been smoking for fifty-five years and I am addicted to it. And, soon you will see that because of the effect of nicotine a member of my body will be paralysed'. This prophesy quickly became true and one of Mírzá Abu'l-Faḍl's arms was paralysed for the next two years. Doctors insisted that he resume smoking to regain the use of his arm, but he refused, saying, 'I prefer to die than to disobey 'Abdu'l-Bahá'.[21]

After ten months, the Master sent him to Cairo and the Al-Azhar University, one of the best-known Islamic centres of learning. 'Abdu'l-Bahá told him not to reveal that he was a Bahá'í, and he quickly became known for his interpretations of religious scriptures. Both scholars and professors were soon sitting at his feet, some believing that he had divine powers. When he finally revealed that he was a Bahá'í, 30 of the students became Bahá'ís. They were all expelled from the university.

Mírzá Abu'l-Faḍl was soon corresponding with people from around the world, as 'Abdu'l-Bahá kept referring questions about interpretation of scriptures to him. The first discussion of the Faith in print was a magazine article he wrote. It provoked severe objections which resulted in his being able to write more. In answer to an attack by Muslim clergy in the Caucasus in 1898, he published an 800-page book called *Faráid* (The Matchless Gems). He wrote only a single draft and needed no margin notes or corrections. Two years later, in 1900, he wrote *Miracles and Metaphors*, which caused an uproar amongst the Muslim clergy.[22]

In December 1900, 'Abdu'l-Bahá sent Laura Barney to escort Mírzá Abu'l-Faḍl to America. The pair tarried in Paris for three months and Mírzá Abu'l-Faḍl was able to help educate the Bahá'ís there, including May Bolles (who would become May Maxwell) and Agnes Alexander, a future Hand of the Cause. Thirty seekers accepted the Faith during his stay in the city. 'Abdu'l-Bahá sent Mírzá Abu'l-Faḍl to America because of the actions of Ibráhím Kheiralla, the man who had introduced the Faith to most of the early American believers. Kheiralla's teachings diverged significantly from those of Bahá'u'lláh, and Mírzá Abu'l-Faḍl was sent there to help deepen the nascent Bahá'í community.[23]

The Master sent Ali Kuli Khán to translate for Mírzá Abu'l-Faḍl and he held regular classes for the American Bahá'ís and seekers so that they would understand the true teachings of the Faith. Beginning his work in Chicago, Mírzá Abu'l-Faḍl later moved to Washington DC and then to Green Acre. Though he was a reclusive scholar and had rarely given large public talks, Mírzá Abu'l-Faḍl rose to the occasion as large crowds attended his talks about the Bahá'í Faith.[24]

'Abdu'l-Bahá was so highly impressed with the brilliance of Mírzá

Abu'l-Faḍl's American work that He asked him to write a treatise about the Faith, which Ali Kuli Khán was to translate into English. The result was *The Bahá'í Proofs*, published in 1902, which explained the 'timeless truths of the Faith, the coming of the Day of God, oneness of religion, also God being absolute unity beyond characterization'.

On 9 November 1903, Mírzá Abu'l-Faḍl left America. He told the crowd who came to see him off that 'Thirty-two years ago when I left my home town I still was a Muslim. My mother, sister and brothers gathered to say goodbye. Three years later when I became a Bahá'í they abandoned me and left me alone. Now consider the bounties of our Master who has granted me hundreds of friends'.[25]

When Mírzá Muḥammad-'Alí and his cohorts were at the height of their rebellion, Mírzá Abu'l-Faḍl would go and talk with them in the hope of bringing them back from spiritual death. One day, 'Abdu'l-Bahá asked, "Why do you go visit Mírzá Muhammad-'Alí (the arch-Covenant-breaker)?" He responded, "Your Excellency, was His Holiness the Exalted One [the Báb] the true One or was He not?" 'Abdu'l-Bahá said, "He was the true One." Mírzá Abú'l-Faḍl then said, "If You say that He was not, I will accept." When 'Abdu'l-Bahá remained silent, the depth of Mírzá Abu'l-Faḍl's faith, certitude, constancy and firmness in the Covenant were proven.

In 1904, 'Abdu'l-Bahá told Mírzá Abu'l-Faḍl, 'If I were in your place, I would go to Egypt and engage in teaching and educating students in the Qur'án. It is not too late. You can do so now'.[26] Because of this request, Mírzá Abu'l-Faḍl established himself in Cairo for the final ten years of his life and became a part of many pilgrims' journeys after they were told by 'Abdu'l-Bahá to visit him and learn more about the Faith. The Master sent Lua Getsinger to him, saying that he would tell her and her companions some of the things they wished to know. He also sent Ethel Rosenberg, Fanny Knobloch, Alma Knobloch, Emogene Hoagg and Ida Finch — interestingly, all women. Besides knowledge, Mírzá Abu'l-Faḍl gave Fanny his prayer beads, his most precious possession, saying, 'My Lord gave them to me'.[27]

When Emogene Hoagg's pilgrimage was over, 'Abdu'l-Bahá suggested that she study with Mírzá Abu'l-Faḍl. Emogene wrote:

> For four weeks Mírzá Abu'l-Faḍl received me at the home of Nurulláh Effendi twice a day, morning and evening, and gave me

such explicit instruction on the Bible that for the first time this Book became an open page. It was not without difficulty that I got the explanation. Sometimes Nurulláh Effendi would give me the meaning in Italian, and at other times Aḥmad Yazdí Effendi would translate into French. Then I would put their words into English. After about two weeks Anton Effendi Haddad was sent to Port Saíd, and he translated directly into English. Almost every evening five or six of the Bahá'í brothers would meet with us to hear Mírzá Abu'l-Faḍl's explanations. Those were wonderful days, – to think that I, an American woman, was able to meet with these Bahá'í brothers of a different nationality and in a foreign country, and to feel so perfectly at home, just as though I had been with my own family! Probably to them it was yet a more novel experience to be able to meet with an unveiled sister. All this has been brought about by the power of Bahá'u'lláh.[28]

When Hooper Harris and Harlan Ober passed through Egypt in 1906 on their way to see 'Abdu'l-Bahá, they visited Mírzá Abu'l-Faḍl specifically to ask about teaching in India because of his experience there. Demonstrating his complete humility, the famous scholar refused to give them advice, saying that 'Abdu'l-Bahá would tell them all they needed to know. When his visitors persisted, Abu'l-Faḍl said, 'When the sun shines, the candles go out'.[29]

Another instance that illustrated Mírzá Abu'l-Faḍl's humility was in 1913 when he was hosting a meeting in his home in Egypt:

> . . . there were about twenty sheiks who had come over from Alexandria to visit him. One who seemed to be the leader was a very learned and gorgeously attired young sheik, who said with some pride that he had been educated in the oldest university in the world. He was the editor of a magazine in Alexandria and had come to interview Mirza Abu'l-Fazl, who for more than an hour had been listened to with absorbed attention. His talk was interspersed with an occasional jest and his sharp eye would glance from one face to another to see if his point was understood . . .
>
> Suddenly Abdul-Baha appeared. Mirza Abu'l-Fazl . . . stood with his head bowed, his whole attitude changed. He immediately became the most humble and respectful of servitors. Then quickly

arranging a chair for Abdul-Baha, he told him . . . the subject under discussion. Abdul-Baha continued the subject . . .[30]

Isabel Fraser frequently visited Mírzá Abu'l-Faḍl in Alexandria and wrote that

> with all his book-learning, he was not at all bookish . . . the same dignity and impressiveness with which he discussed a verse of the Qurán with the learned sheiks, he put into the meeting of some sojourning American, often finishing with a personal pleasantry, for he was a ready humourist and made his guests instantly at ease. He had the placidness of a child and the air of one who was never in a hurry and had plenty of time to make radiantly happy the place where God had placed him.[31]

'Abdu'l-Bahá Himself told a story about Mírzá Abu'l-Faḍl. Apparently Mírzá Abu'l-Faḍl had difficulties with all the questions from American and English women, and their persistence in wanting answers. One day a group of women went to Mírzá Abu'l-Faḍl's home and knocked on the door, but there was no answer. Undeterred, they continued to knock until a voice, obviously Mírzá Abu'l-Faḍl's, spoke in English from the other side of the closed door: '*Abu'l-Faḍl not here*'. This convulsed the women with laughter so much so that the hidden object of their desire was also heard laughing from the inside.[32]

In 1911, a Presbyterian minister, Peter Easton, met 'Abdu'l-Bahá in London. Easton had been a missionary in Iran. After meeting 'Abdu'l-Bahá and reading the newspaper accounts of His visit, Easton launched a vicious attack on the Faith. In writing about Bahá'u'lláh and then 'Abdu'l-Bahá, Easton wrote:

> In short, he was a moral and spiritual monster, who exalted himself against all that is called God or what is worshiped. To become a Bahai means to put this anti-Christ in the place of the God and Father of our Lord Jesus Christ. This is what the people of Great Britain are now invited to do . . .
>
> I am sorry for Abdul Baha. Brought up in this terrible system, he is entangled in its meshes . . . May God in great mercy open his eyes to behold the truth as it is in Jesus . . .[33]

Ḥabíb Mu'ayyad brought Easton's article to Mírzá Abu'l-Faḍl. He wrote that

> I took it to the esteemed Mírzá Abú'l-Faḍl and explained the situation to him, briefly outlining the content of the pamphlet. Residing in a hostel, the honored Mírzá Abú'l-Faḍl was ill and bed-ridden, but immediately rose, placed his 'abá over his shoulders, and instructed me to take pen and paper to take down dictation of his rebuttal. For about one hour he dictated, and I wrote. It was not finished, but he grew very tired and had to return to bed, saying, 'You go now and when I feel better, I will finish composing the reply.'"
>
> The following day, I went to the hostel [to visit Mírzá Abú'l-Faḍl] and he informed me, 'I have completed the reply to Peter Z. Easton. Submit it by post to the presence of 'Abdu'l-Bahá to do with it as He deems appropriate.'[34]

'Abdu'l-Bahá received the long treatise while in New York and immediately ordered it to be translated into English and published. Mírzá Abu'l-Faḍl's answer became *The Brilliant Proof* and was published in 1912.

In late January 1913, while 'Abdu'l-Bahá was in Paris, he received news that Mírzá Abu'l-Faḍl was ill. He sent a cable to Egypt stating: 'He is me', indicating that the Bahá'ís there should treat Mírzá Abu'l-Faḍl as they would him. The Master said, 'Mirza Abu'l-Faḍl is very beloved to me. Mírzá Abu'l-Faḍl and Haji Mirza Heydar Ali are peerless and unique. They are perfect Bahais. They embody in themselves Bahai principles. Their value is not now appreciated. It will become known later'.[35]

With Mírzá Abu'l-Faḍl's health failing, 'Abdu'l-Bahá sent one of His sons-in-law and another believer to care for him. Then he was transferred to the home of a believer who had access to the best doctors. But on 21 January 1914, Mírzá Abu'l-Faḍl passed away at the age of 70. He was buried in the Cairo cemetery.[36]

When 'Abdu'l-Bahá was informed of Mírzá Abu'l-Faḍl's passing during lunch the next day, He immediately went to His room where he stayed until late afternoon. In the evening, 'Abdu'l-Bahá talked about Mírzá Abu'l-Faḍl, but with many silent pauses. Later He said:

> How erudite and learned Abu'l-Faḍl was. He had the knowledge of all religious books and the intricate laws and customs of many countries in the East and the West. He knew the doctrines of every sect and party. In the servitude to the threshold of Bahá'u'lláh he was My partner and associate. During the hours of grief he was the source of My consolation. In his humility he lived in the station of nothingness. I never heard the word 'I' from him. While weak and sick he refused to accept a servant and would prepare tea himself for his visitors. He had been imprisoned several times but I had never heard him complain about his hardship . . . No matter how much We want to console Ourselves, We cannot. While in Alexandria every time my heart was depressed, I used to go and meet him, and at once my depression vanished.[37]

'Abdu'l-Bahá later revealed a Tablet in Mírzá Abu'l-Faḍl's honour:

> This glorious soul was a luminous star, a bright lamp, a blessed and fruitful tree, a billowing ocean of knowledge, a fountain of everlasting life, and well-established in the Ark of Salvation. From the beginning of his childhood, he lived a life of utmost piety and spent all his days in acquiring perfections. He was either engaged in the worship of God or in the acquisition of knowledge and the arts until he heard the Voice of God and His summons and thus he hastened to the kingdom of God. He hearkened to the melody of the Concourse on High and focused all his attention on the 'Abhá Beauty. He became so attracted and so enkindled that all his friends and acquaintances were astonished saying: "What light is it that hath become ignited in this lamp? What grace it is that hath become manifest in this century?" He cut himself utterly from the world of human attachment and turned entirely to the world of Divinity. He closed his eyes to all the comforts, joys and glory of this physical realm and sought attachment only to the fragrances of the All-Merciful and the grace and bounty of the Godhead. He caused everyone who came to see him and ask him questions relating to the abstruse problems of faith to attain satisfaction and his blessed heart was such a fountain of truth and significance that he caused every thirsty one to be filled up. He wrote books and treatises establishing the Cause of the 'Abhá Beauty, some of which are published and

some which are not as yet published. He left his native land in the path of God and traveled in all parts. In every city he raised the cry of the advent of the kingdom of God and he gave the glad tidings as to the light of the Sun of Truth. He put forth proofs, whether rational or traditional, and in all, he had an eloquent tongue and an attractive utterance and illumined heart, an immense intelligence and perspicacity and a wondrous capacity. Until at the end, after many journeys and pilgrimage to the sacred shrines, he came to Alexandria and was My companion for several months and was engaged in his writing. Because of his wish to have a change, he went from Alexandria to Cairo and there he ascended to the Concourse on High. Like unto a nightingale, he flew to the rose garden of the Luminary of the world. Like a thirsty fish, he hastened to the depth of the infinite sea. He caused our hearts to burn with the fire of his bereavement. He caused our souls to shed tears like a candle. From all towns and cities, lamentation and crying hath been raised and eyes are tearful and hearts are burning. Yet that master of the believers in the Lord hath become freed from the narrow confines of this world and hath flown unto the limitless apex of joy. A drop has gone back to the Mighty Ocean. The ray hath returned to the Sun. He is free from the wilderness of separation. He hath ascended to the assembly of the lights of the Lord of the Covenant and is now immersed in His light and established in the 'Abhá Kingdom.[38]

6

MÍRZÁ 'ALÍ-MUḤAMMAD – VARQÁ

(c1856–1896)

The martyrdom of Mírzá 'Alí-Muḥammad, best known as Varqá, and his 12-year-old son Rúḥu'lláh, at the hands of the Persian government, is one of the most powerful stories in a Faith full of powerful stories.

In July 1845, Muḥammad Sháh, the king of Persia, had become very alarmed at the spread of the Faith of the Báb. He sent his most trusted and knowledgeable man, Siyyid Yaḥyá Dárábí, who would become known as Vaḥíd, to investigate and find out the truth about the Cause of the Báb. On his way to Shiraz to question the Báb, Vaḥíd stopped in Yazd and proclaimed his mission. But when Vaḥíd confronted the Báb, he was 'struck dumb' and instead of defeating the Báb, became His ardent follower. Leaving Shiraz, Vaḥíd again passed through Yazd and made another proclamation: that he had become a follower of the Báb.[1]

Many people in Yazd immediately accepted the Báb as a Manifestation of God, including Ḥájí Mullá Mihdí-i-Yazdí, the father of Varqá. Mullá Mihdí soon became a Bábí and began to boldly teach about the new Faith, both in Yazd and around the area. After one teaching trip in about 1877, he held a large meeting with 200 people in his home. Bábí meetings were usually secret but this one immediately attracted the attention of the Muslim clergy and the next day he was summoned to the home of the chief cleric. All the clergy but one demanded that he be executed. In the end, Mullá Mihdí was bastinadoed (where the soles of his feet were whipped) and then expelled from the city.

Taking his eldest son, Ḥusayn, and 22-year-old Varqá, Mullá Mihdí went to Tabríz. While there, they met Mírzá 'Abdu'lláh Khán-i-Núrí, who was the chief attendant of the Crown Prince Muzaffaru'd-Dín Mírzá and also a Bahá'í. 'Abdu'lláh Khán very much wanted Mullá Mihdí and his sons to visit him in his home, but his wife, from a high-class family of the Sháhsavan tribe, was bitterly hostile to Bahá'ís, in spite of her husband. They had one daughter and 'Abdu'lláh Khán's wife desperately wanted another child, but none of the remedies given her had been effective.[2]

Varqá was a poet of outstanding calibre, but was also very knowledgeable in the science of ancient medicine and well-versed in religious subjects.[3] When 'Abdu'lláh Khán learned that Varqá had some knowledge of medicine, he convinced his wife to invite him, along with his brother and his father, to their home for a consultation. She agreed out of desperation. That evening after consulting with her, Varqá prescribed a 'pearly pill'. Later that evening, 'Abdu'lláh Khán, who really wanted to spend time with the visiting Bahá'ís, quietly suggested to his wife that 'maybe they should ask Varqá and the family to stay as their guests to see if the medicine would become effective or not'. When she agreed, her delighted husband invited the visitors to stay in their home.[4]

After a time, 'Abdu'lláh Khán's wife became pregnant, whereupon he told her that 'he had pledged to God that whoever gives them the bounty of another child, he would give his daughter to marry him.' She was not happy about this suggestion because 'the thought of giving her precious daughter to a stranger who was not only a Bahá'í but also considered by her to be below their class, was very hard to swallow'. When 'Abdu'lláh Khán worried that if he didn't keep his pledge to God, they might lose the child, she reluctantly agreed, and Varqá and the daughter were married.[5]

Sometime in 1878 or 1879, Mullá Mihdí, Ḥusayn and Varqá departed on foot to 'Akká on pilgrimage. This was to be the third time that Ḥusayn attained the presence of Bahá'u'lláh, since he had gone twice to Baghdad before 1860 when the Blessed Beauty was there. On one of those visits, he had returned to Yazd with a copy of the *Hidden Words*, the first copy to reach Yazd, and intimated that Bahá'u'lláh Himself was 'Him Whom God shall make manifest'. He also told the Bábís of Mírzá Yaḥyá's defection from the Faith.

Because of bad shoes and walking such a long distance, Mullá Mihdí's feet became infected and by the time they reached Beirut, he was very ill. He insisted that his sons continue without him. After they left, he continued toward 'Akká on his own, almost dragging himself along until he came to Mazra'ih, where he succumbed to his illness. 'Abdu'l-Bahá built his grave with His own hands.[6] Bahá'u'lláh and His companions stopped one day at Mazra'ih, and Bahá'u'lláh revealed a Tablet of visitation that illustrated Mullá Mihdí's exalted rank in the Concourse on High.[7]

When Varqá entered the presence of Bahá'u'lláh, he became 'utterly magnetized by the onrushing forces of Bahá'u'lláh's Revelation. He truly became a new creation'. But the first time he saw Bahá'u'lláh's face, he was quite surprised because he knew that he had seen that face before. One day, after having been in His presence several times, Bahá'u'lláh said to him, 'Varqá! Burn away the idols of vain imaginings!' Immediately, Varqá remembered a long-forgotten dream he had had as a child. In the dream, he had been playing with dolls in a garden when 'God' arrived and took the dolls away from him and burned them in a fire.[8]

Though he should have been quite convinced of Bahá'u'lláh's station, Varqá still wanted further proof. One day while with Bahá'u'lláh, he thought to himself: 'I know that Bahá'u'lláh is the supreme Manifestation of God, but I wish He would give me a sign to this effect'. Instantly, a verse from the Qur'án came into his mind: 'Thou seest the earth barren and lifeless, but when We pour down rain on it, it is stirred to life, it swells, and it puts forth every kind of luxuriant growth in pairs'. Varqá's immediate response was to wish that Bahá'u'lláh would repeat that quotation. Some time later, the Blessed Beauty did just that, but Varqá still wanted more and wondered to himself if it could have just been an interesting coincidence. The moment he had that thought, Bahá'u'lláh turned to him and said, 'Was this not a sufficient proof for you?' Varqá was 'dumbfounded' and 'shaken', but he also understood.[9]

Varqá returned to Tabríz and his wife. His father-in-law introduced him to Crown Prince Muẓaffaru'l-Dín Mírzá, who recognised his knowledge and talents, and he told 'Abdu'lláh Khán to bring Varqá whenever there was a gathering of the learned. Varqá's poetry was very popular at these meetings and the Crown Prince honoured him with awards. At one gathering, one of the learned clergymen stated that

> These Baha'is used to serve dates in their firesides to convert the innocent Muslims. After discovering this, people avoided eating dates in firesides. Now, they have come up with a new trick. They make extract of date into a pill which the speaker holds between his fingers. As their bewitching words make the jaws of the listeners

> drop open, he shoots the pill into each one's mouth, and that is the reason for such a large number of conversions.[10]

Varqá's reply, the first time he had spoken other than to recite his poetry, was that

> I have knowledge of medicine and am aware of many extracts, but never heard about the date extract. Such pill-throwing requires years of practice and marksmanship so they don't miss the mouth, and thirdly, regardless of how eloquent a speaker, seldom does one see every jaw drop in awe, and finally, if the pill gets into the mouth, people still have to swallow it, which no one has reported.[11]

Varqá travelled extensively in teaching the Faith and suffered occasional hostility and opposition, both on the road and at home. In 1883, Varqá returned to his home town of Yazd to see his sister, Bíbí Túbá. Upon his arrival, the same Muslim clergyman who had bastinadoed his father and exiled him from the city, issued a death sentence on Varqá. The government, however, preferred to put him in prison, which it did. After a year in the Yazd prison, he was transferred to Iṣfahán, about 300 km away. He made the seven-day journey with stocks on his feet and chained, riding on a donkey. He avoided abuse from his attendant by pretending to be a deaf-mute.

Soon after his arrival at the Iṣfahán prison, a Bahá'í poet, Sina, who had himself just been released from prison, went to visit him. The guard told Sina that the prisoner was a deaf-mute. When Sina and Varqá saw and recognised each other, Varqá vocally greeted his friend, causing the other prisoners to yell out that the Bahá'ís had performed a miracle.

The prison in Iṣfahán was foul, and Sina set about getting him transferred to a better one. How he did so involved Ẓillu's-Sulṭán (a son of Naṣiri'd-Dín-Sháh and Governor of the province), a confidant of the Prince, Varqá's father-in-law, and Bahá'u'lláh Himself. Ẓillu's-Sulṭán hated the Crown Prince in Tabríz and sent his confidant to Bahá'u'lláh, requesting that the Bahá'ís kill him. Bahá'u'lláh, of course, refused. Later, when the confidant went to Tabríz, the Crown Prince had him arrested and sentenced to be hung. The Crown Prince's chief attendant, Varqá's father-in-law, interceded and the confidant was released. When the Bahá'ís in Iṣfahán learned about this, they went to the confidant and said, 'Varqá, who is in the foul prison, is the son-in-law of the man in Tabríz who saved your life. Now is your turn to return the favor'. Varqá was soon transferred to a prison for dignitaries, though he still wore the stocks and chains.

While in the new prison, Varqá was chained next to a prominent son of a tribal chief. Soon the chain-mate became a Bahá'í. Ẓillu's-Sulṭán would visit him, and Varqá's poetry charmed them both. This led to the stocks being removed from his feet, and eventually his freedom. Thirty years later, Ẓillu's-Sulṭán, shorn of power, visited 'Abdu'l-Bahá and said of Varqá that 'He was one of the greatest men in Iran, if not the greatest'.[12]

In about 1891, Varqá made his second pilgrimage to 'Akká, accompanied by two of his sons, 'Azízu'lláh and Rúḥu'lláh, and his father-in-law, 'Abdu'lláh Khán. Rúḥu'lláh was seven years-old at this time and he had his father's poetic ability. His intense poems demonstrate his purity of soul and his true understanding of the station of Bahá'u'lláh. All three pilgrims were completely enthralled by being in Bahá'u'lláh's presence. Once, when He was not feeling well, the Blessed Beauty asked Varqá, since he knew about medicines, to prescribe something for Him. That evening, Bahá'u'lláh called Varqá and told him that He had taken the medicine and as a patient, He liked His physician.

One day, Bahá'u'lláh talked about the station of 'Abdu'l-Bahá and His 'heavenly qualities':

> He said in the world there exists a phenomenon that in various tablets He had referred to as the Most Great Elixir. Christ had this phenomenon, and see what influence He exerted upon the world after His crucifixion. He truly revolutionized the world. Then He said, 'Look at the Master who so patiently deals with all kinds of people. He also possesses this power.' Varqa then realized who would succeed Bahá'u'lláh, and was filled with joy. He prostrated at the feet of Baha'u'llah, and begged Him to accept him and one of his sons as a sacrifice in the path of Abdu'l-Baha, to which Bahá'u'lláh consented.[13]

On another occasion, Bahá'u'lláh asked Rúḥu'lláh what he had done that day. The boy answered that he had learned about the return of the prophets. When asked what that meant, the boy repeated what his teacher had said. Bahá'u'lláh asked him to explain it in his own words. Seven-year-old Rúḥu'lláh said that 'it is like cutting a flower from a plant this year. Next year's flower will look exactly like this one, but it is not the same'. Bahá'u'lláh praised the answer.[14]

In 1893, Varqá made his third pilgrimage to the Holy Land, along with his sons 'Azízu'lláh and Rúḥu'lláh. Both 'Abdu'l-Bahá and Bahíyyih Khánum, the Greatest Holy Leaf, showed great respect for Rúḥu'lláh. One day, she asked Rúḥu'lláh how he found receptive people to whom he could teach the Faith. He replied that he looked into their eyes. When two of Bahá'u'lláh's sons came in, she asked Rúḥu'lláh to look into their eyes. After doing so, he said, 'They are not worth looking into'. Both sons later broke the Covenant.[15]

After returning to Tabríz, Varqá had serious difficulties with his wife, whose mother was enraged over the fact that both her husband, son-in-law and grandsons were dedicated Bahá'ís. Varqá considered divorce, but 'Abdu'lláh Khán would not allow it and advised him to just keep travel-teaching. When enemies of the Faith poisoned the Crown Prince's mind against his chief attendant, 'Abdu'lláh Khán was forced to flee Tabríz. Then, when his wife realised her husband would not return, she attempted to have Varqá murdered and offered a servant a large fee to kill him. Unbeknownst to her, the servant was a Bahá'í and he revealed the plot to Varqá.[16]

Varqá was forced to make a clandestine escape. In the middle of the night, he lowered all of his Tablets and precious possessions out of the window onto the street. He then left the house, retrieved everything from the street and escaped. The next day, he went back to the house and took 'Azízu'lláh and Rúḥu'lláh with him.[17] When the mother-in-law learned what had happened, she insisted that the local mujtahid issue Varqá's death warrant, dragging Rúḥu'lláh before him to prove the corrupting influence of her son-in-law. She demanded that Rúḥu'lláh say his daily prayer for the mujtahid. When Rúḥu'lláh said the Long Obligatory Prayer in a beautiful voice, the mujtahid rebuked the lady, saying that what she was trying to do to a man who had raised such a wonderful child was 'heinous and unforgivable'. The result was that both Varqá and 'Abdu'lláh Khán divorced their wives.[18]

Varqá managed to keep two of his sons, Ḥusayn and Rúḥu'lláh, with him and later married Liqá'íyyih Khánum, the granddaughter of martyrs. Of his other two sons, who were left with their mother and grandmother, the youngest died young and the other, Valíyu'lláh, was later rescued by an uncle and became a Hand of the Cause and Trustee of Ḥuqúqu'lláh.[19]

Varqá, 'Azízu'lláh and Rúḥu'lláh moved to Zanján and had a couple of tranquil years within a strong and loving Bahá'í community. Rúḥu'lláh, ever forthright and courageous, and his brother one day met a mullá riding a donkey:

> 'Whose boys are you?' Rúhu'lláh, usually being the spokesman, answered, 'Sons of Varqá from Yazd.' 'What is your name?' asked the mullá. 'Rúhu'lláh,' was the answer. The mullá said, 'Wow! What a great name. That is the title of Christ who brought the dead to life.' Rúhu'lláh answered, 'If you stop your donkey, I shall do the same to you.' The mullá, whipping his donkey, said, 'You must be Baha'is.'[20]

At one time, the Governor of Zanján arranged several meetings between the divines of the city and Varqá. Rúḥu'lláh was allowed to attend as well. The Governor brought in Bahá'í books and Tablets and had some read to the divines. Everything the divines objected to was answered, either by Varqá or Rúḥu'lláh, who answered questions with 'amazing courage, eloquence and profundity'. Since the Governor was sympathetic to the Bahá'ís, the divines were not able to attack them overtly.[21]

After two and a half years of more or less serene times, things began to boil again. Zanján had been the site of the massacre of 1,800 Bábís several decades previously, in 1850. 'Abdu'l-Bahá sent a Tablet that 'stressed steadfastness in the face of fierce storms of tests'. Realising that it was time to leave Zanján, Varqá and Rúḥu'lláh prepared to leave. On their final night, Varqá went to the telegraph office to say goodbye to a friend. A hostile mullá saw them there and reported them to the police, who informed the newly arrived Governor, a suspicious man. Father and son departed that night, but the next morning the Governor summoned the Bahá'ís for questioning. Finding that Varqá had left the city, he sent a group of men on fast horses to bring them back.[22]

When they were back in Zanján, the Governor began to verbally abuse them, but Varqá calmed him by saying, 'It is not very becoming of a great man to say such words to a person he does not know'. Impressed, the Governor requested that they be confined in his own quarters, and only put in chains at night. Varqá and Rúḥu'lláh were jailed for 16 days, and put on public display as though they were in a zoo. The Governor arranged meetings between Varqá and the Muslim clergy and delighted in the 'show', even though he sometimes had to intervene when the clergy began to fight over how to respond to Varqá's pronouncements. At one point, a mullá stated that he could reveal passages that were as good as Bahá'u'lláh's. Varqá asked whose words they would be and the mullá replied, 'Mine'. Varqá responded that Bahá'u'lláh always said that His words came from God. This led to a big argument between the divines about which 'proofs' were more important, the words of the Qur'án or the traditions of the Imáms.[23]

The Governor then sent Varqá and Rúḥu'lláh along with Mishkín-Qalam (see Chapter 15) to Tehran so that their fate could be decided by others. On the way, they stopped at a village called Dízij and the prisoners were dragged off and put in front of an assemblage of divines and notables. The group attempted to verbally subdue Varqá, but failing to do so, they turned on the 12-year-old Rúḥu'lláh, who gave them cryptic answers that encouraged them. But when they realised that the boy was actually ridiculing them, 'their wrath knew no bounds', saying 'This child is insulting holy divines'. The divines called for their deaths, but the soldiers escorting them instead took them to Tehran.[24] By the time the soldiers had delivered their prisoners to Tehran, the officer in charge had become a Bahá'í.

Their prison in Tehran contained 60 robbers and murderers. The three prisoners were brought in and chained together using the heaviest chain, known as Qara Guhar, which weighed 50 kilograms and was the very same chain that had been placed on the neck of Bahá'u'lláh. Ḥájí Ímán, Varqá's new father-in-law, was brought in and added to the chain. It was so heavy that Rúḥu'lláh could not support it, so they put a wooden support under it for him. They were also given no food.[25]

On 1 May 1896, Náṣiri'd-Dín Sháh went to the Shrine of Sháh 'Abdu'l-A'zím in Tehran as was his wont each Friday. Inside the shrine, an assassin pretended to present him with a petition then suddenly pulled out a pistol and shot him point-blank in the heart.[26]

When Hájibu'd-Dín heard of the assassination, he was incensed. Hájibu'd-Dín was with Náṣiri'd-Dín Sháh 44 years earlier when the misguided Bábís had attempted to kill the Sháh, and he had been extremely frustrated at not having been able to murder Bahá'u'lláh. In his rage and without authority, Hájibu'd-Dín 'barged into the prison like a mad dog with his face red with rage. He shouted that all prisoners should be locked in chains and stocks. The terror-stricken prisoners, not knowing what had happened, went numb'.

The four chained Bahá'ís were taken out into the yard and saw soldiers with weapons pointed at them and executioners dressed in red. Varqá and Rúḥu'lláh were unchained and taken away, leaving Mis͟hkín-Qalam and Ḥájí Ímán alone. When soldiers appeared with Varqá's clothes, they knew what had happened and expected the same to happen to them. Mis͟hkín-Qalam later wrote that 'As we sat down, stunned and unable to talk, the attendants surrounded us, discussing with laughter which piece of our clothing each one would be getting tomorrow. We were so numb that we did not care'.[27]

He asked one of the guards what had happened and was told the story. Varqá and Rúḥu'lláh had been taken into a room and as soon as Hájibu'd-Dín saw Varqá, he shouted,

> 'You finally did what you did.' Varqa, not knowing about the assassination, quietly answered he was unaware of having done anything wrong. Then Hajib asked Varqa, 'Do you want me to kill you first, or your son?' Varqa answered, 'It does not matter.' The fiend pulled his dagger, and plunged it into Varqa's stomach, and asked him, 'How are you feeling?' Unshaken and undaunted, that symbol of courage, that steadfast hero, with his last breath, exclaimed, 'I feel much better than you do.'[28]

Varqá's body was then dismembered in front of Rúḥu'lláh and he cried out 'Oh, dear father, oh dear father, take me, take me with you'. Hájibu'd-Dín told him that he would take him home with him, give him an allowance and get him a post with the king. But Rúḥu'lláh said, 'I do not want your allowance or the post. I wish to join my father'. Defied and rejected by one so young, Hájibu'd-Dín had him strangled.

Not having satisfied his blood lust, Hájibu'd-Dín ordered that Mis͟hkín-Qalam and Ḥájí Iman be brought in. But as soon as the door was opened, Rúḥu'lláh's body leaped up and jumped across the room. This terrified Hájibu'd-Dín and he dashed out in panic.[29]

The next day, the Bahá'ís were found to be innocent of the S͟háh's assassination. The new king, Muzaffaru'd-Dín S͟háh, was the Crown

Prince to whom Varqá used to read poetry in Tabríz. He was moderate and tolerant in his views and met another Apostle of Bahá'u'lláh, Mírzá Maḥmúd-i-Furúghí (see Chapter 7), from whom he learned about the Faith of Bahá'u'lláh directly.[30]

Varqá was named a Hand of the Cause of God by Shoghi Effendi and his son, Válíyu'lláh Varqá and grandson, Dr 'Alí Muḥammad Varqá, were both also named Hands of the Cause. His son and grandson also held the post of Trustee of Ḥuqúqu'lláh, one after the other.

7

MÍRZÁ MAḤMÚD-I-FURÚGHÍ

(?–1928)

Mírzá Maḥmúd-i-Furúghí came from the village of Dúghábád, which Bahá'u'lláh later designated as Furúgh, meaning splendour, light. His father, Mullá Mírzá Muḥammad, had been an influential and very respected clergyman who insisted on actual justice, no matter who the accused was. His enemies were not happy with his high reputation and schemed to bring about his downfall. Pretending to be interested in the claims of the Báb, they asked Mullá Mírzá Muḥammad to investigate for them. Mullá Mírzá Muḥammad and a group of men left Dúghábád and went in search of Mullá Ḥusayn. As they travelled, more and more of the group became tired or disenchanted, but five stayed the course until they found Mullá Ḥusayn at the fort of Shaykh Tabarsí. Mullá Ḥusayn and Quddús convinced them of the truth of the Báb and they all became Bábís. Not only did they become Bábís, they all stayed at the fort to defend it against the Persian army.[1]

Mullá Mírzá Muḥammad, who had never wielded a sword in his life, became a fierce fighter and was wounded by bullets or swords on five occasions, but survived to return to Dúghábád, where he began to teach the new Faith. At some point after 1863, Aḥmad of Yazd, the recipient of Bahá'u'lláh's *Tablet of Aḥmad,* visited Mullá Mírzá Muḥammad and his brothers in Dúghábád. Aḥmad recounted that

> I went to Furughí (Province of Khurasan) in the garb of a dervish, and spoke about 'Him Whom God shall make manifest' to Mulla Mírzá Muḥammad and his brothers. In the course of our discussions they became aggressive and fiercely assaulted me. In the struggle which ensued they broke my tooth. When the fighting had stopped and emotions subsided, I resumed my discussion, saying that the Báb had specifically mentioned that 'Him Whom God shall

> make manifest' would appear by the name of Bahá. They promised to accept the claims of Bahá'u'lláh should I be able to verify my statement. I asked them to bring the Writings of the Báb to me. They made an opening in the wall and took out all the Writings which were hidden for fear of the enemy. As soon as I opened one of them, we found a passage which indicated that 'Him Whom God shall make manifest' would bear the name of Bahá. They happily embraced the Faith of Bahá'u'lláh and I left them and travelled to other towns.[2]

Mullá Mírzá Muḥammad later suffered imprisonment in Mas͟hhad.

Mírzá Maḥmúd-i-Furúg͟hí followed in his father's outspoken footsteps. Described as:

> Of middle height, he was a dignified figure possessed of an attractive and handsome face, a thick beard which was dyed and a commanding voice. Dressed in the garb of the divines, his speech and his demeanour reflected his inner strength. One particular distinction of this man was the fact that he never, never engaged in backbiting, and no one in his presence ever committed backbiting, so much was he held in high respect. And if anyone wanted to break the code, he was denied the chance to proceed; for in whatever meeting Furúg͟hí was present, from start to finish, he kept people entranced by the recital of scriptures, the narration of the services and sufferings of early believers, and by relating something of his own life.[3]

When he was just a youth, Mírzá Maḥmúd went on his first travel teaching trip in his native province of K͟hurásán with another Bahá'í. Upon his return, he received a Tablet from Bahá'u'lláh that read: 'Verily, We were with thee when thou didst journey away from home, and didst travel in the land to propagate the Cause of thy Lord, the Ruler of this world and the Kingdom. We heard thy call giving the Most Great Announcement, and thy words regarding this wronged Exile'.[4]

In 1890, Mírzá Maḥmúd's teaching efforts in Dúg͟hábád raised a furore among the divines. The Governor had him arrested and sent to Mas͟hhad, but Mírzá Maḥmúd managed to secretly send a letter to Náṣiri'd-Dín S͟háh. The letter was written with a twig, using coal instead of ink, and so touched the S͟háh's heart that Mírzá Maḥmúd was freed.[5]

The divines in Mashhad, however, caused him to be banished to Kalát-i-Nadírí, 150 km north of Mashhad near the Turkmenistan border, where he was imprisoned for two years. During this time, Bahá'u'lláh ascended and the news devastated Mírzá Maḥmúd-i-Furúghí. He began fasting and on the fourth night, Bahá'u'lláh appeared to him in a dream and gave him new life. The Governor of Kalát became very friendly and asked him to preach from the pulpit each day. Because of the power of his speech, the divines demanded his exile, claiming that he 'had robbed half of the inhabitants of Kalát of their true faith'. The Governor weakly acquiesced and Mírzá Maḥmúd-i-Furúghí went to Bájgírán, near 'Ishqábád.[6]

Mírzá Maḥmúd made several pilgrimages during 'Abdu'l-Bahá's ministry. The date of the first one is not known, but 'a few years later' he went on his second, which was in 1894 or 1895. The first pilgrimage, therefore, was probably in the early 1890s. Immediately prior to the second pilgrimage, Mírzá Maḥmúd fell deathly ill, with a physician declaring his case to be 'beyond hope'. In spite of his illness, he asked for permission to go to the Holy Land, and was again with the Master.[7]

At this time, 'Abdu'l-Bahá was concealing the nefarious Covenant-breaking activities of Mírzá Muḥammad-'Alí and his followers. During this visit, Mírzá Maḥmúd was so upset by the grief of the Master at the activities of the Covenant-breakers that he offered his life as a ransom. 'Abdu'l-Bahá answered that 'You wish to be relieved of this world and repair at the earliest to the presence of Bahá'u'lláh. But, no, you must live. And the Covenant-breakers will soon receive their deserts'. 'Abdu'l-Bahá also unexpectedly asked what he had said to Áqá Jamál-i-Burújirdí. Some time previously, Mírzá Maḥmúd had been with Jamál, who had been involved in moving the sacred remains of the Báb with Ḥájí Ákhund in 1867, when Jamál made a disparaging comment about something 'Abdu'l-Bahá had said. Mírzá Maḥmúd had leaped to his feet in anger, and said 'You have waxed so insolent as to match the perspicuous text with your puny understanding', and yanked away the pillow Jamál was sitting on. When he told the Master, 'Abdu'l-Bahá replied that 'The Blessed Perfection inspired you to do what you did. He has joined the Covenant-breakers. Tell the friends to beware of him and not to be beguiled by him'.[8]

One day, one of Mírzá Muḥammad-'Alí's sons came with a bowl of fruit, saying:

Mírzá Maḥmúd soon departed for Yazd, where he arrived on 10 June.

Sometime later, Mírzá Maḥmúd went to Egypt at the request of 'Abdu'l-Bahá, visiting Port Said and Alexandria before arriving in Cairo[16], where he was able to be with Mírzá Abu'l-Faḍl. During a talk on the Covenant, he became very outspoken, so much so that Mírzá Abu'l-Faḍl (see Chapter 5) interrupted and asked him to show more restraint. Mírzá Maḥmúd replied that he had a Tablet from 'Abdu'l-Bahá telling him to 'be a leader of this legion'. Immediately, Mírzá Abu'l-Faḍl said 'I am the very first person to kiss the knee of this commander!' The two men then embraced and kissed each other's cheeks.[17]

From Egypt, Mírzá Maḥmúd went to Tehran, where his arrival prompted hundreds of Bahá'ís to gather to hear him speak. The enthusiastic response of the Bahá'ís to his talks alarmed Kámrán Mírzá, the Náyibu's-Saltanih, or Governor, of Tehran, who was also the son of Náṣiri'd-Dín Sháh. He sent spies to see what was happening. At one meeting where Mírzá Maḥmúd was speaking, one of the spies counted 900 pairs of shoes. Kámrán Mírzá ordered Mírzá Maḥmúd's arrest, but found only a servant in his house. After questioning the servant, who gave convincing arguments supporting the Bahá'í Faith, Kámrán Mírzá sent him with a message that he wanted to meet Mírzá Maḥmúd.[18]

Three days later, Mírzá Maḥmúd met with the Governor, who remarked on his guest's fearlessness and the fact that he had not run away after being summoned. At one point, the Governor referred to Bahá'u'lláh as Mírzá Ḥusayn-'Alí, which greatly angered Mírzá Maḥmúd: 'Upbraiding the Prince for his display of irreverence, he asked for the knife. "What do you want it for?" Náyibu's remarked. "To cut my throat, that you may drink my blood" was Furúghí's answer. "It seems that your thirst has not been slaked; perchance, drinking my blood may give you satisfaction."' Mírzá Maḥmúd then explained that Bahá'u'lláh lived on two planes, one human and one divine. The Governor then asked, 'I am told that you are convening many meetings; do you intend to cause mischief?'[19] Mírzá Maḥmúd's response was that

> Our books are in your possession; you can easily verify what they teach. Moreover, our community is composed of all sorts of people. Within every community you find both good men and bad men. We hold our meetings to warn the wayward, to still uncontrolled passions, to help the people distinguish clearly that which is right

> from that which is wrong. These are our reasons for holding meetings, for bringing men together, and not to foment discontent and disorder. Holding these meetings is also to your advantage. In the early years of this Faith, some of its followers, because of their ignorance of the true purport of the teachings of the Bab, made an attempt on the life of the sovereign which led to great upheavals and suffering. That event was never repeated, because at our meetings we help the people to be on their guard and not to slip into negligence and waywardness.[20]

Shortly after the death of Náṣiri'd-Dín Sháh in 1896, Mírzá Maḥmúd was able to meet with the new king, Muzaffaru'd-Dín Sháh. Suspicion for Náṣiri'd-Dín Sháh's death had fallen on the Bahá'ís. The king's Chancellor, 'Alí Atábac Saḍr-i-A'ẓam, who was sympathetic to the Bahá'ís, summoned Mírzá Maḥmúd and asked if the Bahá'ís were grateful or not for his support. Mírzá Maḥmúd replied that of course they were grateful. The Chancellor then noted someone was gathering large numbers of people together and asked if Mírzá Maḥmúd would meet with the Sháh and allay his fears that the Bahá'ís were involved.

Mírzá Maḥmúd agreed and, two days later, was escorted by two servants on horseback to the presence of the King. The King asked if he was the one attracting large numbers to his gatherings and Mírzá Maḥmúd said that he was. The Sháh was surprised at his fearlessness. Mírzá Maḥmúd replied that fear belonged to nonbelievers and people who have behaved wrongly. The Sháh then asked why he was holding the gatherings. Mírzá Maḥmúd listed the benefits: 1) the people are ignorant and need to be educated to behave well and develop trustworthiness, faithfulness, truthfulness and all the attributes of God; 2) they need to learn to avoid betrayal, sedition and corruption, and to work day and night for what is pleasing to God; and 3) that as people change their behaviour and develop their spiritual qualities and avoid negative behaviours, the world will become a heavenly realm and the people of the world will live in peace and harmony.[21]

The Sháh was pleased with his answer, but still had some reservations. Mírzá Maḥmúd replied that 'Either I am a wise and sane man or I am a madman. If I am insane there is nothing to discuss here anymore but if I am a sane man, then I am bound by the teachings of a religion that teachers trustworthiness, truthfulness, loyalty, enlightenment, purity of heart and discourages backbiting and dishonesty.'[22] Mírzá Maḥmúd then listed the qualities that determine the human station as given in the Bahá'í Writings and concluded by asking:

> If someone believes in a religion, do you think they would behave against the teachings of that religion? God Forbid God Forbid. If it is the will of the King that we should not have any gatherings, we will abide by the will of the King immediately.
>
> O Thou kind King if you see any shortcomings from any of the believers of the Baha'i faith please don't think that it is the religion that is wrong. In every religion, there are people that are wise and behave according to the teachings of the religion and there are also people that are ignorant, and don't understand the essence of the religion and they may behave wrongly. They may use force because they don't know how to behave better but please don't think that any of these behaviours belong to the Faith of Baha'u'llah.[23]

Afterwards, 'Abdu'l-Bahá said: 'Consider how a servant of the Abhá Beauty, all alone, outwardly bereft of all aid and assistance, converseth in the way he did with such a person, proveth equal to the task, and causeth wonder'.[24]

Mírzá Maḥmúd-i-Furúghí constantly travelled to teach the Faith with his outspoken style. Though the Bahá'ís may have been uplifted by his visits, others were not so happy. When he returned to Dúghábád in 1910, a mob set upon him, beating him severely and forcing him to leave the town. In October, when he was in Mashhad for the marriage festival of his daughter, a gunman fired several shots at his chest at close range, but only succeeded in wounding him a couple of times in the shoulder. Afterwards, Mírzá Maḥmúd wrote to 'Abdu'l-Bahá, who responded by reminding him that the chest of His Holiness The Báb was the target of such bullets and that the incident he had suffered was proof of the care and loving kindness with which he was encompassed.[25]

After having been shot and beaten, he travelled to 'Ishqábád and then, in November 1913, to Egypt while 'Abdu'l-Bahá was there. The Master then sent him to Haifa to announce His upcoming return, after which he stayed in Haifa for 80 days. When Mírzá Maḥmúd arrived back in Persia, he survived a second assassination attempt in Mashhad and then retired to Dúghábád, where he had to suffer constant attacks from his enemies.[26]

In 1922, Mírzá Maḥmúd was able to go on pilgrimage to meet Shoghi Effendi. He was described as 'Old in body, and young in heart, he has visited many towns and cities during the past year and now he is getting younger still by his having the privilege of being with the Guardian of the Cause, beloved Shoghi Effendi'. During the visit, Mr Faizi recounted that

> After he had attained the Guardian's presence for a whole week, he had heard nothing from the beloved Guardian's mouth other than descriptions of institutions of the Faith and how to strengthen them.
>
> Finally, the day arrived when, in the reception room, he found himself seated across from the Guardian. With his impressive and awe-inspiring figure, he was still the picture of devotion and surrender. Placing hands on his knees, he pleaded to the Guardian in a loud and eloquent tone: 'Beloved Guardian, during the time of the Master, he often bestowed verbal and written honorifics, but so far your honeyed tongue has not granted any such favours.'
>
> The beloved Guardian, with a winning smile and in utmost kindness and affection asked: 'For example, what title was granted to you?' Mr. Furúghí replied in his deep voice: 'He addressed me as the general of 'Aramram Army.'
>
> The Guardian responded in utter humility: 'I am one of the soldiers of this army. What can I say?" Mr. Furúghí was deeply moved by this heavenly reply; tongue-tied he quietly left the Guardian's presence and on foot went to Mt. Carmel to pay pilgrimage to the Shrine of the Báb. In a remote spot he prostrated and, seeking forgiveness with tears in his eyes, he kept saying: "Please forgive me; I was ignorant, now I know."[27]

As he left the Holy Land, the Guardian asked him to visit various communities on the way home and he faithfully did so. One of his first stops was Alexandretta in Turkey, where he stayed for two weeks at the request of the Bahá'ís. His arrival was announced in the newspapers and all the 'leading notables of the town, the mayor and the French Governor, called on him' and heard him speak of the grandeur of the Cause. The French battleship, Lorraine, was in port at the time and Mírzá Maḥmúd was invited aboard for tea.[28]

Mírzá Maḥmúd then went to Constantinople, where he spent a few months, after which he journeyed to Baku on the Caspian Sea. While in

Baku, he spent all his time teaching the Faith, holding several meetings each day, to the delight of the Bahá'ís.[29]

On 1 July 1927, while living in Dú<u>gh</u>ábád, Mírzá Maḥmúd was invited by a purported friend to a feast. But instead of friendship, he received poison with his meal. This caused a serious illness that he, in his advanced age, could not survive. He died a short time afterwards.[30]

8

MULLÁ 'ALÍ-AKBAR-I-SHAHMÍRZÁDÍ – ḤÁJÍ ÁKHUND

(1842–1910)

The future Hand of the Cause of God, Mullá 'Alí-Akbar-i-Shahmírzádí, better known as Ḥájí Ákhund, was born in the village of Shahmírzád in the province of Khurásán around 1842. His father had become a Bábí in Karbilá, but after the defeat of the Bábís at Fort Shaykh Tabarsí in 1848, his faith had weakened, with the result that his son Ḥájí Ákhund had heard of the Faith but was not a Bábí. As a young man, Ḥájí Ákhund married and, as he was eager for the knowledge of religious subjects, he went to Mashhad.[1]

Ḥájí Ákhund soon became very acquainted with the learning of the day, with secular studies, philosophy, and religious jurisprudence. He frequented the gatherings of philosophers, mystics, and Shaykhís, thoughtfully traversing those areas of knowledge, intuitive wisdom, and illumination; but he thirsted after the wellspring of truth, and hungered for the bread that comes down from Heaven. No matter how he strove to perfect himself in those regions of the mind, he was never satisfied; he never reached the goal of his desires; his lips stayed parched; he was confused, perplexed, and felt that he had wandered from his path. The reason was that in all those circles he had found no passion; no joy, no ecstasy, no faintest scent of love. And as he went deeper into the core of those manifold beliefs, he discovered that from the day of the Prophet Muḥammad's advent until our own times, innumerable sects have arisen: creeds differing among themselves; disparate opinions, divergent goals, uncounted roads and ways. And he found each one, under some plea or other, claiming to

> reveal spiritual truth; each one believing that it alone followed the true path . . .[2]

Ḥájí Á<u>kh</u>und first encountered the Bábís in 1861, when he was about 19 years old, and was given a copy of the *Kitáb-i-Íqán*. Reading it, and the discussions he then had with Bábís like Mullá Sádiq Muqaddas, the father of Ibn-i-Aṣdaq (Ch 21), 'ignited the fire of faith in his pure heart' and he accepted the Báb to be a Manifestation of God. 'Abdu'l-Bahá wrote that 'Like a fountain, his heart welled and jetted forth; meaning and truth, like soft-flowing crystal waters, began to stream from his lips.'[3]

Ḥájí Á<u>kh</u>und was not a reluctant warrior for the Cause. On the contrary, he tossed away all caution and charged out into the world to tell others of this new Faith. 'Abdu'l-Bahá wrote that 'For the sake of God he cast all caution aside, as he hastened along the ways of love. He became as one frenzied, as a vagrant and one known to be mad . . . Whenever trouble broke out, he was the one to be arrested first. He was always ready and waiting for this, since it never failed.'[4]

His teaching efforts brought large numbers of people into the Faith, but it also aroused the wrath of others and made persecution a conspicuous part of his life. Angered by his teaching, the students at his theological college forced Ḥájí Á<u>kh</u>und to flee Ma<u>sh</u>had for his home village of <u>Sh</u>ahmírzád. Unfazed, Ḥájí Á<u>kh</u>und openly taught the Faith in the town and soon had many enemies who compelled him to abandon it for Tehran, leaving his wife and child behind until things quieted. Things didn't change in Tehran. He unambiguously shared the teachings widely and, again, the clergy reacted with fury. As Ḥájí Á<u>kh</u>und walked the streets of the city, people would point and call him a Bahá'í.[5]

In 1867, Bahá'u'lláh instructed Ḥájí Á<u>kh</u>und and Áqá Jamál-i-Burújirdí to remove the casket containing the sacred remains of the Báb and secretly transfer it elsewhere for safe-keeping. Their first problem was that they couldn't find the casket. The two who had been told its location had died. Mírzá Músá knew its approximate location, but the person sent to find it could not. Eventually, an elderly Bahá'í located the precious remains.[6]

With the casket in their possession, Ḥájí Á<u>kh</u>und and Jamál-i-Burújirdí began to look for a safe place. To be discreet, they sent their wives on a scouting trip to the Shrine of 'Abdu'l-Azím in a village near Tehran to look for possible places. In the guise of pilgrims to the shrine, the women reconnoitred the area but were unable to find a suitable site. The two men disguised the casket as luggage, rejoined their wives who had been unsuccessful in their quest, and continued until they saw a run-down mosque. In preparation, they opened the casket, wrapped the sacred remains in a new silk shroud and returned them to the casket, which was then placed inside a new casket. After dark, they interred the casket in what they thought was a judicious manner. Their efforts, however, were not as clandestine as they thought. When the men went back the next day, they discovered the casket out and open.[7] Fortunately, the only thing missing was a piece of the shirt the Báb had been wearing when He was martyred. Because of this attempted robbery, a non-Bahá'í family came into possession of the cloth fragment. Initially, they refused to part with it, but when a Bahá'í doctor helped them, they gave him the sacred relic and it is now in the International Bahá'í Archives.[8]

Ḥájí Á<u>kh</u>und and Jamál-i-Burújirdí quickly headed back to the city with the casket in front of them on a mule. Approaching the city, they became very worried that the guards would examine what they carried, but a fortuitous thunderstorm sent a swarm of people through the gate, Ḥájí Á<u>kh</u>und and Jamál-i-Burújirdí with them. They soon found a house whose Bahá'í owner had recently died, and they concealed the casket in the basement. Ḥájí Á<u>kh</u>und quickly rented the house and lived in it to protect his precious charge.[9] Jamál-i-Burújirdí later broke the Covenant.

Ḥájí Á<u>kh</u>und guarded his treasure for the next 14 months, trying to keep it secret. He was not overly successful and more and more people would come to the house to pray. It was even suggested that it be turned into a permanent shrine for the Báb. In desperation, Ḥájí Á<u>kh</u>und wrote to Bahá'u'lláh asking what he should do. Bahá'u'lláh sent Ḥájí <u>Sh</u>áh Muḥammad-i-Man<u>sh</u>ádí to Tehran to secretly remove the casket and Ḥájí Á<u>kh</u>und was specifically told not to ask where it was to be taken. In complete obedience, Ḥájí Á<u>kh</u>und did not even look to see which direction Bahá'u'lláh's trustee went when he left the house.[10]

In 1868, Ḥájí Mullá Aliy-i-Kaní, the highest religious leader in Tehran, was the first to order Ḥájí Á<u>kh</u>und to be imprisoned. This mullá had been involved in the decision to martyr the Báb and was the recipient of a Tablet from Bahá'u'lláh in which he was strongly condemned and rebuked for his actions in relation to the Bahá'ís. It isn't known how long Ḥájí Á<u>kh</u>und was imprisoned this time, but it was probably not too long.[11]

Ḥájí Á<u>kh</u>und continued his teaching activities in Tehran for the next several years and became a well-known figure within the Bahá'í community. His teaching efforts were also directed towards his family and he was able to bring his father back into the Faith along with two brothers and four sisters.[12]

Badí', who delivered Bahá'u'lláh's Tablet to Náṣiri'd-Dín <u>Sh</u>áh, was tortured and killed for that act in July 1869 (see Chapter 2). Taherzadeh wrote that after the delivery of this Tablet, which clearly enunciated the teachings and principles of Bahá'u'lláh's revelation and the failure of the <u>Sh</u>áh and the Persian people to respond, a divine chastisement was sent down in the form of a severe famine. The famine was so devastating, that Ḥájí Á<u>kh</u>und wrote to Bahá'u'lláh and 'begged forgiveness for the people of Persia and asked for relief in their sufferings'. In His reply, Bahá'u'lláh 'affirms that the famine was God's punishment for the martyrdom of Badí' and that He had warned the Persians. He also wrote that had it not been for the Bahá'ís, He would have struck down the whole country. But He also 'responded favourably to Ḥájí Á<u>kh</u>und's intercession'.[13]

Then in about 1870,[14] Ḥájí Á<u>kh</u>und went on his first pilgrimage and spent six months under the love and guidance of Bahá'u'lláh Himself. While he was gone, his wife passed away and sometime after his return to Tehran, he married Fáṭimih <u>Kh</u>ánum, a descendent of the Safavid kings, who became his close companion for the rest of his life. When they married, Ḥájí Á<u>kh</u>und was living in a dilapidated room with a sheepskin and a kettle as his only possessions. Three days after the marriage, he was arrested in Tehran and thrown into prison for a second time.[15]

This time, it was Kámrán Mírzá, the Náyibu's-Saltanih or Governor of Tehran, and the son of Náṣiri'd-Dín <u>Sh</u>áh, who ordered his imprisonment. Ḥájí Á<u>kh</u>und was kept in a small cell with a chain around his neck and his feet in stocks for seven months. After his release, Ḥájí Á<u>kh</u>und travelled through the northern part of Persia to raise up the believers and encourage them into action.[16]

In 1882, Ḥájí Á<u>kh</u>und was back in prison in Tehran, again, but this time for two years, along with Mírzá Abu'l-Faḍl and Mullá

Muḥammad-Riḍáy-i-Yazdí. Their jailor, Náyibu's-Saltanih again, was impressed with the learned Bahá'ís and would invite them to explain the Faith to him. Some of these session lasted for hours. The prisoners were even able to prove the validity of Bahá'u'lláh's claims and explain His teachings. The knowledge of Mírzá Abu'l-Faḍl, the audacity of Mullá Riḍá and the spiritual qualities of Ḥájí Ákhund were a powerful combination that was able to proclaim the Faith at the highest levels.[17]

Ḥájí Ákhund's obvious spirituality impressed the Sháh, but the King was too afraid to meet him face to face, in spite of assurances from his son that Ḥájí Ákhund was not dangerous. Finally, the Sháh looked in at Ḥájí Ákhund through a window. Ḥájí Ákhund's calmness and dignity strongly affected the Sháh and he sent a photographer to capture the image of this man who was completely unperturbed by his fate.[18]

During these imprisonments and the ones to yet to come, Ḥájí Ákhund endured 'in a spirit of joy, of pride and of thankfulness to his Lord'. When an uproar happened, he would 'put on his turban, wrap himself in his 'abá and sit waiting for his enemies to rouse and the farráshes to break in and the guards to carry him off to prison'.[19] Other Bahá'ís tried to get him to be more careful or to hide himself away during certain times, but Ḥájí Ákhund replied:

> It is true that in the Holy Tablets we are commanded to observe wisdom. By wisdom is not meant to be fearful or to have no reliance upon God. It means to act with thoroughness, and to conduct oneself with truthfulness, benevolence and patience; it means to sow the seed of the teachings of God in the pure and goodly soil of the hearts. It does not mean fear or hiding.
>
> When I was a child, I fell into a river and was carried down the stream for a few miles. People were sure that I was drowned, but somehow I was thrown on the bank almost lifeless, and in the end I recovered. God saved me. On another occasion, I fell twice on a mountain, from a height of about one hundred metres. I survived, for it was meant that I should live. Besides, I have been captured many times, and from periods of six months up to three years I have been imprisoned, chained and fettered. On each of these occasions there was no hope of freedom. And yet many souls who were not as famous as I, but were worthy to lay down their lives in the path of God, have been martyred. But so far I have not. If it is the will

> of God, and if this incomparable bounty of laying down my life becomes mine, imagine what a great gift that would be! Furthermore, is it possible or conceivable to be able to run away from God's decree? On the contrary one has to speed up towards Him.[20]

The fact that Bahá'u'lláh wrote in one of his Tablets that the 'inmates of the highest Paradise have raised their voices and announced the glad-tidings that 'Alí-Akbar had entered the prison in the path of God', illustrates Ḥájí Á<u>kh</u>und's special station.[21] 'Abdu'l-Bahá further emphasised Ḥájí Á<u>kh</u>und's protection in *Memorials of the Faithful*: 'But observe the power of God! In spite of all this, he was kept safe. "The signs of the knower and lover is this, that you will find him dry in the sea." That is how he was. His life hung by a thread from one moment to the next; the malevolent lay in wait for him; he was known everywhere as a Bahá'í – and still he was protected from all harm. He stayed dry in the depths of the sea, cool and safe in the heart of the fire, until the day he died'.[22]

In 1887, Ḥájí Á<u>kh</u>und was imprisoned again, along with a number of other Bahá'ís, though it isn't known for how long. In October of that year, Bahá'u'lláh directed that Ḥájí Á<u>kh</u>und be sent a copy of the Obligatory Prayers revealed in the *Kitáb-i-Aqdas*. Though the *Kitáb-i-Aqdas* had been revealed in 1873, Bahá'u'lláh had withheld the publication of some of its laws, including those relating to the Obligatory Prayers. Ḥájí Á<u>kh</u>und had requested them and Bahá'u'lláh had acquiesced.[23]

In 1888, after leaving prison, Ḥájí Á<u>kh</u>und made his second pilgrimage to 'Akká and the Blessed Beauty. Bahá'u'lláh appointed him a Hand of the Cause at about this time.[24]

Ḥájí Á<u>kh</u>und regularly wrote to Bahá'u'lláh and received many Tablets in return. In one of his letters, Ḥájí Á<u>kh</u>und complained about something. Bahá'u'lláh's reply was that 'he had no right to complain, for so much spiritual food and imperishable benefits had been showered upon him from the heaven of divine bounty that he would be unable to reckon them'. He added that Ḥájí Á<u>kh</u>und should 'thank' – repeating the word nine times – his Lord for the blessings he had been given.[25]

In 1891, Ḥájí Á<u>kh</u>und was once more thrown into prison, though for the last time. On the orders of Náṣiri'd-Dín <u>Sh</u>áh and his son, Kámrán Mírzá, the Governor of Tehran, he was first imprisoned in Tehran and then in Qazvín. This time, one of his fellow prisoners was Ḥájí Amín (see Chapter 4). They were incarcerated for 18 months.[26] Upon news of their arrest, Bahá'u'lláh revealed the *Lawḥ-i-Dunya*, whose opening paragraph illuminated the spiritual nature of Ḥájí Á͟k͟hund and Ḥájí Amín:

> Praise and thanksgiving beseem the Lord of manifest dominion Who hath adorned this mighty Prison with the presence of their honours 'Alí-Akbar and Amín, and hath illumined it with the light of certitude, constancy and assurance. The glory of God and the glory of all that are in the heavens and on the earth be upon them.[27]

The Tablet also contains the well-known prayer for the Hands of the Cause (Light and glory, greeting and praise be upon the Hands of His Cause . . .).

Náṣiri'd-Dín S͟háh, who had already taken a photograph of an unperturbed Ḥájí Á͟k͟hund in chains, had another photograph taken of Ḥájí Á͟k͟hund and Ḥájí Amín together, both with chains around their necks and their feet in stocks. As in the first photo, the men show 'absolute resignation and calm, unperturbed by their afflictions'. 'Abdu'l-Bahá so admired the photograph that He placed a copy in the hallway across from His room in 'Akká.[28]

Bahá'u'lláh ascended in 1892, while Ḥájí Á͟k͟hund was still in prison in Qazvín. Upon his release in 1894, Ḥájí Á͟k͟hund made the long journey to 'Akká. When he arrived, he learned of the betrayal of Mírzá Muḥammad-'Alí, Bahá'u'lláh's half-brother. Ḥájí Á͟k͟hund promptly went and tried to convince him of his error but was unsuccessful. Ḥájí Á͟k͟hund returned to Tehran and spent the next years emphasising the importance of the Covenant of Bahá'u'lláh and countering the activities of the Covenant-breakers.[29]

In 1897, 'Abdu'l-Bahá instructed the four Hands of the Cause, Ḥájí Á͟k͟hund, Mírzá 'Alí-Muḥammad (see Chapter 19), Ibn-i-Abhar (see Chapter 11), and Ḥájí Mírzá Ḥasan-i-Adíb (see Chapter 16), who were all living in Tehran at that time, to gather together and consult about what would become the beginning of the Bahá'í Administrative Order. Two years later, they formed the Central Spiritual Assembly in Tehran that consisted of the four Hands and nine other men elected by a group of specially selected electors appointed by the Hands. Over the following years, the Central Spiritual Assembly transformed into the Local Spiritual Assembly of Tehran.[30]

Ḥájí Á<u>kh</u>und lived the rest of his life in Tehran. After his passing on 4 March 1910, ‘Abdu’l-Bahá wrote in *Memorials of the Faithful*:

I loved him very much, for he was delightful to converse with, and as a companion second to none. One night, not long ago, I saw him in the world of dreams. Although his frame had always been massive, in the dream world he appeared larger and more corpulent than ever. It seemed as if he had returned from a journey. I said to him, ‘Jináb, you have grown good and stout’. ‘Yes’, he answered, ‘praise be to God! I have been in places where the air was fresh and sweet, and the water crystal pure; the landscapes were beautiful to look upon, the foods delectable. It all agreed with me, of course, so I am stronger than ever now, and I have recovered the zest of my early youth. The breaths of the All-Merciful blew over me and all my time was spent in telling of God. I have been setting forth His proofs, and teaching His Faith’. (The meaning of teaching the Faith in the next world is spreading the sweet savors of holiness; that action is the same as teaching.) We spoke together a little more, and then some people arrived and he disappeared.

His last resting-place is in Ṭihrán. Although his body lies under the earth, his pure spirit lives on, ‘in the seat of truth, in the presence of the potent King’. I long to visit the graves of the friends of God, could this be possible. These are the servants of the Blessed Beauty; in His path they were afflicted; they met with toil and sorrow; they sustained injuries and suffered harm. Upon them be the glory of God, the All-Glorious. Unto them be salutation and praise. Upon them be God’s tender mercy, and forgiveness.[31]

9

MULLÁ MUḤAMMAD – NABÍL-I-AKBAR – FAḌL-I-QÁ'INÍ

(1829–1892)

Mullá Muḥammad, best known as Nabíl-i-Akbar, the title given to him by Bahá'u'lláh, and also known as Faḍl-i-Qá'iní, was a great scholar who was instrumental in bringing Mírzá Abu'l-Faḍl into the Faith. When Mírzá Abu'l-Faḍl was still a Muslim, but was studying the Bahá'í Faith with Nabíl-i-Akbar, he is reported to have said of Nabíl-i-Akbar, 'By God, no one could withstand the power of this great man of knowledge'.[1]

Nabíl-i-Akbar was born on 29 March 1829 in the village of Naw-Firist, near Bírjand, in the centre of Iran. The men in his family had long been important Muslim clerics and Nabíl-i-Akbar followed the same religious path. When he was 17, he moved to Sabzivár in the province of Ma<u>sh</u>had to study with Ḥájí Mullá Hádí, the most eminent Persian philosopher in the country. Five years later, he returned home, but not for long. After heated arguments with his father over religious understandings, Nabíl-i-Akbar left home again and returned to his most recent teacher. Ḥájí Mullá Hádí insisted that he write a letter to his father asking for guidance. Forgiving him, his father advised him to go to Karbilá and Najaf, which were the centres of Islamic learning at that time. He even sent money, a horse and a servant to ensure he arrived safely.[2]

Nabíl-i-Akbar didn't make it to Karbilá or Najaf that summer. Passing through Tehran as the summer of 1852 began, he decided to stay there for a time and attend theological classes. Before long, he had become his teacher's favourite student, something that upset those students who had been studying with him longer. On 15 August, two deluded Bábís attempted to assassinate Náṣiri'd-Dín <u>Sh</u>áh and suddenly the whole country was in an uproar. Bábís everywhere were being attacked, persecuted and killed. Nabíl-i-Akbar's jealous classmates took revenge for his usurping of their teacher's attention by accusing him of being a Bábí. It worked, and he was quickly arrested.

Taken to the house of Tehran's mayor, Maḥmúd-Khán-i-Kalantar, Nabíl-i-Akbar was detained along with other Bábís. Screams echoed through the house as Maḥmúd-Khán tortured his captives. After finishing with one Bábí, Maḥmúd-Khán sat down opposite Nabíl-i-Akbar. Without permission, Nabíl-i-Akbar walked over to him and told him he was not a Bábí. The mayor paid no attention to him. Luckily, however, as he was arrested, Nabíl-i-Akbar managed to send a message to his teacher. Soon after, the secretary of the school's principal arrived and delivered a note to Maḥmúd-Khán. Abruptly, the mayor told Nabíl-i-Akbar: 'Apparently the honorable principal expects you, so may I ask that, without any delay, you go and see him', and escorted him to the door as a sign of respect.[3]

Returning to school, Nabíl-i-Akbar learned that the clergy and students really did think that he was a Bábí and would keep their distance. Nabíl-i-Akbar shared a room at the school with one of the other students who studied there, Siyyid Ya'aqub, who had also come from Qá'in. One night, Siyyid Ya'aqub, who was secretly a Bábí, jokingly told Nabíl-i-Akbar, 'Do you know that you are known as a Babi?' Nabíl-i-Akbar denied the charge, saying:

> 'I have never met a single one of them or read a line from their writings' . . . Siyyid said, 'Well, it does not make any difference, and by the way, I have come across some of the writings of the Bab which are too heavy for me to understand. I thought I should bring them to you so with your degree of learning you could explain them to me'. He placed the papers on the table and left.
>
> Faḍl [part of Nabíl-i-Akbar's other title] states, 'To please the Siyyid, I scanned the papers, but since they did not appear to be in my style, which was that of philosophers, they did not impress me. Finding them not worthy of my time, I hid them under some books and papers so no one would find such incriminating material in my room'.
>
> The next night Siyyid came back. I told him I found them worthless, and how I felt sorry for the foolish and gullible who

> had embraced that Cause to the point of giving their lives for it. Worse than them, I said, were those learned people who should have known better than to become overzealous followers of the Bab, misleading the innocent Muslims.
>
> Upon hearing my words, Siyyid's face showed his deep emotional despair. He lowered his head. After a long pause, he raised his head a few times as if he were going to say something but held it back. Finally on the way to the door, he recited this poem, 'How often knowledge and intelligence turn into a monstrous thief robbing the wayfarer'. As the final word, Siyyid said, 'Turn your heart to the truth in these words' and left.[4]

Nabíl-i-Akbar deduced from the Siyyid's behaviour that he was a Bábí, and that he was trying to entrap him. He intended to elude the trap, but didn't realise how subtle it was. He still had the Bábí writings so decided to vanquish them with logic. Nabíl-i-Akbar thought that his intelligence was more than enough to disprove the writings. As he noted, 'My motivation was not to learn, but to find faults to prove the fallacy of the Báb's claim'. But instead, he wrote that 'With every line I read a new door of knowledge opened before my eyes. Sleep escaped me and I was led into a new world. All night I read the Báb's writings with increased enthusiasm discovering gems previously hidden from me. The first rays of the sun found my vision, my soul, and my heart totally changed and refreshed'. By morning, Nabíl-i-Akbar was a Bábí.[5]

As autumn approached, Nabíl-i-Akbar decided to continue with his plan to study in Karbilá and Najaf, so that no one could say, 'If he knew better, he would not have become a Bábí'. His goal was to obtain a doctorate degree in Islamic law and he studied under one of the greatest of the Islamic divines, Shaykh Murtidá-i-Ansárí, who was later praised by both Bahá'u'lláh and 'Abdu'l-Bahá. After six years, Shaykh Murtidá gave him some questions and Nabíl-i-Akbar wrote a book of a few thousand verses in answer. The Shaykh was highly impressed and wrote of his astonishment and praise for Nabíl-i-Akbar's depth of learning in the margin of the book. Other students, who were taking much longer than six years, were jealous and upset that their illustrious teacher would give praise to a Bábí. Shaykh Murtidá challenged them to write a similar book if they wished to have his signature. Receiving his signature was far above normal approval; only two other people ever gained a similar degree from Shaykh Murtidá and one of them was Mírzá-i-Shírází, a Bahá'í.[6]

Nabíl-i-Akbar obtained his degree in 1858 and decided to go to the Shrine of the Imam Ḥusayn in Karbilá. While there, he encountered a Persian Bábí who told him about the exiled community of Bábís in Baghdad, and praised Jináb-i-Bahá, who would become known as Bahá'u'lláh. When asked about the supposed successor to the Báb, Mírzá Yaḥyá, the Persian Bábí made no comment.

Arriving in Baghdad, Nabíl-i-Akbar went to the house of Bahá'u'lláh to meet Him. When he entered, Bahá'u'lláh said, 'Don't you know that in the eyes of the government of Iran We are considered to be the enemy of the state and therefore have been cast out? People, too, regard us as outlaws. You are a learned man, a mujtahid who is highly respected. How, then, did you dare to come to Us?' Bahá'u'lláh then invited the young man to stay as His guest.[7]

Nabíl-i-Akbar recognised Bahá'u'lláh as a very spiritual person, but no more. Then one afternoon, he was talking with Muḥammad-Ṣádiq-i-Khurásání, known as Mullá Ṣádiq and renowned for his learning and stature (also the father of Ibn-i-Aṣdaq, see Chapter 19), when Bahá'u'lláh entered the room and the young mullá learned about humility:

> Mullá Ṣádiq, who was the embodiment of dignity and solemnity, immediately rose to his feet and prostrated himself at the feet of Bahá'u'lláh. This action did not please Bahá'u'lláh Who angrily rebuked Mullá Ṣádiq and ordered him to rise immediately.
>
> I was amazed and bewildered at such behaviour on the part of Mullá Ṣádiq as I had never expected such an important person to act in this mannerI expressed my disapproval of Mullá Ṣádiq's behaviour and admonished him for it, saying: 'You are a man who occupies an exalted position in the realm of knowledge and learning and, above all else, you had the honour of attaining the presence of the Báb Himself. Your rank is next to the Letters of the Living and you are one of the Witnesses of the Dispensation of the Báb. It is true that Bahá'u'lláh is an eminent person Who belongs to the nobility and His ancestors have occupied high positions in the government. It is also true that He has suffered persecution and imprisonment as a result of embracing the Cause of God, that all His possessions have been confiscated and that He has finally been exiled to this land.

Yet, your behaviour towards Him this afternoon was like that of an unworthy servant towards his glorious Lord'.

Mullá Ṣádiq refrained from answering me. He was in a state of spiritual intoxication, his face beaming with joy; he merely said to me, 'I beseech God to tear asunder the veil for thee and shower His bounties upon thy person through His abundant grace'.

After this incident, I decided in my heart to investigate and began to observe the person of Bahá'u'lláh and His actions very carefully. The more I observed the less I discovered any sign which could point to His claiming a station. On the contrary, I observed in Him nothing, either in word or deed, except humility, self-effacement, servitude and utter nothingness. As a result, I was led into grievous error, believing that I was in every way superior to Bahá'u'lláh, and preferred my own self to Him.

It was through my vain imagining that in the gatherings of the friends I always used to occupy the seat of honour, assume the function of the speaker and would not give an opportunity to Bahá'u'lláh or anyone else to say anything. One afternoon, Bahá'u'lláh arranged a meeting in His house and a number of friends had gathered, as usual, in the same large room, a room around which, according to the Pen of the Most High, circle in adoration the people of Bahá. Again, I occupied the seat of honour. Bahá'u'lláh sat in the midst of the friends and was serving tea with His own hands.

In the course of the meeting, a certain question was asked. Having satisfied myself that no one in the room was capable of tackling the problem, I began to speak. All the friends were attentively listening and were absolutely silent, except Bahá'u'lláh Who occasionally, while agreeing with my exposition, made a few comments on the subject. Gradually He took over and I became silent. His explanations were so profound and the ocean of His utterance surged with such a power that my whole being was overtaken with awe and fear. Spellbound by His words, I was plunged into a state of dazed bewilderment. After a few minutes of listening to His words – words of unparalleled wonder and majesty – I became dumbfounded. I could no longer hear His voice. Only by the movement of His lips did I know that He was still speaking. I felt deeply ashamed and troubled that I was occupying the seat of honour in that meeting. I waited impatiently until I saw that His lips were no longer moving when I knew that

> He had finished talking. Like a helpless bird which is freed from the claws of a mighty falcon I rose to my feet and went out. There three times I hit my head hard against the wall and rebuked myself for my spiritual blindness.[8]

Nabíl-i-Akbar was suddenly aware of the truth of Bahá'u'lláh's station. To confirm his understanding, he wrote a letter to Bahá'u'lláh, which he gave to 'Abdu'l-Bahá to deliver. In His reply, Bahá'u'lláh alluded to His Station, and Nabíl-i-Akbar understood. He wrote a second letter to Bahá'u'lláh in which he acknowledged that He was the Supreme Manifestation of God and begged to be guided to serve Him. At this point, his true mission in life was set.[9]

Bahá'u'lláh directed him to return to Persia. He was welcomed back to his hometown of Naw-Firist by a large number of divines, students and merchants who travelled out of the town to meet the now-acclaimed mujtahid. Even the Amír, or ruler, of the district of Qá'in came and hailed him. The divines secretly tested him by sending their most learned one to question him. That one reported to the others that Nabíl-i-Akbar's knowledge was even better than his own. The jealous local clergy were not happy to see someone else steal their prestige and popularity.

Nabíl-i-Akbar had no trouble bringing people into the Bábí Faith and that upset the clergy even more. One of Nabíl-i-Akbar's relatives, who was also a cleric, soon became a Bábí. One day in his sermon, the relative inserted some passages from the Báb into his message. The assemblage quickly became agitated and asked where these new words came from. Fearing for himself, he said that he had heard them from Nabíl-i-Akbar. This was just the thing that the jealous local mullás were waiting for, and they used it to turn the Amír against him.

Soon afterwards, when he was returning to the town, Nabíl-i-Akbar was accosted on the road by the Amír's agents. They ordered Nabíl-i-Akbar to dismount from his horse, and took off his boots, filled them with gravel and hung them around his neck, forcing him to walk the rest of the way barefoot. There, he was incarcerated for two months with his feet in stocks. He was then transferred to Bírjand and confined in the police chief's house (the homes of police chiefs were usually large compounds with many rooms).[10]

Nabíl-i-Akbar's time in Bírjand was short due to a dream the police chief's mother had. Before his arrival, she had dreamed that 'the sun descended from the sky right into our house and set in a corner of a certain room'. The following day, Nabíl-i-Akbar arrived. When the police chief's mother first saw him through a window, he was sitting in the exact corner where she had seen the sun set. She shared this with her son, and the police chief quickly returned his prisoner to Naw-Firist with the hope that he would keep a low profile.[11]

Nabíl-i-Akbar's bitterest enemy in Naw-Firist was Abu'l-Talib, who did not want the young mujtahid there. First, he had Nabíl-i-Akbar arrested and taken to Mashhad, bribing the agents to torture him on the way. The Governor-General of Mashhad, however, was a fair man who treated Nabíl-i-Akbar well and gave him an allowance. After a time, the Governor encouraged him to return to his hometown. This did not make Abu'l-Talib happy, and he sent complaint after complaint to Tehran until finally Nabíl-i-Akbar was taken there.[12]

Nabíl-i-Akbar was set free in Tehran in 1869 and stayed in the city for three and a half years, becoming very well known and highly respected. He also got married at this time. But the Muslim clergy in Tehran became fearful of his influence and began plotting his murder. Hearing of the plot, Nabíl-i-Akbar disguised himself in part by changing his mullá's turban for an ordinary hat.[13]

'Abdu'l-Bahá described the time:

> He was pursued by the watchmen; guards looked everywhere for him, asking after him in every street and alley, hunting him down to catch and torture him. Hiding, he would pass by them like the sigh of the oppressed, and rise to the hills; or again, like the tears of the wronged one, he would slip down into the valleys. He could no longer wear the turban denoting his rank; he disguised himself, putting on a layman's hat, so that they would fail to recognize him and would let him be.[14]

Two of the highest clergymen in the city turned the King against him and soon the police were searching for him in every corner of the city, but without success. They arrested Nabíl-i-Akbar's 15-year-old brother and tortured him, but he gave nothing away. As the King's noose drew ever closer, Nabíl-i-Akbar decided to leave. This was just one month after his wedding. His departure, however, did not stop his enemies. Since he was so well known by this time, they sent notices to the authorities of his possible stopping places in the hope of arresting him.[15]

In 1873, Bahá'u'lláh invited Nabíl-i-Akbar to come to 'Akká. While there, Bahá'u'lláh honoured him with the title Nabíl-i-Akbar. Nabíl means 'noble and learned' and Akbar means 'great'. The Blessed Beauty also revealed the *Lawḥ-i-Ḥikmat*, the *Tablet of Wisdom*, in his honour.[16]

After leaving Bahá'u'lláh's presence, Nabíl-i-Akbar travelled extensively across Persia, educating and uplifting the Bahá'ís. He lived in Tehran and then spent a number of years in Qazvín, where he married again and had a daughter.[17]

When Nabíl-i-Akbar travelled and taught the Faith, the authorities were ever in pursuit. Finally, the King himself ordered his arrest. Nabíl-i-Akbar and his nephew, Shaykh Muḥammad-'Alí (see Chapter 17), were travelling together to Sabzivár, where Nabíl-i-Akbar had received his early education. Though in disguise, they were recognised and arrested, his nephew writing: 'Fadl and I were approaching Sabzivár-when we decided not to enter the city in order to avoid recognition. Therefore we went to a caravanserai and lodged for in a room. Our disguise in civilian clothing had worked so far. However, at midnight an agent came and told my uncle, "you are Fadl, and I am ordered to take you to the governor"'.

When Nabíl-i-Akbar entered the presence of the Governor, the Governor simply said, 'Without a doubt, you are the celebrated Faḍl'. Then he angrily denounced him, saying that he couldn't understand why anyone with a family and education such as his could possibly give his allegiance to Bahá'u'lláh. Nabíl-i-Akbar calmly responded that

> Your highness knows that it is a natural instinct for everyone to want to be respected, particularly the higher class and the learned. I was no exception to the rule. When I met Bahá'u'lláh for the first time I considered myself way superior to Him, but in the course of events when I heard His outpouring of gem-like utterances, I was convinced that He was the ocean and I was but a lowly drop. I find myself to be a helpless bird in the claws of the mighty falcon. He rules my heart and my soul. This is my confession. Do with me what you have to do. Kill me on the spot, put me in chains and stocks, or transfer me to Tehran for execution.[18]

So impressed was the Governor with this answer, that he told Nabíl-i-Akbar that he would pretend that he had never seen him. He ordered him to leave the city, warning him to be careful because there were spies everywhere. Nabíl-i-Akbar and his nephew, Shaykh Muḥammad-'Alí, wasted no time in leaving, bought two donkeys and headed for the Russian border.

They arrived at the border, but had no passports. Nabíl-i-Akbar simply dismounted from his donkey and walked up to the office, reciting a prayer from the Báb. The Persian customs chief greeted him and offered him tea, which he declined, and the Russian side passed them through without asking for any documents. They were soon in 'Ishqábád.[19]

It was 1892 when they arrived in 'Ishqábád. Nabíl-i-Akbar had no income and consequently lived in poverty. One night, a Bahá'í invited Nabíl-i-Akbar for dinner and recorded that 'Before dinner was served, I saw Faḍl picking up a dry piece of bread in the corner of the room and, with a sigh, began to eat it. I learned that Faḍl had not eaten a few meals'. After a time, Nabíl-i-Akbar accompanied by Mírzá Abu'l-Faḍl, went to Bukhárá in Uzbekistan. There, on 6 July 1892, five weeks after the ascension of Bahá'u'lláh, Nabíl-i-Akbar died, ending his 30 years of service and reuniting with his heart's desire. 'Abdu'l-Bahá described him in *Memorials of the Faithful*:

> A sign of guidance, he was, an emblem of the fear of God. For his Faith, he laid down his life, and in dying, triumphed. He passed by the world and its rewards; he closed his eyes to rank and wealth; he loosed himself from all such chains and fetters, and put every worldly thought aside. Of wide learning, at once a mujtahid, a philosopher, a mystic, and gifted with intuitive sight, he was also an accomplished man of letters and an orator without a peer. He had a great and universal mind.
>
> Praise be to God, at the end he was made the recipient of heavenly grace. Upon him be the glory of God, the All Glorious. May God shed the brightness of the Abhá Kingdom upon his resting-place. May God welcome him into the Paradise of reunion, and shelter him forever in the realm of the righteous, submerged in an ocean of lights.[20]

10

ḤÁJÍ MÍRZÁ MUḤAMMAD-TAQÍ-I-AFNÁN – VAKÍLU'D-DAWLIH – VAKÍLU'D-HAQQ

(1830–1909)

Ḥájí Mírzá Muḥammad-Taqí-i-Afnán, a cousin of the Báb and later known as Vakílu'd-Dawlih, directed the construction of the first Mas͟hriqu'l-Ad͟hkár of the Bahá'í world in 'Is͟hqábád. He was born in 1830 in Shiraz, the second son of Ḥájí Mírzá Siyyid Muḥammad, the maternal uncle of the Báb for whom the *Kitáb-i-Íqán* was written.

Vakílu'd-Dawlih spent his childhood and adolescence in Shiraz in a family known for its nobility and for belonging to the lineage of the Prophet Muḥammad. He became a merchant in Shiraz and later went to Bus͟hihr.[1] He would sometimes visit his aunt, the mother of the Báb. He and the Báb were close childhood friends and often played games together.[2] On one visit in 1844, the Báb, who had not yet declared His station, was there and writing prayers. He recalled that

> Melon was placed before Him, and with the tip of a knife, He graciously offered me a piece. I ate it. He handed me a page of a prayer, and, after I had read it, He asked, 'What manner of supplication do you perceive this to be?' I was familiar with the *Sahífihy-yi Sajjádíyyih*, recited each day of the week and, therefore, replied, 'It is similar to the prayer of *Sahífih*'.[3]

The *Sahífih* was a book of prayers written by the Fourth Imám of Shi'a Islam and is considered to be the oldest Islamic prayer book and thus highly revered. Even at such a young age, Vakílu'd-Dawlih's spiritual nature and perception were obvious.

In 1854, he moved to Yazd and quickly became a prominent merchant. He was visited in Yazd by Mullá Muḥammad-i-Qá'iní, the great theologian known to many as Nabíl-i-Akbar (see Chapter 9), who talked to him about the Bábí Faith. Three years later, in 1857, Vakílu'd-Dawlih travelled to Baghdad and met Bahá'u'lláh, Who confirmed his belief in the Báb. Back in Yazd, he became the Consular Agent for Russia, gaining the title of Vakílu'd-Dawlih which meant 'Representative of the Government'. Bahá'u'lláh gave him the slightly different title of Vakílu'd-Haqq, 'Representative of the True One'.[4]

At some point during these years, Vakílu'd-Dawlih married his cousin, Bíbí-Zahrá Bigum.[5]

In mid-January 1861, Vakílu'd-Dawlih received a letter from his father, Ḥájí Mírzá Siyyid Muḥammad, the uncle of the Báb, in which he enigmatically began with: 'If you wonder over our state . . .' His father had just been given what at that time was called the *Treatise for the Uncle* in response to his questions about the station of the Báb. This 51,000-word document, written in early January 1861 over just two days, is now known as the *Kitáb-i-Íqán*.[6]

Sometime later, Vakílu'd-Dawlih was given a copy of the *Kitáb-i-Íqán*. Upon reading it, he immediately recognised the truth of the Cause and rushed to Baghdad. 'Abdu'l-Bahá wrote that

> He was among those souls who, after one reading of the Book of Íqán, became believers, bewitched by the sweet savors of God, rejoicing at the recital of His verses. His agitation was such that he cried out, "Lord, Lord, here am I!" Joyously, he left Persia and hurried away to 'Iráq. Because he was filled with longing love, he sped over the mountains and across the desert wastes, not pausing to rest until he came to Baghdád.
>
> He entered the presence of Bahá'u'lláh, and achieved acceptance in His sight. What holy ecstasy he had, what fervor, what detachment from the world! It was beyond description. His blessed face was so comely, so luminous that the friends in 'Iráq gave him a name: they called him "the Afnán of all delights."[7]

Being in the presence of Bahá'u'lláh transformed Vakílu'd-Dawlih, and he recognised the station of Bahá'u'lláh before He Himself had had revealed it. His love for Bahá'u'lláh was such that as he 'walked in the streets of Baghdad, he radiated such heavenly joy that the believers of that city used to refer to him as the "delightful Afnán."'[8]

Yazd had long been a city whose fanatical inhabitants attacked first the Bábís and then the Bahá'ís. On 19 May 1891, Maḥmúd Mírzá, the governor of Yazd and the son of the Bahá'ís' inveterate foe, Ẓillu's-Sulṭán, put to death in 'horrible circumstances' seven Bahá'ís in that city. The martyrdoms so affected Bahá'u'lláh that He 'withheld' the revelation of His words for nine days and then revealed the *Lawḥ-i-Dunyá*, which gives the details of the deaths. In another Tablet, the *Tablet of the Times*, Bahá'u'lláh states that the martyrdoms of the seven in Yazd, along with the imprisonment of Ḥájí Á<u>kh</u>und (see Chapter 8) and Ḥájí Amín (see Chapter 4) in Qazvín, 'created the most joyous jubilation among the Concourse on High. He describes in glowing terms the festive mood among the inmates of the highest paradise as they rejoice and celebrate with exceeding gladness the victory of the triumphant martyrs over their adversaries'.[9]

Vakílu'd-Dawlih avoided arrest at this time, possibly because he was the Russian Consul, but those around him feared for his safety. The head of the British Legation in Tehran sent a message stating that, 'Three days ago seven people of the Babi sect were killed in Yezd'. He sent a second message describing the deaths and said that 'Ḥájí Mírzá Muḥammad Taki, Russian Agent, is unsafe . . .' The Dutch Chargé d'Affairs also sent his account and noted that 'The principal merchants here are Bábis and several amongst them are decidedly more or less in danger; especially Ḥájí Mírzá Md. Takki, Shirazi and his son Ḥájí Mírzá Md'.[10]

The next year, 1892, T.E. Gordon, a British army officer and diplomat in Tehran, visited Yazd to appoint a British Consular Agent there. He wrote that, 'I met many of the Yezd merchants, Mohamedan and Parsee, during my visit there in April last, and among them, Ḥájí Mírzá Mohamed Taqi-Shirazi (old Shiraz Family) the first Mahomedan merchant there. He is the Russian Agent in Yezd. He and all his family are of the Babi sect. He is an old man of over 70 [actually, he was 62] with a fine presence and most agreeable manners'.[11]

Though to outward appearances, he was a businessman, in reality, he was a dedicated teacher of the Faith:

> During his days in Yazd he was, outwardly, engaged in commercial pursuits, but actually teaching the Faith. His only aim was to exalt

> the Word of God, his only wish, to spread the Divine sweet savors, his only thought, to come nearer and ever nearer to the mansions of the Lord. There was no remembrance on his lips but the verses of God. He was an embodiment of the good pleasure of Bahá'u'lláh; a dawning-point of the grace of the Greatest Name. Many and many a time, Bahá'u'lláh expressed to those about Him, His extreme satisfaction with the Afnán; and consequently, everyone was certain that he would in future initiate some highly important task.[12]

During the 1880s, Russia began building a new city close to the Persian border, calling it 'Ishqábád. Escaping the persecution in Persia, many Bahá'ís moved to the new city. Before the ascension of Bahá'u'lláh, Vakílu'd-Dawlih had purchased some properties there and the Blessed Beauty told him to reserve a portion of these for a Mashriqu'l-Adhkár. Then at the turn of the century, 'Abdu'l-Bahá asked Vakílu'd-Dawlih to go to 'Ishqábád and take charge of the construction of the first Mashriqu'l-Adhkár in the world.[13]

Bowing to the Master's request, in 1900 Vakílu'd-Dawlih concluded all his business affairs in Yazd, sold everything and departed for 'Ishqábád. Beginning the construction work was expensive and financing the effort difficult. Vakílu'd-Dawlih sacrificed everything for the House of Worship. One night in 'Akká, 'Abdu'l-Bahá told the resident believers his story:

> Although the scope of Jináb-i-Ḥájí Vakílu'd-Dawlih's business activities has become severely restricted, nevertheless, having estimated the total worth of his wealth to be some twenty thousand túmáns, he has decided to consecrate the whole sum to the construction of the Mashriqu'l-Adhkár. Moreover, despite his state of health and weakened condition, he has taken it upon himself to begin construction activities and has therefore started on the excavation work. I have written to him that the construction of this type of public Bahá'í institution requires the participation of the entire Bahá'í community.[14]

One day, 'Abdu'l-Bahá was going over receipts for expenditures and contributions for the construction. He commented on the 'participation of the entire Bahá'í community' and that the amounts of the contributions were negligible. Today I realized the truth of something they have frequently written to me from 'Ishqábád. They wrote that the construction of the Mashriqu'l-Adhkár has become a real test. Those from whom much was expected have not assisted at all, or contributed very little, while on the contrary, those from whom nothing was expected have truly sacrificed everything they had, especially the poor and the downtrodden. They have truly done their utmost. Even the very poor gave a few *shahi* or a few *qeran*. I sign their receipts with pleasure and joy.[15]

Construction on the nine-sided House of Worship began on 31 October 1902. Vakílu'd-Dawlih laid the foundation stone, but then word was received that General Subotich, the Governor-general of Turkistan, was coming to lay the cornerstone on behalf of the Czar. On 19 November 1904:

> The Governor of the State, escorted by a company of officers and soldiers together with the foreign Minister and the local Consul, all dressed in uniform and decorated with royal medals, came to the blessed grounds of the Mashrak-el-Azcar to express his congratulations. . . The grounds were especially adorned and the most exquisite rugs were spread. Shady arbors and bowers were erected, each having nine columns. In the parlors two tables were set, one of them covered with many kinds of sweetmeats, most luscious fruits and flowers of all kinds; on the other were placed the Holy Scriptures, the sketch of the Mashrak-el-Azcar, and both Russian and Persian translations of the history and the date of the building being newly erected . . .
>
> At half past three that afternoon the Government carriages approached, and, at the first gate of the grounds they stopped [and] alighted at the gate. They walked over the beautiful rugs and came to where the believers were assembled. There were from six to eight hundred of the people of Bahá and about the same number of Russians, Armenians . . . (and other nationalities).
>
> Then the Governor removed his overcoat and gloves, the officers all following his example, and came to the appointed place for his work . . .
>
> Then the silver box (containing a description of the construction

> methods and the materials to be used in the building) was brought and presented to the Governor who took it in his hand and began the work. While he was laying the corner stone he spoke the following words which were translated by the interpreter, word for word: 'It gives me great pleasure to realize the House of Worship of the Bahais is being erected in my days, and my hope is that I will see it when it is finished'.[16]

When the Mas͟hriqu'l-Ad͟hkár was completed in 1907, it towered over the rest of the city. It was surrounded by luxurious and verdant gardens, and bordered on each side by tree-lined avenues. Additionally, Bahá'í schools, a medical dispensary and an inn for travellers were built. Nearby was the Ḥaẓíratu'l-Quds (Bahá'í administrative centre) and the residence of the grounds keeper.[17]

Having completed his work, Vakílu'd-Dawlih handed over the affairs of the Mas͟hriqu'l-Ad͟hkár to his son, Ḥájí Mírzá Maḥmúd. In 1907, 'Abdu'l-Bahá called Vakílu'd-Dawlih to 'Akká, so he departed to spend his remaining days close to the Master. At one point during these years in 'Akká when the Master's life was threatened, 'Abdu'l-Bahá wrote a Tablet to Vakílu'd-Dawlih instructing him to arrange for the election of the Universal House of Justice, should he be killed.[18]

Vakílu'd-Dawlih's final two years were spent in tranquillity in 'Akká. Occasionally, during these troublesome years, he hosted the pilgrims. In 1908, Mason Remey stayed with him for two days and nights.[19]

Vakílu'd-Dawlih died in 1909 and was buried in the Bahá'í cemetery at the foot of Mount Carmel.[20]

'Abdu'l-Bahá designated Vakílu'd-Dawlih to be one of the 'four and twenty elders which sat before God on their seats' mentioned in the Revelation of St John in the Bible. Of the other 23, only the Báb and the 18 Letters of the Living have been identified. In *Memorials of the Faithful*, 'Abdu'l-Bahá wrote that

> he passed his days, holy and pure, supplicating and entreating the Lord. God's praise was always on his lips, and he chanted prayers with both his tongue and heart. He was wonderfully spiritual, strangely ashine. He is one of those souls who, before ever the drumbeat of "Am I not your Lord?" was sounded, drummed back: "Yea, verily Thou art!" It was in the 'Iráq period, during the years between

the seventies and the eighties of the Hijra, that he first caught fire and loved the Light of the World, beheld the glory dawning in Bahá'u'lláh and witnessed the fulfillment of the words, "I am He that liveth in the Abhá Realm of Glory!"

The Afnán was an uncommonly happy man. Whenever I was saddened, I would meet with him, and on the instant, joy would return again. Praise be to God, at the last, close by the Shrine of the Báb, he hastened away in light to the Abhá Realm; but the loss of him deeply grieved 'Abdu'l-Bahá.[21]

11

ḤÁJÍ MULLÁ MUḤAMMAD-TAQÍ-I-ABHAR – IBN-I-ABHAR

(mid 1800s–1917)

Ḥájí Mírzá Muḥammad-Taqí-i-Abhar, more commonly known as Hand of the Cause Ibn-i-Abhar, was imprisoned seven times for his faith, but never stopped teaching. He was born sometime in the mid 1800s in Abhar, a village between Zanján and Qazvín. His father, Mírzá Ibráhím-i-Abharí, was a leading Muslim cleric who became an early follower of the Báb[1], so Ibn-i-Abhar grew up in a Bábí household. The family moved to Qazvín in 1868 because of persecution. When Bahá'u'lláh declared His Mission, Ibn-i-Abhar was initially unsure, but his father, who had already accepted Him, told his son to carefully read the *Bayán*. After doing so, he quickly embraced the Faith of Bahá'u'lláh.[2] Ibn-i-Abhar suffered the first imprisonment for his faith when he was jailed in Tehran in 1873 for 14 and a half months.[3]

The next year his father died from having been poisoned, and Ibn-i-Abhar was afflicted by plots against him and the confiscation of all his possessions by his enemies. Because of this, he moved to Zanján.

In 1876, uncertain of the best path to follow in service to the Faith, Ibn-i-Abhar wrote to Bahá'u'lláh, asking 'whether it was more meritorious to lay down one's life for the love of God or to teach the Cause with wisdom and the power of utterance'. Bahá'u'lláh indicated that his path should be one of teaching with wisdom, advising that after the death of Badí', who had been martyred after delivering Bahá'u'lláh's Tablet to the Sháh of Persia, the believers should act with prudence and not volunteer to be martyrs. At some point, Ibn-i-Abhar moved back to his hometown of Abhar.

In about 1886, Ibn-i-Abhar was able to go on pilgrimage for the first time and attain the presence of Bahá'u'lláh, who 'showered His bounties upon him'. It was on this visit that Bahá'u'lláh designated him as a Hand of the Cause. After returning home, the Blessed Beauty sent him a Tablet in which He told him to 'pass through the cities, and even as a breeze that stirs at the break of dawn to shed upon whomsoever will turn to him the sweet savours of His loving kindness and favours'. This became Ibn-i-Abhar's guide for the rest of his life.[4]

Because of the opposition he faced in Abhar, Ibn-i-Abhar moved again to Zanján, along with his uncle, 'Abu'l-A'ẓím, and two others. His mission was to revive the community there, which had been struggling against the Covenant-breaking efforts of the Azalís, those who supported Bahá'u'lláh's Covenant-breaking half-brother Mírzá Yaḥyá. During the day, the Bahá'ís would visit the mullás, the Governor and other educated people to ensure they understood the difference between the Azalís and the Bahá'ís. Then at night, Ibn-i-Abhar would clandestinely go to the homes of the Bahá'ís and educate them as well. After four months of intense work, all but two of the Azálís had returned to the Faith.[5]

In 1890, political unrest washed across Persia and, as was usual, along with the political rabble-rousers, many Bahá'ís were also arrested, including Ḥájí Á<u>kh</u>und (see Chapter 8), Ḥájí Amín (see Chapter 4), Mírzá Maḥmúd-i-Furú<u>gh</u>í (see Chapter 7) and Ibn-i-Abhar.

After Ibn-i-Abhar returned to Abhar, the enemies of the Faith increased their efforts. They convinced Prince Ruknu'd-Dawlih, one of Náṣiri'd-Dín <u>Sh</u>áh's brothers, that the Bahá'ís were dangerous, and as a result, some of the believers were thrown into jail. Abú'l-Ṭálib, an inveterate enemy of the Faith, began writing to one of Ibn-i-Abhar's cousins and bitterest enemies, the Imám-Jum'ih, who Bahá'u'lláh had given the name of the She-Serpent. Abú'l-Ṭálib and Imám-Jum'ih ridiculed Ibn-i-Abhar before the Governor and wrote incendiary letters to the fanatical mullás, saying that he was 'hostile to religion'. At first the Governor, who was Ibn-i-Abhar's friend, laughed these accusations off, saying, 'It was written through jealousy and a misunderstanding. I have neither seen nor heard anything from Ebn Abhar which is hostile to religion'. His comments, however, created an uproar and the Governor, realising that people were threatening to murder the Bahá'ís, ordered that Ibn-i-Abhar be brought in along with any Bahá'í Tablets found in his home. Since he was found to have many Tablets, the Governor repudiated their friendship, out of fear, and condemned Ibn-i-Abhar to death.[6]

That evening, a group of soldiers came to Ibn-i-Abhar's house and demanded to see him. About 50 soldiers surrounded the house, and this drew a crowd of curious onlookers. To get rid of the crowd, the soldiers began firing their guns and the people scattered. Then the soldier's leader, Mírzá Jalíl Khán, handed Ibn-i-Abhar a letter which read:

> Your Excellency! For the purpose of investigating certain matters your presence is necessary in this city. Mírzá Jalil Khan, with ten soldiers has been commanded to bring you. With Mírzá Abdul Azeem and Kerbelaiy Mehdi Milani you must start for Zanján that the matter may be investigated in your very presence. Kindly see to it that you do not fail to start; otherwise the affair may become serious.[7]

Two soldiers prepared to put a large chain on Ibn-i-Abhar and his brother, Mírzá 'Abdu'l-'Aṭúf, for the night so that they couldn't escape, but after the payment of 50 túmáns, they were allowed to sleep unchained. During the night, the soldiers frequently fired their guns and made threats.

The next morning, Imám-Jum'ih's brother took Mírzá Jalíl Khán aside and offered him 'earthly and spiritual advantages' if he would torture the captives while they travelled. Imám-Jum'ih himself made 'calumnious accusations against [Ibn-i-Abhar] and against the Revealer of the Cause' and then also tried to persuade him to torture Ibn-i-Abhar:

> Tell him that you will bind his shoulders, chain him, put his feet in stocks and ride him on a bare-backed mule. Undoubtedly, to escape such ignominy he will pay you a large sum of money. After obtaining the money then act to the very limit of your power in order to secure your heavenly recompense, for these transgressors lead the people astray and the more scornfully they are treated the more the people will fear to follow them. Then, how great will be your station in the sight of the Great Father Mohammed in the day of resurrection! Proceed at once to Zinjan, and make this matter seem very important before the Governor. As soon as he arrives there let the Governor purify the province of Kamsare from his ignoble presence – (let him be killed).[8]

Mírzá Jalíl Khán, however, responded that he had listened all night to Ibn-i-Abhar as he 'gave us the story of the prophets in detail exhorting us to live in peace with all the people of God'. He said that 'there is an immense difference between your statements and his . . . Alas for me! That I must bring about the murder of such a prisoner'. Mírzá Jalíl Khán then went to Ibn-i-Abhar and said, 'I thought all Bahais were the enemies of God and of His prophet and I intended to torture and kill you. But since last night, and especially, today, I have changed my mind and am anxious to gain a thorough knowledge of your purpose. I am resolved to do nothing which may cause me to be ashamed in the presence of God and of His prophet'.[9]

The next day, Mírzá Jalíl Khán asked Ibn-i-Abhar 'Why are these cousins so opposed to you, seeking to destroy you?' He replied that: 'The uncles of His Holiness Mohammed were against him, and his cousins sought to martyr his descendants. The citizens of Galilee were opposed to Christ. In Moses time his relatives arose and drove him out. The family of Abraham caused his expulsion. And was not Joseph cast into the pit. By whom? – his wicked brethren.'[10]

It was the fourth day of Muharram, the month during which the faithful Shi'a beat themselves in atonement for the death of the Imám Ḥusayn. The streets were lined with groups of men and soldiers ready to beat the prisoners, while others scorned or cursed them. Before they departed, some of Ibn-i-Abhar's aunts and nieces offered the soldiers a sum of money if they could see him one more time. The soldiers refused, but when the offer was increased, they relented and brought out Ibn-i-Abhar, bound hand and foot in chains. During all this, Ibn-i-Abhar's mother remained emotionless, but then told her son: 'O my dear! You know how precious you are to me; but the most glorified One is the Blessed Perfection. I dedicate you to be a sacrifice in his Cause. Go! Be steadfast! Sacrifice yourself in the Cause of God and fear no one. The Koran says: Do they think that those who are killed in the path of God are dead? Nay, they are alive and in the presence of their Lord and are supping with Him'.

The group then began their journey, with Imám-Jum'ih leading them along the most public route as the crowds hurled ridicule, curses and stones. At one point, the prisoners told the soldiers to stop so that the crowd could 'satisfy their curiosity'. Two miles out of Zanján, Mírzá Jalíl Khán stopped the group to rest, sending seven of the guards who had persecuted the prisoners ahead. He kept the other three guards, who were friendly towards them, with the prisoners.[11]

When the party reached the house of Mírzá Jalíl Khán, they stopped, took off Ibn-i-Abhar's chains and summoned a group of Bahá'ís to consult about what to do. But after two hours, they were interrupted by two deputies and 20 farrashes (servants) who re-chained Ibn-i-Abhar and with 'utmost roughness and disrespect' dragged him to the government office. The warden took Ibn-i-Abhar's 'abá and emptied his pockets, then threw him into a hole dug into the ground and covered by a large millstone. The space was about 30 feet square with a ceiling so low that standing was not possible. It was also filled with fleas, ants and lice. The millstone was moved once a day for two hours so that fresh air could replace the stench. Ibn-i-Abhar spent over four months in this subterranean prison.

Being thrown into a dark hole in the ground didn't stop Ibn-i-Abhar from teaching. He spoke about the Faith to the other prisoners, both Bahá'í and non-Bahá'í. One day, the very intoxicated warden wanted to know how the farráshes were treating Ibn-i-Abhar, so he sent a new farrásh to find out. Ibn-i-Abhar recounted that

> This one also in that dark cell became captive to the Mount of God. He stood like a statue, listening eagerly. The warden, wondering why no sound reached him from the dungeon came, stealthily, near, and stood by the opening listening for the cruel treatment of the prisoners. Hearing nothing he rushed in angrily and found that all the prisoners had gathered around this prisoner and were listening to the words of life. He had a heavy club of almond wood in his hand and with it started beating the head jailer striking him and his assistants so severely that the club broke in two. Then, with the remaining piece, he came toward me and began striking me, saying, "O you devil! Can you not keep silent even here? Do you want to lead astray the prison force?"

After striking Ibn-i-Abhar with the remains of his club, the warden then called for a heavy chain to be brought. He handed the chain's collar to Ibn-i-Abhar, ordering him to put it around his neck. Ibn-i-Abhar was so numbed from the beating, that he tried to put the collar on over his head so that it sat like a cap. The warden burst out laughing at this and then ordered that the non-Bahá'í prisoners be kept in separate cells 'lest all should become Bahais'.[12]

Transferred to a prison in Tehran, Ibn-i-Abhar spent the next four years in a cell. Prison food was very poor, but two Bahá'í women posed as his sisters and brought him food and necessities. He had no paper for writing, but was able to use the wrappers from sugar cones, tea or candles. He wrote letters, some of them quite long, in a very tiny script and would send them out with the two women, who would forward them on.[13]

Ibn-i-Abhar was in this prison when Bahá'u'lláh ascended. It was a devastating time for him, and he finally wrote to 'Abdu'l-Bahá asking for help to overcome the loss. The Master's reply 'brought great comfort and consolation to him'. 'Abdu'l-Bahá suggested that he read the Qur'án, which in any case was the only book available in the prison.[14]

A photograph of Ibn-i-Abhar, in chains, with two guards was taken at some point. When 'Abdu'l-Bahá saw it, He wrote:

> O thou who art steadfast in the Covenant,
>
> A few days ago I was glancing at some photographs of the friends. By chance I came across thy photograph. As I beheld thy person standing poised and in the utmost dignity with chains around thy neck, I was so affected that all sorrow was turned into joy and radiance, and I praised God that the world's Greatest Luminary hath nurtured and trained such servants who, while tied in chains and under the threat of the sword, shine forth in the utmost exultation and rapture. And this is but a token of the grace of thy Lord, the Merciful, the Compassionate.[15]

During some of his time in the prison in Tehran, Ibn-i-Abhar wore the same monstrous chains that had been inflicted on Bahá'u'lláh in 1852 when He was in the Síyáh-<u>Ch</u>ál.[16]

Upon his release in 1895, Ibn-i-Abhar journeyed to 'Akká to meet 'Abdu'l-Bahá. While there, the subject of marriage was broached. A Persian woman named Fáizih <u>Kh</u>ánum had told the Master that it was time for Ibn-i-Abhar to get married and had even suggested a wife, Munírih <u>Kh</u>ánum, the daughter of Hand of the Cause Mullá 'Alí-Akbar. 'Abdu'l-Bahá sent one of his sons-in-law to 'convey to him the timeliness of his getting married'. Ibn-i-Abhar refused because, while in prison, he had made a vow not to marry, but to expend everything on teaching the Faith. Marrying, he said, would involve saddling himself with obligations that would make teaching more difficult. So adamant was he that 'Abdu'l-Bahá finally called him into His presence and told him to return to Tehran and marry Munírih Khánum. Ibn-i-Abhar protested and mentioned his vow, whereupon 'Abdu'l-Bahá nudged him with His shoulder and said, 'My good man! I am the Centre of the Covenant; when I say you will not break your vow by marrying, you will not!' Ibn-i-Abhar returned to Tehran and married Munírih Khánum. 'Abdu'l-Bahá sent money for the wedding feast, and the Greatest Holy Leaf sent a dress for the bride.[17]

In 1897, 'Abdu'l-Bahá directed the four Hands of the Cause to gather in Tehran and begin building the Bahá'í Administrative Order. They were able to form the Central Spiritual Assembly in Tehran in 1899, consisting of the four Hands and nine other men. This body evolved over the years into the Central Spiritual Assembly which then became the Local Spiritual Assembly of Tehran.[18]

Ibn-i-Abhar went on pilgrimage 11 times and was in 'Akká in 1899 when the first Western pilgrims arrived. This was also the time when Ibrahim Kheiralla, who had been helping to raise up the American Bahá'í community, began his rebellion against 'Abdu'l-Bahá. Kheiralla argued with many believers while in 'Akká, including Hand of the Cause Ibn-i-Abhar. The Hand had seen through Kheiralla's façade and lack of understanding, and had tried to guide him back to the correct path. His efforts, however, did not work and one discussion became so acrimonious that 'Abdu'l-Bahá Himself had to intercede.[19]

During the following years, Ibn-i-Abhar travelled extensively throughout Persia to spread the Teachings. In 1907 he accompanied Harlan Ober, Hooper Harris and Mírzá Maḥmúd-i-Zarqání on a teaching trip across India.[20]

Late in life, even blindness couldn't stop Ibn-i-Abhar from teaching. One of the believers recalls seeing the blind Ibn-i-Abhar sitting up in bed while an 'aged Seyid who had come from far away seeking Ebn Abhar to teach him the Bahai truths' sat, in Oriental fashion, on the floor at the foot of the bed.[21]

Ibn-i-Abhar died in Tehran in 1917. Over the course of his life, he received at least 30 Tablets from Bahá'u'lláh, some as short as four lines and some as long as 15 pages. Most of the longer Tablets were revealed by Bahá'u'lláh, but signed by Mírzá Aqá Jan. The short ones were written by Bahá'u'lláh Himself.[22]

'Abdu'l-Bahá once told Anton Haddad:

> Perhaps you have heard something about Ibn-Abhar. He is a Persian teacher and one of the greatest in knowledge and spirituality and holds a very high position among the believers; still, when asked by anyone about any other certain believer he generally says, 'I am not worthy to unloose the latchet of his shoes'. This teaches us humility and that we ought to speak very well of others, even to prefer them to ourselves . . .[23]

12

MULLÁ MUḤAMMAD-I-ZARANDÍ – NABÍL-I-AʻẒAM

(1831–1892)

Mullá Muḥammad-i-Zarandí, better known as Nabíl-i-Aʻẓam or simply Nabíl, wrote the seminal Baháʼí history, *The Dawn-Breakers*. He was born in Zarand, a town southeast of Yazd, on 29 July 1831. In his youth, Nabíl worked as a shepherd, and wrote that

> I longed to devote more time to my studies, but was unable to do so, owing to the exigencies of my situation. I read the Qur'án with eagerness, committed several passages to memory, and chanted them whilst I followed my flock over the fields. I loved solitude, and watched the stars at night with delight and wonder. In the quiet of the wilderness, I recited certain prayers attributed to the Imám 'Alí, the Commander of the Faithful, and, as I turned my face towards the Qublih, supplicated the Almighty to guide my steps and enable me to find the Truth.[1]

In 1847, while visiting the village of Rubát-Karím with his uncle, he overheard two men talking about the Báb:

> 'Have you heard,' one of them remarked, 'that the Siyyid-i-Báb has been conducted to the village of Kínar-Gird and is on his way to Tihrán?' Finding his friend ignorant of that episode, he proceeded to relate the whole story of the Báb, giving a detailed account of the circumstances attending His Declaration, of His arrest in Shíráz, His departure for Iṣfahán, the reception which both the Imám-Jum'ih and Manúchihr Khán had extended to Him, the prodigies and wonders He had manifested, and the verdict that the 'ulamás

of Iṣfáhán had pronounced against Him. Every detail of that story excited my curiosity and stirred in me a keen admiration for a Man who could throw such a spell over His countrymen. His light seemed to have flooded my soul; I felt as if I were already a convert to His Cause.

My father remarked upon my restlessness, and expressed his surprise at my behaviour. I had lost my appetite and sleep . . . I remained in that state until a certain Siyyid Ḥusayn-i-Zavári'í arrived at Zarand and was able to enlighten me on a subject which had become the ruling passion of my life. Our acquaintance speedily ripened into a friendship which encouraged me to share with him the longings of my heart. To my great surprise, I found him already enthralled by the secret of the theme which I had begun to disclose to him. 'One of my cousins,' he proceeded to relate, 'Siyyid Ismá'íl-i-Zavári'í by name, convinced me of the truth of the Message proclaimed by the Siyyid-i-Báb. He informed me that he had several times met the Siyyid-i-Báb . . . and had seen Him actually reveal . . . a commentary . . . The rapidity of the Báb's composition, and the force and originality of His style, had excited his surprise and admiration. He was amazed to find that, whilst revealing His commentary, and without lessening the speed of His writing, He was able to answer whatever questions those who were present were moved to ask Him.[2]

Hearing of the battle at Shaykh Tabarsí at the beginning of 1849, 17-year-old Nabíl and his teacher, Siyyid Ḥusayn-i-Zavári'í, were preparing to join the defenders when they learned that they were too late.[3]

Nabíl went to Tehran instead and stayed at the same religious college as Mírzá Aḥmad, the Báb's amanuensis. There he met many Bábís, including Bahá'u'lláh, though he did not recognise His station at that time.[4] In early 1851, Nabíl headed home to Zarand and, after the martyrdom of the Seven Martyrs in Tehran, went to Kirmánsháh, where he met Mírzá Aḥmad again.[5] He was there in late June when the Letter of the Living Mullá Báqir, arrived with a coffer sent by the Báb to Mírzá Aḥmad. Opening the coffer,

We marvelled when we beheld, among the things which that scroll of blue paper, of the most delicate texture, on which the Báb, in

> His own exquisite handwriting, which was a fine Shikastih script, had penned, in the form of a pentacle, what numbered about five hundred verses, all consisting of derivatives from the word 'Baha'. That scroll was in a state of perfect preservation, was spotlessly clean, and gave the impression, at first sight, of being a printed rather than a written page. So fine and intricate was the penmanship that viewed at a distance, the writing appeared as a single wash of ink on the paper. We were overcome with admiration as we gazed upon a masterpiece which no calligraphist, we believed, could rival. That scroll was replaced in the coffer and handed back to Mírzá Aḥmad, who, on the very day he received it, proceeded to Tihrán. Ere he departed, he informed us that all he could divulge of that letter was the injunction that the trust was to be delivered into the hands of Jináb-i-Bahá [Bahá'u'lláh] in Tihrán.[6]

Nabíl stayed in Kirmánsháh until Bahá'u'lláh passed through on His way to Karbilá in August 1851. Bahá'u'lláh told Nabíl to return to Tehran and take Mírzá Yaḥyá to a fort near Sháhrúd, northeast of Tehran. Mírzá Yaḥyá, however, refused to go and told Nabíl to go to Qazvín and deliver some letters to his friends.[7] Returning to Tehran after going to Qazvín, Nabíl spent his time transcribing and distributing the Writings of the Báb.[8]

In 1852, two fanatical Bábís tried to assassinate the Sháh and this resulted in the imprisonment and exile of Bahá'u'lláh, the martyrdom of Ṭáhirih, the murder of countless Bahá'ís, and Mírzá Yaḥyá, Bahá'u'lláh's half-brother, going into hiding out of fear for his life. Most of the Letters of the Living had also been martyred by this time. With the Bábí community disillusioned and apparently leaderless, a deluded Nabíl claimed that he was 'Him Whom God shall make manifest', passing around some of his own writings as proof.[9]

Nabíl obviously wasn't totally convinced of his own claim because some time later while Bahá'u'lláh was in Sulaymaniyyih, Nabíl went to Baghdad to see Mírzá Yaḥyá, who some Bábís thought was the Báb's designated successor. When he arrived, Mírzá Músá, Bahá'u'lláh's brother, told him that Mírzá Yaḥyá refused to meet anyone. Nabíl did receive a note from Yaḥyá urging him to leave Baghdad, go to Karbilá and seek out Siyyid Muḥammad-i-Isfahání, which he did. But the 'riotous behaviour and childish pranks' of the Siyyid, who would later be named the Antichrist of the Bahá'í Dispensation after the passing of Bahá'u'lláh, completely disillusioned Nabíl.[10]

When Bahá'u'lláh returned to Baghdad from His self-imposed exile in 1854, Nabíl quickly recognised His true station and 'prostrated himself at His feet and begged forgiveness for his presumption' of claiming to be a Manifestation of God. As repentance, he cut off his beard, the symbol of a man's dignity in those days, made a brush from the hair and used it to sweep the approach to Bahá'u'lláh's house. From then on, he was one of Bahá'u'lláh's most dedicated servants.[11]

Three months after attaining Bahá'u'lláh's presence, the Blessed Beauty directed Nabíl to teach the Faith in Qazvín. As he was leaving, a messenger caught up with him to give him money from Bahá'u'lláh for the journey. He took only a little of the money and wrote that 'Every instant a new door would fling open before me. It was as if I had wings to soar in the Heaven of the Beloved. I felt no need to have a companion on the road and I had no fear of highwaymen'.[12]

After completing his travel-teaching, Nabíl returned to Baghdad. Bahá'u'lláh told him and Áqá Siyyid Ismá'íl-i-Zavári'í to review a manuscript of the *Qayyúmu'l-Asmá*, the commentary on Joseph revealed by the Báb on the night of His declaration, to make sure it was accurate. It took them 18 days to do so.[13] During this time, Nabíl wrote that 'the words of Bahá'u'lláh were revealed in great profusion', and that He would reveal the equivalent of the Qur'án each day over a two year period. Much of what He revealed was not recorded.[14]

In 1860, two implacable enemies of the Faith, Mírzá Buzurg Khán-i-Qazvíní, the Persian Consul, and Shaykh 'Abdu'l-Ḥusayn, a Persian mujtahid, who were both incensed at Bahá'u'lláh's increasing prestige, began to threaten the Bábís. Since most of the Bábís were Persian, they were under grave threat of being sent back to Persia by the Consul. To protect them, Bahá'u'lláh told all the Bábís to get Ottoman citizenship. Over the course of three weeks, the Bábís went in twos and threes with Áqá Muḥammad Riḍáy to apply for Ottoman passports. Nabíl was one of them. With that done, the Bábís, as Ottoman citizens, were protected from the Persian Consul.[15]

When Bahá'u'lláh proclaimed that He was 'Him Whom God shall make manifest', Nabíl was already a believer. After the Ottoman Government sent Bahá'u'lláh to Constantinople, Nabíl, unable to endure His absence, followed Him in the guise of a dervish. He joined

Bahá'u'lláh's party while it was travelling, and remained with it until it arrived in the Ottoman capital.[16]

Bahá'u'lláh departed Constantinople for Adrianople on 1 December 1863. The night before leaving, Bahá'u'lláh directed Nabíl and Mírzá Áqá to return to Persia and spread the tidings of His announcement.[17] When Nabíl reached Shiraz and told a gathering of Bábís of Bahá'u'lláh's station, Khadíjih-Bagum, the widow of the Báb, was in the next room behind a curtain. Upon hearing of His declaration, she immediately put her forehead on the ground and told her nephew, Áqá Mírzá Áqá, who also accepted Bahá'u'lláh's station, to 'Offer at His sacred threshold my most humble devotion'.[18]

In about 1865, while in Adrianople, Bahá'u'lláh wrote a Tablet addressed to Nabíl in which He

> directs Nabíl to travel throughout the land, meet the sincere souls among the community, and rend asunder the grievous veils that have hindered them from recognizing the Countenance of Glory the mission of Nabíl and other disciples of Bahá'u'lláh at this period was primarily to teach His Cause to the members of the Bábí community. But He warns him not to associate with, and even to flee from, those who show enmity towards Him. This is mainly a reference to the Bábís who were unfaithful to the Cause and were drawn to Mírzá Yaḥyá.[19]

Nabíl was in Khurásán in the spring of 1866. While there, he introduced the use of 'Alláh'u'Abhá' as a greeting amongst the Bahá'ís, replacing the Islamic 'Alláh'u'Akbar'. This gave the Bahá'ís a distinct greeting and separated them from the Bábís, who still used the older term. In the autumn, Nabíl went to Shiraz and Baghdad with two Tablets called the *Súriy-i-Ḥajj* I and II, the Tablets of the Pilgrimage. In Shiraz, he did the rites of pilgrimage and read the Tablet at the House of the Báb. Reaching Baghdad, he did the same thing at the House of Bahá'u'lláh, thereby becoming the first person to complete a pilgrimage to both holy sites.[20] He also delivered gifts from Bahá'u'lláh to Khadíjih-Bagum, the wife of the Báb.[21]

Near the end of His confinement in Adrianople, probably in early 1868, Bahá'u'lláh sent Nabíl on a mission to Egypt to appeal to the Khedive in Cairo on behalf of seven Bahá'ís, including Mírzá Ḥaydar-'Alí, who had been imprisoned there by the hostile Iranian Consul-General, Mírzá Ḥasan Khán-i-Khú'í.[22] Nabíl arrived in Cairo to find that the prisoners had been sent to Sudan. He then had a dream in which Bahá'u'lláh warned him that something bad was afoot. The next day, he was taken before the Consul on fabricated charges, put in chains, thrown into prison and interrogated several times. On one occasion, he was shown a photograph and asked who it was. He truthfully answered that it was 'Abdu'l-Bahá. Then they showed him a copy of the *Kitáb-i-Íqán* and told him to read it. Feeling ill, he said someone else should read it. The part read was about the detachment and self-sacrifice of the Bábís, which asks 'if they were not right, then by what proofs could one demonstrate the rightness of the Cause.' The reader jokingly asked, 'Why did you become a Bábí? Had the Cause of the Báb been true, I should have become a Bábí, because I am both a siyyid and a Shírází'. Nabíl answered 'But neither has it been proved that I am a Bábí, nor that you are not one.' The Consul didn't like the answer and sent him back to prison.[23]

Nabíl was then transferred to a prison in Alexandria. In that prison, he met a Christian physician named Fáris Effendi, who had been jailed for financial reasons. Fáris was attracted to Nabíl. At first Fáris tried to convert Nabíl to Christianity, but soon found himself enamoured by Nabíl's description of the Revelation of Bahá'u'lláh, and joyously became a Bahá'í.[24]

While in the Alexandria prison, Nabíl had another dream in which Bahá'u'lláh appeared to him and said that his imprisonment would end 81 days later, on 27 August 1868. When that day arrived, Nabíl went up onto the roof of the prison to see what would happen. Suddenly, he saw Bahá'u'lláh's caterer, Muḥammad Ibráhím, on the street below. Bahá'u'lláh's ship had arrived in Alexandria that day from Gallipoli and he had gone ashore for supplies. Calling out to him, Nabíl was able to have a short visit with him in the prison. Muḥammad Ibráhím pointed out Bahá'u'lláh's ship in the harbour and told him that Bahá'u'lláh was headed for 'Akká.

That night, Nabíl and Fáris wrote a letter to Bahá'u'lláh and gave it to a Christian youth the next day to deliver to Bahá'u'lláh's ship. The youth headed for the ship in a row boat, but the ship began to sail away before he was able to reach it, to the great dismay of Nabíl and Fáris. But then, mysteriously, the ship stopped just long enough for the letter to be delivered and for Bahá'u'lláh to reveal a Tablet to the two prisoners. That Tablet bestowed Bahá'u'lláh's bounties on Fáris and 'fanned into flame the fire of faith which had been ignited by Nabíl'. Both prisoners were freed soon thereafter.[25]

From Alexandria, Nabíl went to Cyprus and then to 'Akká to attain the presence of Bahá'u'lláh. He went disguised as a man from Uzbekistan, arriving in October 1868, but was recognised by Siyyid Muḥammad-i-Isfahání, an enemy of the Faith, and expelled from the city. For the next four months, Nabíl lived in the caves of Mount Carmel and roamed the nearby countryside. In February 1869, he again tried and was able to enter the city of 'Akká and meet a few of the Bahá'ís, but was unable to be with Bahá'u'lláh. Not until 1 May 1869, was he finally able to enter Bahá'u'lláh's presence.[26] Nabíl remained in 'Akká for the rest of his life, basking in the light of the Blessed Beauty on a regular basis.[27]

In 1871, Bahá'u'lláh declared that the Badí' Calendar would begin in 1844. He asked Nabíl to transcribe the text of the Calendar and then instruct the believers on how to use it. The names of the months came from a Shí'á prayer in which there are 19 invocations, each using one of God's names. The Báb had taken these names in the same order for the names of the months of His calendar.[28]

On 22 January 1872, three Covenant-breakers, including the Antichrist of the Bahá'í Dispensation, Siyyid Muḥammad-i-Iṣfahání, were murdered by seven Bahá'ís who could no longer tolerate their incessant efforts to undermine Bahá'u'lláh. Bahá'u'lláh was put in custody, and 'Abdu'l-Bahá jailed. Even Nabíl was put in jail for a few days until it was determined that they were innocent. Although released, he was sent away from Akká for a time.[29]

In September 1879, Nabíl and Ḥájí Muḥammad-Ṭáhir-i-Málmírí were living in adjacent rooms in 'Akká that overlooked the street Bahá'u'lláh passed along on His way to the Mansion. One evening, two hours after sunset, Nabíl and Muḥammad-Ṭáhir saw Bahá'u'lláh ride by on His white donkey. Nabíl suggested that they follow, and circumambulate the Mansion. Keeping about 50 steps behind, they followed the Blessed Beauty to the Mansion, which was illuminated by a large oil lamp. When Bahá'u'lláh entered the building, Nabíl and Muḥammad-Ṭáhir walked toward the Mansion to start their circumambulation, but as they drew near, they found the pathways full of people. Muḥammad-Ṭáhir wrote that

The footpaths around the walls of the Mansion were packed with people, who were standing. Crowds had assembled around the four sides of the Mansion and we could hear their murmuring as well as their breathing. Of course we knew that no one had come from 'Akká to circumambulate the Mansion, and we two had gone there without permission. Anyhow, since there was no room to walk on the footpath we stepped back, and at a distance of about thirty steps from the Mansion we circumambulatedAs we circled the Mansion we could sense the presence of the multitude on the four sides of the building at some distance from us. In the end we prostrated ourselves on the ground opposite the Gate of the Mansion, and returned to 'Akká

When we arrived home, Nabíl suggested that we ought not to sleep that night and instead keep vigil. He said to me, 'I will compose poems and you make tea.' I made tea several times during the night and Nabíl was engaged in writing poetry . . . By the morning, he had produced poems written on both sides of a large sheet of paper. We sent a copy of his poems, together with two sugar cones, to the Blessed Beauty. His poems were mainly about history, the history of Bahá'u'lláh's imprisonment, His banishment to Baghdad, Istanbul, Adrianople and 'Akká, the sufferings He had endured in the barracks, the story of the building of the Mansion by 'Údí Khammár, and 'Abdu'l-Bahá renting it to serve as a residence for the Blessed Perfection.

He then described the events of the evening Bahá'u'lláh went to the Mansion, and how we both followed Him, the account of our circumambulation when we saw the souls of all the Prophets and Messengers and the Concourse on high assembled outside the Mansion, circumambulating the throne of their Lord. In these poems Nabíl described in detail our keeping vigil, his own writing poems, and my making tea.

When His Blessed Person received the poems of Nabíl, He revealed a Tablet in honour of Nabíl and myself. In it He graciously accepted our pilgrimage to the Mansion, conferred upon Nabíl the title of Bulbul (Nightingale) and upon myself Bahháj (the Blissful).[30]

With Nabíl and Muḥammad-Ṭáhir sharing two rooms, practical jokes were common. One day, Nabíl took Muḥammad-Ṭáhir's prayer beads and hung them high up near the ceiling where they were out of reach. Soon thereafter, Bahá'u'lláh arrived and 'asked Nabíl in an amused tone, "Whose prayer beads are those that you have imprisoned here?"'[31]

Nabíl began what became his greatest work, *The Dawn-Breakers*, in 1887 in collaboration with Mírzá Músá (see Chapter 1), Bahá'u'lláh's faithful brother. The text was completed in approximately a year and a half, and the draft submitted to Mírzá Áqá Ján. Ten months later, a corrected copy was returned to him, and Nabíl made the alterations Unfortunately, following the passing of Bahá'u'lláh, the Covenant-breakers stole two satchels of documents, including the corrected version of Nabíl's manuscript. This updated version of the manuscript has never been found. What Shoghi Effendi later translated was the original uncorrected version of the book. The full manuscript contained the history of the Faith up to the passing of Bahá'u'lláh in 1892,[32] but Shoghi Effendi's translation only covers the time up to 1852.

During Bahá'u'lláh's final days in the physical world, Nabíl was allowed a final private audience with Him. When Bahá'u'lláh ascended on 29 May 1892, Nabíl was completely devastated and inconsolable. 'Abdu'l-Bahá asked him to select a text for recitation at His tomb and he chose four passages from Bahá'u'lláh's own Writings. This is now the *Tablet of Visitation*.[33]

For Nabíl, life without Bahá'u'lláh was not worth living and on 20 December 1892, he walked into the sea and drowned. He left a note for 'Abdu'l-Bahá that formed his own epitaph:

Nabíl hath been immersed in the ocean
Of the Mercy of his Glorious Lord.
Open Thou a way for a consumed heart to see,
Drowned – drowned in this year let me be![34]

13

SHAYKH MUḤAMMAD KÁẒIM-I-QAZVÍNÍ – SAMANDAR

(1844–1918)

Shaykh Muḥammad Káẓim-i-Qazvíní, commonly known as Samandar, was a pillar of the Faith of Bahá'u'lláh in Qazvín, and a man of knowledge who put the Faith before everything else in his life. In his early days, he was a merchant by profession, but that did not divert his attention from service. He was very aware of the injunction of the Qur'án: 'Men whom neither merchandise nor traffic beguile from the remembrance of God'[1]. His father, Ḥájí Shaykh Muḥammad Qazvíní, had asked Siyyid Káẓim-i-Rashtí to pray that he be given a son. When this son was born he called him Káẓim.[2]

Shaykh Káẓim was born in Qazvín on 6 February 1844 with an impressive lineage. His grandfather, Ḥájí Rasúl, lived in Karbilá and was the first in the family to meet the Báb, encountering Him before His declaration. He met Him 'oftentimes in the Shrine of Imám Ḥusayn' and was 'enchanted with His grandeur and majesty'. When told that his son had become a Bábí, Ḥájí Rasúl said, speaking of the Báb, that 'I have never met any blessed Being possessed of such humility and such nobility'. Samandar's father was introduced to the Faith by a Letter of the Living and had visited the Báb in Tabríz, Mákú and Chihríq, receiving a Tablet from the Báb while He was in Mákú.[3] The Báb gave him his title of Nabíl.

One of Samandar's earliest memories was of the time when Ṭáhirih came to Qazvín in 1847. Amid the tension of her presence, Ṭáhirih's uncle, Mullá Taqí, who was highly antagonistic towards the Faith, was murdered by a Shaykhí baker when he said that those who followed the Shaykhí beliefs 'were the very embodiments of error'. The authorities didn't believe anyone as lowly as the baker could murder such an important cleric, and

Samandar's father was blamed, even though he had been out of town at the time. Warned upon his return, Ḥájí Shaykh Muḥammad went into hiding, with the authorities in angry pursuit. Samandar wrote that

> Witnessing the state my mother was in, I realized that my father had come home. But instead of joy, sorrow and lamentation prevailed. My mother was bemoaning the return of my father. My late aunt kept striking her head and breast, telling my father: 'Why did you return at such a time? . . . Alas! it is too late . . . They have put your name at the top of the list of wanted men and are all looking for you. So demanding are they that even your brother, who does not share your beliefs and for that reason is hostile towards you, has found living so constricted that, terror-stricken, he has gone into hiding in a subterranean place. Make haste; there is no time to tarry.'
>
> He consented, and was taken to the home of Mashhadí Báqir-i-Sabbágh . . . they had a subterranean room . . . which could be reached only in the centre of an upper room. A plank was placed over the entrance . . .
>
> Within two hours a number of *farrashes*, accompanied by an executioner and a certain Siyyid Muhsin, appeared outside our house, knocking furiously at the gate which was not opened to them. Then they brought a ladder, stormed the house, poured over the wall and the roof, searched everywhere, and found no one. When they came over the wall and the roof, I, a little boy, was in the courtyard, trembling from head to foot.[4]

Ṭáhirih left Qazvín, and things calmed down so that Samandar's father could resume his business. But soon, the mujtahid summoned him and, after but a few words, ordered his minions to beat him. Though he was being severely battered, Ḥájí Shaykh Muḥammad focused his thoughts on the Báb, and soon noticed that one of his nails was about to fall off. Completely detached from the beating, Ḥájí Shaykh Muḥammad began to smile. At that point, the superintendent arrived and seeing the smile, said in astonishment, 'They are killing you and you are smiling!' He intervened and Ḥájí Shaykh Muḥammad was released. He then moved to Tabríz. When he later went to see the Báb, the Báb told him that 'They scourged you and you suffered for My sake; in truth, it was I who was scourged'.

The young Samandar also suffered for his father's strong faith, and told a story about going to the grocers:

> I went to make some purchases from a grocer's shop at the end of our lane. A few men were idling their time around that shop. They saw me approaching from afar, and decided amongst themselves to do me some harm. As I neared the shop, one of them who was a well-built man, to do a good deed approached me and, without saying a word, slapped me hard on the face. I remember that the grocer, knowing that I had come to make purchases at his shop, stopped them and told them to leave me alone. Since I had gone to buy some provisions from him, I went forward and gave him the money. Whilst he was weighing the things, I could hear those men talking about me. I heard one of them say, 'Is he a bastard or not?' Another said in reply: 'If he was conceived prior to his father's ratting and becoming a Bábí, then he is not a bastard; but he is one if his conception took place when his father had already become a Bábí.'[5]

In his early years in Qazvín, Samandar met some of the most well known Bábís such as Mulla Ḥusayn, Vaḥíd, Mullá Jalíl-i-Urúmí, one of the Letters of the Living, and others. At the age of fifteen, he went with his father to Tabriz, where, following in his father's footsteps, he learned how to be a merchant. Samandar loved to learn new things. Two of his teachers were Bahá'u'lláh's uncle, Zaynu'l-Muqarrabín (not to be confused with the Apostle of Bahá'u'lláh Zaynu'l-'Ábidín Muqarrabín) and Ḥájí Á<u>kh</u>und, who became both a Hand of the Cause and an Apostle of Bahá'u'lláh (see Chapter 8). Samandar studied for two years with Ḥájí Á<u>kh</u>und.[6]

When Samandar was eighteen, his father passed away and it fell upon him to take care of his father's business in Tabríz, Qazvín and Lahíján. His deep grief at the death of his father was replaced by joy when he received a Tablet of condolence from Bahá'u'lláh wherein he was asked to forget his sorrow and grief because his father had ascended to the Divine Kingdom and now abided under the shadow of Divine Grace. In the year 1865, Samandar married <u>Kh</u>ánum Fáṭima Sulṭán and a year later she gave birth to a son who they named 'Abdu'l-Ḥusayn.[7]

When Bahá'u'lláh unveiled His true station in the Garden of Riḍván in 1863, it was only to a few people. Later, He revealed the *Súriy-i-Aṣḥáb*, which proclaimed His Revelation clearly and openly. When the Tablet arrived in Qazvín, Samandar, whose name was mentioned in the Tablet, wrote that 'it precipitated a great upheaval and created a severe convulsion [among the community]. After discussions, talks, investigations and references to the Holy Writings, each one in the community, somehow in some way, through the bounty of God was guided [to the truth] and reached the stage of steadfastness'. Samandar was one of them.[8]

Many were challenged by Bahá'u'lláh's declaration that He was the One Whom God shall make manifest. These included such illustrious Bábís as Ḥájí Á<u>kh</u>und. Bahá'u'lláh commanded Samandar to take a message to him and through Samandar's efforts, Ḥájí Á<u>kh</u>und soon recognised the Blessed Beauty.

Some still erroneously thought that Mírzá Yaḥyá was the appointed heir to the Báb. One Bábí wrote to Mírzá Yaḥyá with a question about whether it was lawful to eat the meat of snakes:

> One of the questions which he had asked was this: some physicians prepare pills with the flesh of serpents, and sometimes they mix it with other ingredients and make an electuary. At other times they prescribe the cooked meat of a serpent to cure certain ailments. Is it lawful to partake of such flesh? That man, Azal, had written an answer in Arabic. These were his words: 'Is there a dearth of things to eat, that you wish to eat serpents and scorpions?' Yes, that answer made me [Samandar] see that that man [Mírzá Yaḥyá] was more stupid than I had ever thought him.[9]

In 1866/67, Samandar wrote a treatise that denounced and rebutted Mírzá Yaḥyá and his rebellion against Bahá'u'lláh. Bahá'u'lláh referred to the treatise in His Tablet called the *Lawḥ-i-Siráj* and reportedly gave him his title of 'Samandar', meaning 'phoenix', because of it. In the *Tablet of Salmán*, Bahá'u'lláh confirms Samandar's efforts in his treatise, writing: 'It is incumbent upon all men, each according to his ability, to refute the arguments of those that have attacked the Faith of God'.[10]

In March 1874, Samandar and Ḥájí Nasír, a survivor of <u>Sh</u>ay<u>kh</u> Tabarsí, were able to attain the presence of Bahá'u'lláh in 'Akká.[11] Samandar described their pilgrimage, saying that in October 1873,

> this servant, with bales of merchandise consisting of silk and coarse silken material, left Qazvín for Ras͟ht, accompanied by Ḥájí Muḥammad-Ḥasan, the goldsmith, my own maternal uncle (who had his wife and mother-in-law with him), Ḥájí Mullá Bábá, Kallih-Darri'í, and Áqá 'Abdu'lláh . . . There we attended to our business concerns, and took with us Ḥájí Muḥammad-Nasír who was in charge of the trading-house in Ras͟ht, and went on our way. In those days there was as yet no railway between Bádkúbih and Tiflís. We travelled by commercial cart. The late Ḥájí Nasír and I stayed in Istanbul for trading purposes. Others in our company went on pilgrimage to the Holy Land, while we two asked once again for permission. When it came, we left Istanbul with Mansúr-i-Uskú'í. We reached 'Akká on [28 February 1874], coinciding with the period of fasting. We were in His sacred presence throughout Naw-Rúz and Riḍvan. Another pilgrim at the time was Ismu'lláhu'l-Aṣdaq [Ibn-i-Aṣdaq's father (see Chapter 19)]. He spoke to us about what they had experienced in Mázindarán. Ḥájí Nasír was there too.
>
> One day the Blessed Perfection, Who was staying in the house of Áqáy-i-Kalím at the K͟hán-i-['Avámíd] addressed Ḥájí Nasír in words such as these, as far as I can remember: 'Jináb-i-Ḥájí! You have toiled much and suffered much in the path of God. If you yourself have forgotten what you have done and endured, God has not. But the worlds of God are not confined to this world. Were it so, the Exalted Prophets would not have consented to bear such adversities wrought by men; the Manifestation who preceded Me would not have consented to be suspended and martyred with volleys of malice and malignity; and I would not have consented to be dragged, bare-headed and barefooted, in utmost degradation, from Níyávarán to Tihrán to bear untold blows.' In brief, He expounded this theme in most excellent words. He was telling the Ḥájí that he will be recompensed in the worlds to come.[12]

The French Emperor Napoleon III had died while Samandar was in Istanbul and he wanted to ask Bahá'u'lláh 'why it was that those who had persecuted the Faith, its Founders and followers were still enjoying power while Napoleon III had gone the way predicted in the Tablet addressed to him'. Before he could ask, however, Bahá'u'lláh spoke about the French Emperor and the other Kings that He had addressed:

> Napoleon, Baha'u'llah said, was godless. Intellect was his god, and he believed that he himself was the wisest of all men. As soon as he was challenged and found wanting, the hand of God seized him and struck him down. Then He spoke of developments in Persia and Turkey and told Samandar that the oppressors of these lands would also, in due time, receive their deserts. Two years later, 'Abdu'l-'Azíz of Turkey met his doom, and in 1896, Náṣiri'd-Dín of Iran, on the very eve of his Jubilee celebrations, fell before the bullet of an assassin.[13]

In 1883, Samandar employed a tutor for his son. This man, Mullá 'Alí, lived in Samandar's home for many years. Mullá 'Alí's nephew was an enemy of the Faith and did not want his uncle living in a Bahá'í home, so he accused Samandar of kidnapping his uncle:

> He carried on his vendetta to such an extent that the government became really suspicious. 'My uncle', he said, 'has been kept a prisoner by this Babi. He does not allow him to leave the house.' Therefore the governor sent his *farrásh-báshí* and a number of *farráshes,* together with the plaintiff himself, to put the matter right. As it happened, the Mu'allim [Mullá 'Alí] had gone on a journey with Áqá Muḥammad-i-Qá'ní, known as Fáḍil, to accompany him part of the way, leave him at a certain spot, and return [to Qazvín] . . .
>
> All that while the nephew of Mullá 'Alí was lashing him with his waspish tongue. But Samandar kept calm and told his tormentors that they could search everywhere in the house for Mullá 'Alí, but they would be wasting their time because the Mu'allim was not there; he had been there, but had gone away. He was returned to his home, while the search went on, which was in vain. Samandar's household was naturally alarmed, the women and children distressed, but he asked for a hubble-bubble to be brought for him and the *farrásh-báshí.* They sat down quietly by the flower-bed and had a smoke together, while the intense search continued for Mullá 'Alí. Once the *farráshes* were satisfied that the man whom they sought was indeed not in that house, they prepared to leave, taking Samandar with them. They realized they had made a great mistake, but no one was prepared to admit it. In the meantime the rabble was growing in number, and the ill-intentioned nephew of Mullá 'Alí was becoming

> louder with his denunciations. Samandar was threatened with death, but as dignified as ever he kept calm and unruffled. While the mob was thickening and chaos increased, the deputy-governor made his appearance. He and the *farrá<u>sh</u>-bá<u>sh</u>í* took counsel together and came to the conclusion that Samandar was telling the truth and others were prevaricating. He was allowed to return home . . .[14]

In 1891, Samandar made his second pilgrimage to 'Akká and was again enveloped in the light of Bahá'u'lláh. He was accompanied by his son, Ṭaráẓu'lláh Samandarí, the future Hand of the Cause, and the teacher, Ḥájí Nasír.[15] They had travelled via Istanbul and Alexandria, Egypt. One day, just as he was leaving Bahá'u'lláh's presence, Samandar heard Him say, 'You are going to 'Akká; go into the presence of Sarkár-i-Áqá'. Sarkár-i-Áqá was one of the titles 'Abdu'l-Bahá was known by, and Samandar was 'greatly surprised' by Bahá'u'lláh's emphatic command. It was only later, when Mírzá Muḥammad-'Alí broke the Covenant, that he understood that Bahá'u'lláh had been telling him to turn to 'Abdu'l-Bahá for guidance. Samandar was allowed to spend two months in 'Akká. When he departed, he travelled back to Iran with Varqá (see Chapter 6) and his two sons, 'Azízu'lláh and Rúḥu'lláh.[16]

Attacks on the Bahá'ís in Tehran were increasing dramatically and Samandar was warned to take precautions, so he left one night and went into hiding. As he lay low, his business in Ra<u>sh</u>t came under attack. Another businessman in Ra<u>sh</u>t had sold Samandar some goods worth 100 túmáns and, at the instigation of his enemies, refused Samandar's cheque and demanded the money in cash instantly. The sum was large and Samandar didn't have that much readily available in Ra<u>sh</u>t (and he was in Qazvín), so the other man complained to the authorities, who then raided Samandar's offices in Ra<u>sh</u>t, arresting Ḥájí Nasír, his pilgrimage companion, and Nasír's son. They were both thrown into prison, and the stress was so great that the very elderly Ḥájí Nasír died in his cell. When his body was taken out, the 'rabble of the town' took it, defiled it and then dragged it to a 'ruined' spot and threw stones at it until it was buried. When things calmed down, Samandar's innocence was proved and the Governor decided to arrest Mullá 'Alí's nephew, who fled the town. Years later, he returned and, full of remorse over what he had done, apologised.[17]

In 1900, Samandar, along with his son Áqá <u>Gh</u>ulám-'Alí, and the son of Ḥájí Nasír, Áqá 'Alíy-i-Arbáb, went on pilgrimage to see 'Abdu'l-Bahá. While there, Samandar attempted to get his daughter, Thurayyá, away from the Covenant-breakers. She had been married to Mírzá Ḍíyá'u'lláh, one of Bahá'u'lláh's sons allied with the Covenant-breaking Mírzá Muḥammad-'Alí, and was living in the Mansion of Bahjí. Ḍíyá'u'lláh had died and Samandar wanted to take his daughter home. A meeting was arranged within the Shrine of Bahá'u'lláh:

> The infamous crew, entrenched in the Mansion of Bahjí, made this meeting after long years between a distraught, uncertain, grief-stricken woman and her caring, sorrowing parents, a scene of sordid revenge and conflict. Thurayyá, her tears flowing, complained bitterly that they had unjustly neglected her. Samandar tried gently to reason with her and asked her to come away with them, but Thurayya refused: she would never depart from the vicinity of her husband's grave. Ḍíyá'u'lláh was buried in a room next to the inner Shrine of Bahá'u'lláh [his body was later removed]. An old hajj had been sent to watch the meeting between Thurayyá and her parents. As soon as Mírzá Ghulám-'Alí caught hold of his sister's hand to lead her to the Pilgrim House nearby, the old woman shouted horribly at Thurayyá, who screamed in return. At that, a number of Mírzá Muḥammad-'Alí's partisans rushed in and dragged Samandar and those who were with him into the Mansion, cursing and beating him all the while. There they were detained, howled at and jeered by a mob. Mírzá Áqá Ján, the faithless amanuensis of Bahá'u'lláh, and Javád-i-Qazvíní were foremost amongst them. And in the meantime, the fickle Mírzá Badí'u'lláh, the youngest son of Bahá'u'lláh, and Mírzá Ḥusayn-i-Khartúmí . . . hastened to the Seraye [Government House] in 'Akká, shamelessly reporting to the authorities that a group of people had come ostensibly to visit the Shrine of Bahá'u'lláh . . . in order to kidnap a woman. The Mutasarrif sent an interrogator with a number of horsemen to Bahjí. They put Samandar, his wife, son and two others who were with them in a carriage and took them to 'Akká. There they were driven straight to the Master's house and left. When informed of the base behaviour of the Covenant-breakers, 'Abdu'l-Bahá Himself went to see the Mutasarrif and informed that official of the truth of the matter. The Mutasarrif said that Thurayyá should be brought out of the

> Mansion and united with her parents, but 'Abdu'l-Bahá forbade it. Upon Samandar, who intended to take his case to the courts, He laid the same injunction. He, the very manifestation of mercy, told Samandar that any action to retrieve Thurayyá would greatly sadden Mírzá Ḍíyá'u'lláh's mother, who was still grieving over his death. The interrogator who had gone out to Bahjí, when apprised of the facts of the case advised strongly that Samandar should take action, but again 'Abdu'l-Bahá would not allow it. They had been vindictive and foolish, He said, but we should be forgiving.[18]

Samandar kept a detailed record of the 31 journeys he made between the ages of 11 and 74. He recorded that in 1895, he spent 20 days in Tehran meeting with the Bahá'ís. In 1903, he made a 70-day journey to Zanján, Azerbaijan, and Tabríz and his next trip was to Rasht. His 26th journey was for two and a half months to Tehran. Immediately following this, he went to Rasht. Soon after arriving there, Samandar was informed that Hand of the Cause Ibn-i-Abhar (see Chapter 11) had received a Tablet from 'Abdu'l-Bahá directing him, Samandar and Áqá Mírzá Na'ím to work together and write a book refuting one just published by Prof E. G. Browne which contained two misleading introductions. Samandar stayed in Rasht for three weeks, then went to Qazvín.[19]

On 2 November 1914, Samandar received a Tablet from the Master directing him to go to Tehran and help 'in reconciling the members of that Spiritual Assembly, who apparently had been at 'loggerheads'. He left immediately for Tehran and successfully carried out the mission with 'tact and understanding'.[20]

Samandar's last journey, at the age of 71, was to Rasht in September 1915. He spent about six months there with his family, meeting enquirers about the Faith. His son, Áqá Ghulám-'Alí lived in Rasht, and other family members living in Qazvín came over to be with him. He stayed until 20 March 1916.[21]

With failing eyesight and increasing weakness, he was mostly confined to home. In the winter of early 1918, Samandar died in Qazvín.

14

MUḤAMMAD MUṢṬAFÁY-I-BAGHDÁDÍ

(1838–1910)

Muḥammad Muṣṭafáy-i-Baghdádí, an Arab, was born in 1838 in Baghdad, the son of Shaykh Muḥammad Shibl, a high-ranking 'ulamá. Shaykh Muḥammad had been a student of Síyyid Káẓim Rashtí, who along with Shaykh Aḥmad, had correctly predicted the coming of the Báb. Shaykh Muḥammad Shibl moved to Baghdad in about 1827 and became Síyyid Káẓim's personal representative there. When Ṭáhirih arrived in nearby Karbilá in 1843, he became one of her followers.[1] It was during this time that Ibn-i-Aṣdaq (see Chapter 17), while travelling with the Sháh of Persia, came into contact with Ṭáhirih.

After the declaration of the Báb, Shaykh Muḥammad Shibl was helped to recognise the station of the Báb through the efforts of Letter of the Living Mullá 'Alí Bastámí. When 'Alí Bastámí arrived in Baghdad, he was imprisoned and Shaykh Muḥammad Shibl visited him every day. This allowed him to hear 'the Word of God from him for three months' and he became an ardent Bábí. Shaykh Muḥammad Shibl took what he learned from 'Alí Bastámí and shared it with those searching for spiritual enlightenment, and soon there were a large number of Bábís in Baghdad.[2]

When Ṭáhirih was expelled to Baghdad in December 1845, she stayed with Shaykh Muḥammad Shibl and 7-year-old Mírzá Muṣṭafá for ten weeks. The young boy carried Ṭáhirih's messages from place to place.[3] 'Abdu'l-Bahá described him:

> Muḥammad-Muṣṭafá was a blazing light. He was the son of the famous scholar Shaykh Muḥammad-i-Shibl; he lived in Iráq, and from his earliest youth was clearly delete 'ali'unique and beyond compare; wise, brave, deserving in every way, he was known far and

> wide. From childhood, guided by his father, he had lit the light of faith in the chapel of his heart. He had rid himself of the hindering veils of illusion, gazed about with perceptive eyes, witnessed great new signs of God and, regardless of the consequences, had cried aloud: 'The earth hath shone out with the light of her Lord!'[4]

In March 1847, when Ṭáhirih was forced to return to Persia, she was accompanied by a 'group of about thirty armed Arabs' that included Shaykh Muḥammad Shibl, who covered most of the expenses of the journey, and 10-year-old Mírzá Muṣṭafá. When they reached Kirmánsháh, Shaykh Muḥammad Shibl acted as one of Ṭáhirih's translators for her talks. Father and son followed Ṭáhirih onward to Qazvín in about September 1847. Mírzá Muṣṭafá served as a courier between his father and Ṭáhirih, delivering his father's questions to her and her answers back to him.[5]

A month later, she instructed Shaykh Muḥammad Shibl and Mírzá Muṣṭafá to go to Tehran to meet Mullá Ḥusayn, the first person to accept the Báb. Years later in April 1890, Prof E. G. Browne, returning from his historic meeting with Bahá'u'lláh, met Mírzá Muṣṭafá in Beirut and asked him about the physical appearance of Mullá Ḥusayn. Mírzá Muṣṭafá said that he was 'lean and fragile to look at, but keen and bright as the sword which never left his side. For the rest, he was not more than thirty or thirty-five years old, and his raiment was white'.[6]

After a time in Tehran, father and son returned to Baghdad where Shaykh Muḥammad Shibl spent the remainder of his days. He passed away just two days after receiving news of the Bab's martyrdom in July 1850.

Mírzá Muṣṭafá was in Baghdad when Bahá'u'lláh arrived as an exile from Persia in 1853. He quickly recognised Bahá'u'lláh's majesty and was one of those who recognised His station as Him Whom God shall make manifest, even before He had made His declaration. Because of his deep attachment to Bahá'u'lláh, and 'renowned for his strength and courage, many Bahais took shelter with him whenever they were harassed or in trouble'.[7] 'Abdu'l-Bahá again describes Mírzá Muṣṭafá's powerful character:

> Gracious God! The opposition was powerful, the penalty obvious, the friends, every one of them, terrified, and off in some corner

> hiding their belief; at such a time this intrepid personality boldly went about his business, and like a man, faced up to every tyrant. The one individual who, in the year seventy, was famed in 'Iráq for his love of Bahá'u'lláh, was this honored person. A few other souls, then in Baghdád and its environs, had crept away into nooks and crannies and, imprisoned in their own lethargy, there they remained. But this admirable Muḥammad Muṣṭafá would boldly, proudly come and go like a man, and the hostile, because of his physical strength and his courage, were afraid to attack him.
>
> After Bahá'u'lláh's return from His journey to Kurdistán, the virile strength and bearing of that gallant individual was still further enhanced. Whenever leave was granted, he would attend upon Bahá'u'lláh, and would hear from His lips expressions of favor and grace. He was the leader, among all the friends in 'Iráq, and after the great separation, when the convoy of the Beloved left for Constantinople, he remained loyal and staunch, and withstood the foe. He girded himself for service and openly, publicly, observed by all, taught the Faith.[8]

Ustád Muḥammad-'Alíy-i-Salmání, Bahá'u'lláh's barber, wrote that he 'had known a few quick-tempered people in my time – such as Nabíl-i-Zarandí [Nabíl-i-A'ẓam] and Mírzá Muṣṭafá of Baghdad, who were both thunderbolts'.[9]

Virtually nothing is known about Mírzá Muṣṭafá's life between 1853 and 1872. We do know that in 1872 he was nearly beaten to death by an angry mob and that two years later, he was exiled to Mosul and imprisoned there for eight months.[10] Sometime after his release from prison, between 1875 and 1880, Mírzá Muṣṭafá could no longer stay away from Bahá'u'lláh, so finally made the journey to 'Akká. After meeting Bahá'u'lláh, he asked permission to stay somewhere in the 'Akká area, and Bahá'u'lláh allowed him to settle with his family in Beirut.[11] There, he opened a trading business with a branch in Iskandarún, Turkey.[12]

Mírzá Muṣṭafá spent the next 30 years in Beirut and became well-known to pilgrims during the time of both Bahá'u'lláh and 'Abdu'l-Bahá. In 1900, William Hoar, a future Disciple of 'Abdu'l-Bahá, was told to find Mírzá Muṣṭafá in Beirut before continuing to 'Akká. Not speaking Persian or Arabic, William ended up being led to a shop where he met Mírzá Muṣṭafá's son, Zia Bagdadi, and Youness Khan, who were two of the very few people in the city who could speak English. Zia would later become very well-known to the Bahá'ís in North America. Zia took William to his father and the elder Ba<u>gh</u>dádí entertained him and gave him a tour of the city.[13]

Bahá'u'lláh revealed over 150 Tablets addressed to Mírzá Muṣṭafá, most of which have yet to be translated. Shoghi Effendi placed part of one, however, in *Gleanings from the Writings of Bahá'u'lláh*:[14]

> It is Our wish and desire that every one of you may become a source of all goodness unto men, and an example of uprightness to mankind. Beware lest ye prefer yourselves above your neighbours. Fix your gaze upon Him Who is the Temple of God amongst men. He, in truth, hath offered up His life as a ransom for the redemption of the world. He, verily, is the All-Bountiful, the Gracious, the Most High. If any differences arise amongst you, behold Me standing before your face, and overlook the faults of one another for My name's sake and as a token of your love for My manifest and resplendent Cause. We love to see you at all times consorting in amity and concord within the paradise of My good-pleasure, and to inhale from your acts the fragrance of friendliness and unity, of loving-kindness and fellowship. Thus counseleth you the All-Knowing, the Faithful. We shall always be with you; if We inhale the perfume of your fellowship, Our heart will assuredly rejoice, for naught else can satisfy Us. To this beareth witness every man of true understanding.[15]

In January 1899, the casket containing the sacred remains of the Báb was brought to Mírzá Muṣṭafá's home in Beirut. For 12 days, the casket was hidden there while 'Abdu'l-Bahá arranged for its safe transfer to 'Akká.[16] Somehow, the Covenant-breakers learned of the impending arrival of the casket, and hoped that if they could capture it, they could gain financially through blackmail. They bribed the telegram operators to notify them of all communications to and from 'Abdu'l-Bahá. The Master used this to his benefit. First, He messaged Mírzá Muṣṭafá to send the casket by land, and animals were made ready to pull a carriage. Just before they started, 'Abdu'l-Bahá sent another message telling Mírzá Muṣṭafá to send the casket by sea. This lulled the Covenant-breakers because the next boat to 'Akká was not due to leave for several days. But a small Turkish boat unexpectedly arrived and Mírzá Muṣṭafá and his group immediately took advantage of it. After it sailed, 'Abdu'l-Bahá sent a third message telling Mírzá Muṣṭafá to wait in Beirut – this being sent as the boat arrived in 'Akká. Because 'Abdu'l-Bahá's signals confused the Covenant-breakers, Mírzá Muṣṭafá was able to successfully deliver his precious cargo to the Master in 'Akká.[17]

Youness Khán, who had been serving as one of 'Abdu'l-Bahá's secretaries, moved to Beirut to study medicine in about 1905. Supporting himself financially as a student was difficult until one day he was summoned by Mírzá Muṣṭafá, who was then housebound and semi-blind. Mírzá Muṣṭafá suggested that Youness Khán set up a bank account at his business. That way, funds sent to Youness could easily be deposited there.[18]

As Mírzá Muṣṭafá's health continued to fail, 'Abdu'l-Bahá directed him to move to Alexandretta, Turkey.[19] He spent his final days there, passing away in late 1910.[20]

Following his passing, 'Abdu'l-Bahá Himself 'personally instructed the setting of the tombstone and conveyed its epitaph'. During his eventful lifetime, Mírzá Muṣṭafá received more than 150 Tablets from Bahá'u'lláh, ten in His own hand, and 250 Tablets from 'Abdu'l-Bahá, all of which were written by the Master Himself.[21] In *Memorials of the Faithful*, 'Abdu'l-Bahá wrote about Mírzá Muṣṭafá:

> When the Sun of Truth had set and the Light of the Concourse on high had ascended, Muḥammad-Muṣṭafá remained loyal to the Covenant. He stood so firm against the waverers that they dared not draw a breath. He was like a shooting star, a missile hurled against the demons; against the violators, an avenging sword. Not one of the violators so much as dared pass through the street where he lived and if they chanced to meet him they were like those described in the Qur'án: 'deaf, dumb, blind: therefore they shall not retrace their steps from error!' He was the very embodiment of: 'The blame of the blamer shall not deflect him from the path of God, and the terrible might of the reviler shall not shake him.'
>
> Living in the same manner as before, he served the believers with a free mind and pure intent. With all his heart, he assisted the travelers to the Holy Land, those who had come to circumambulate that place which is ringed around by the Company on high. Later he moved from Beirut to Iskandarún, and there he spent some

time, until, drawn as if by a magnet to the Lord, detached from all save Him, rejoicing in His glad tidings, holding fast to the cord that none can sever – he ascended on the wings of the spirit to his Exalted Companion.[22]

15

MÍRZÁ ḤUSAYN-I-IṢFAHÁNÍ – MISHKÍN-QALAM

(1825–1911)

Mírzá Ḥusayn-i-Iṣfahání, better known as Mishkín-Qalam, was a long-time companion of Bahá'u'lláh, from the time of His exile in Adrianople. He was born in Shiraz in about 1825 [1] and lived in Iṣfahán. Naturally artistic, his calligraphy was second to none and it led him to a respected position in the court of Náṣiri'd-Dín Sháh in Tehrán. This came to pass one day when Mishkín-Qalam was sitting in the shop of a friend and the Prime Minister walked by. With lightning speed, Mishkín-Qalam drew a quick sketch of him with his thumbnail. It was an amazingly accurate portrayal and when the Prime Minister returned, the shop keeper showed him the sketch and Mishkín-Qalam was soon appointed as the tutor of the Crown Prince in Tabríz. The Sháh himself gave him the title of Mishkín-Qalam, which meant the 'musk-scented, jet-black pen'.[2]

In Tabríz, Mishkín-Qalam stayed in the house of Ḥájí Mírzá Hedi and started tutoring the Crown Prince and other members of the reigning family in the art of calligraphy. During that period, he had the occasion to visit Iṣfahán and Tehrán. When his work finished in Tabríz, Mishkín-Qalam returned to Iṣfahán where he was introduced to the Faith by one Áqá Mírzá Siyyid Mehdi. Immediately, his heart was set ablaze with the love of God. From Iṣfahán he went to Baghdad and met with Nabíl-i-A'ẓam (see Chapter 12) and Zaynu'l-Muqarrabín (see Chapter 18). Together they read and studied many sacred Tablets. Meantime, Bahá'u'lláh departed from Baghdad and went to Constantinople, after which he was further exiled to Adrianople. Mishkín-Qalam decided to go to Adrianople at this time.[3]

The trip was arduous and he became seriously unwell in Aleppo, Syria. 'Abdu'l-Bahá wrote that 'By now he was reeling to and fro like a drunkard in his love for God, and because of his violent desire and yearning, his mind seemed to wander. He would be raised up, and then cast down again; he was as one distracted'.[4]

In Aleppo, Mishkín-Qalam taught the children of the Governor, Shawkat Pasha, the art of calligraphy. Soon he was joined by Nabíl-i-A'ẓam, and the two of them went to Adrianople and attained the presence of Bahá'u'lláh, arriving in the late summer or early autumn of 1867.[5]

After attaining the presence of Bahá'u'lláh, 'Abdu'l-Bahá wrote that:

> Here he reached the heights of faith and assurance; here he drank the wine of certitude. He responded to the summons of God, he attained the presence of Bahá'u'lláh, he ascended to that apogee where he was received and accepted . . . He spent some time under the sheltering grace of Bahá'u'lláh, and every day new blessings were showered upon him. Meanwhile he produced his splendid calligraphs; he would write out the Most Great Name, Yá Bahá'u'l-Abhá, O Thou Glory of the All-Glorious, with marvelous skill, in many different forms, and would send them everywhere.[6]

It was a life-changing experience and Mishkín-Qalam became Bahá'u'lláh's devout follower.

Mishkín-Qalam arrived at the time of great tension between Bahá'u'lláh and His brother Mírzá Yaḥyá. In the September of 1867, Mírzá Yaḥyá challenged Bahá'u'lláh to a face-to-face public confrontation. When Bahá'u'lláh immediately accepted, Mírzá Yaḥyá, in fear of the consequences, failed to appear, though he was given several further chances.[7]

After a time, Mishkín-Qalam, along with Mírzá 'Alíy-i-Sayyáh and Áqá Jamshíd-i-Gurjí went to Constantinople. Balyuzi wrote that it was not known why they went, but Ustád Muḥammad-'Alíy-i-Salmání, Bahá'u'lláh's barber, wrote that he and Sidq-'Alí Darvish went there to sell three of Bahá'u'lláh's horses and that Mishkín-Qalam and Áqá Jamshíd went because they thought they could earn a good living with Mishkín-Qalam's calligraphy. 'Abdu'l-Bahá simply wrote that Mishkín-Qalam was 'directed' to go.[8]

Initially, Mishkín-Qalam received great acclaim for his beautiful calligraphy and became close to the Persian Ambassador, Ḥájí Mírzá Ḥusayn Khán. At first, Mishkín-Qalam

> occupied himself with the art of calligraphy in the capital of the king of the empire, became known amongst the people for his piety and worship, for striving at all times to bring about reform and for his efforts to plant harmony in the hearts of the heads of the different faiths. He, furthermore, encouraged friendship between strangers and education amongst the people of his country. He was a refuge to the poor and needy, a treasure to the destitute and a guide to the wanderer. His sole aim unity of the human world, he harboured no enmity or hatred. Meanwhile, the Ambassador of Iran in Constantinople wielded a great leverage and a strong relationship with the ministers. He influenced many of the eminent people of the Turkish capital to attribute every libel and vilification to the Bahá'í community in their meetings and opportunities. Spies surrounded Jinab Mi<u>sh</u>kín-Qalam and with instigation from the Ambassador, the opponents and mischievous presented complaints of falsehood accusing Mi<u>sh</u>kín-Qalam to kindle the fire of dissention and corruption in the country, and that he is a tyrant oppressor to the government and disobedient stubborn individual.[9]

Mi<u>sh</u>kín-Qalam began to 'boldly and eloquently' teach the Faith, but was also 'talking unwisely in the circles to which he had found access, particularly in the presence of the Persian Ambassador'. Shoghi Effendi wrote that 'The indiscretion committed by some of [the Faith's] over-zealous followers aggravated an already acute situation'.[10]

These indiscretions resulted in the Persian Ambassador telling the Sulṭán's viziers that

> This man is an agitator, sent here by Bahá'u'lláh to stir up trouble and make mischief in this Great City. He has already won over a large company, and he intends to subdue still more. These Bahá'ís turned Persia upside down; now they have started in on the capital of Turkey. The Persian Government put 20,000 of them to the sword, hoping by this tactic to quench the fires of sedition. You should awaken to the danger; soon this perverse thing will blaze up here as well. It will consume the harvest of your life; it will burn up the whole world. Then you can do nothing, for it will be too late.[11]

In April 1868, Mi<u>sh</u>kín-Qalam, and Áqá Jam<u>sh</u>íd-i-Gurjí were arrested and put in one prison, and Ustád Muḥammad-'Alíy, Sidq-'Alí Darvish, and Mírzá 'Alíy-i-Sayyáh in another, but at Mishkín-Qalam's request, they were later brought together. This was a particularly difficult time for Mishkín-Qalam, and Ustád Muḥammad-'Alíy noted that he 'kept carrying on and complaining to them that unless he could do his calligraphy his head would never quiet down. "Bring me a pen case," he would say, "and let me write!" Finally, they brought him writing materials and he set to work quietly'.[12]

After several months in prison, Mishkín-Qalam was taken to Gallipoli, arriving on 16 August. Bahá'u'lláh, 'Abdu'l-Bahá and their companions in exile arrived the following day. At the end of August, Mishkín-Qalam, along with Mírzá 'Alíy-i-Sayyáh, Áqá 'Abdu'l-Ghaffár, Muḥammad-Baqír-Qahvih-chí and arch-breaker of the Covenant Mírzá Yaḥyá were sent to Famagusta on the island of Cyprus, while Bahá'u'lláh and the others proceeded to 'Akká.[13]

For the next ten years, Mishkín-Qalam was a prisoner in Famagusta. Áqá 'Abdu'l-Ghaffár escaped from the island in 1870 and Mírzá 'Alíy-i-Sayyáh and Muḥammad-Baqír-Qahvih-chí died in 1870 and 1871, respectively, leaving Mishkín-Qalam as the sole Bahá'í on the island and stuck in the same city as Mírzá Yaḥyá.[14]

In 1978, the British took jurisdiction over Cyprus, but didn't allow Mishkín-Qalam to leave. The Bahá'ís may have held him in high esteem but, to the civil authorities, he was just an elderly man. Their attitude reflected the material world he had to live in. The British Commissioner, in a report, wrote that

> Maskin Kalam. From Korassom [Khurásán]. Allowed Pias. 660 per month. Sentence – for life. Been here 11 years. Came here at same time as Subhe Ezel [Mírzá Yaḥyá]. Sentenced for religious offenses against Porte [Ottoman government]. 53 years old. Has two families, one here and one in Persia. In appearance is a dried-up, shrivelled old man, with long hair almost to the waist.[15]

The family in Cyprus was actually that of Mírzá 'Alíy-i-Sayyáh. Mishkín-Qalam had married 'Alíy-i-Sayyáh's wife upon his death in order to support her. In 1879, Mishkín-Qalam was allowed to move from Famagusta to Nicosia. In August of that year, he petitioned the High Commissioner 'begging to be released from his confinement in order that he could rejoin his [Persian] family after 12 years of exile'. Endless delays afflicted the application. In 1885 he moved to Larnica and was employed by a Mr Cobham. It wasn't until 15 September 1886 that he was finally allowed to leave Cyprus.[16]

Mishkín-Qalam described his departure from that long-time prison:

> I boarded a ship destined for 'Akka. The sea was very turbulent and I noticed the captain paced the deck in a most agitated condition as he wondered what may befall us. In order to alleviate his distress and to calm him a little, I called him forth and showed him the portrait I had just drawn using my fingernail. He found it unbelievable that under such unfavorable conditions and using only my nail, I was able to produce such exquisite and matchless work of art. Therefore, I said to him, 'If you do not believe it, stand still and observe.'
>
> He consented. Within a few minutes, I produced a drawing of his face through making impressions on paper by my nail only, which caused him extreme excitement. He invited me to his quarters and asked if I was willing to draw the impressions of his wife and children during the few days of the journey. I complied with his request.
>
> During the final days that I was on board, he proposed, 'Come with me to England where I will contract you for three thousands liras a year.' 'I would not be prevailed upon even for a hundred thousand liras,' I responded, 'as I have a Beloved Whose nearness I would not barter for all the riches of the earth.'[17]

Mishkín-Qalam was once again in His Beloved's presence.

Pilgrims coming to 'Akká to meet Bahá'u'lláh sometimes had the additional bounty of having Mishkín-Qalam teach them calligraphy. When Mírzá Ḥabíbu'lláh Afnán was on pilgrimage in 1891, he and other pilgrims would go to a classroom on the ground floor of the Mansion at Bahjí and Mishkín-Qalam would instruct them in that delicate art of writing.[18]

While in Cyprus, Mishkín-Qalam had corresponded with 'Abdu'l-Bahá. The Master's Tablets in reply contain references to His love and encouragement during that long captivity, but His sense of humour also came through. In a Tablet to welcome Mishkín-Qalam to 'Akká, 'Abdu'l-Bahá praised him, but also added a gentle warning about keeping his stories focused on Bahá'u'lláh during Bahá'í meetings and not to get side-tracked in telling funny stories:

> O thou divine Mis<u>h</u>kín!
> A thousand praises be to the One True God that for years thou didst suffer in the path of Heavenly Beauty, enduring separation, affliction and captivity, and no sooner was there some respite in restrictions, than thou didst hasten to the Most Great Prison, turned thy face away from all else but Him, melted away in the fires of His love, sought His good-pleasure and recognised the Candle of the Covenant. Through the bountiful grace of the Blessed Beauty, mayest thou adorn and revive the gatherings of the friends, and cause the hearts of His loved ones to be united. This however is on the condition that at such meetings thou makest mention of naught but the soul-stirring remembrance of the Ancient Beauty.[19]

Mírzá Ḥabíbu'lláh Afnán was again in 'Akká in 1901 and had brought a piece of marble from Áqá Siyyid Muṣṭafá in Rangoon, who hoped to make a sarcophagus for the sacred remains of the Báb. 'Abdu'l-Bahá was impressed with the stone and said that 'you can see the sun's rays through this stone. It is the finest piece of stone excavated from the mine and purposed for this sacred sarcophagus'. Mis<u>h</u>kín-Qalam offered to draw a design for the Greatest Name to adorn the sarcophagus. 'Abdu'l-Bahá jokingly replied: 'You want your name to be preserved for as long as the earth and heavens endure!', to which the famous calligrapher said, 'It is entirely possible if I am favoured by the Master's boundless grace'. When Mis<u>h</u>kín-Qalam completed the engravings, he signed them 'The servant of 'Abdu'l-Bahá, Mis<u>h</u>kín-Qalam'. 'Abdu'l-Bahá, however, was indignant and said: 'Who told you to sign them in such a way?! I do not wish for anything to be written at all!' Mis<u>h</u>kín-Qalam took hold of the 'hem of His garment and, with great fervor and intense wailing, begged forgiveness for his misdeed. He sobbed and pleaded with much intensity until the ocean of absolution of his compassionate Master was aroused' and 'Abdu'l-Bahá said, 'If you sign your name in the same manner that you did during the time of the Blessed Beauty, then I will accept'. Mis<u>h</u>kín-Qalam obediently changed it to 'The servant of the Threshold of Bahá, Mis<u>h</u>kín-Qalam'.[20]

As noted above, one of Mis<u>h</u>kín-Qalam's talents was drawing with his long middle fingernail. Mírzá Ḥabíbu'lláh Afnán related, following one of his pilgrimages, that Mishkín-Qalam

> would hold a paper between his thumb and the middle finger, and then using his left hand, would move the paper [thereby imprinting impressions]. In this manner he would exhibit the sacred Verses in an embossed fashion on the paper. Verily, it is a most miraculous achievement and is accomplished in such a distinguished and beautiful way that one finds it hard to believe that this particular vestige has been produced in such a manner. Particularly the word 'al-Hikmat' [wisdom] that was protuberant on two pieces of paper – the letters are so precisely identical that they give the false notion that the word is copied over itself or a printing devise used to produce such impressions.[21]

In 1906, when Jináb-i-Azíz'u'lláh Azízí was on pilgrimage, 'Abdu'l-Bahá appeared withdrawn and 'immersed in an ocean of thought'. This obvious grief bothered Mishkín-Qalam greatly. And one day, 'with agitation and profound sadness', he told the other Bahá'ís 'I have made up my mind that, either I will be expelled from His presence this very day and be debarred forever from gazing upon His loving face, or I will take Him out of this tremendous grief and sadness'. Mishkín-Qalam was not a handsome man. He had delicate features and was nearly beardless, 'having only a few threads on his chin'. He was, however, well-spoken and very humorous, and would make funny faces while speaking. 'The most stoic of listeners had no choice but to break out in laughter'.[22] So, one day when 'Abdu'l-Bahá met with the Bahá'ís and pilgrims, Mishkín-Qalam

> very soberly – and without advance permission – stepped forward and with a very earnest expression on his face, started to talk. But what he was saying would make no sense. His words were nonsense – some Persian, some Arabic. His Holiness Abdul-Baha was listening intently to see what he was trying to say, and was unaware that something was going on. Mishkin-Qalam was talking very seriously and in between sentences would tell a joke and make funny faces. Suddenly, losing his composure, Abdul-Baha started to laugh out loud. As a result of this display of laughter and happiness, everyone present was affected as well. Still, Mishkin-Qalam was carrying out

> his plot a little further to the point where everybody lost control and broke out in riotous laughter.[23]

In addition to his other activities, Mishkín-Qalam transcribed many Tablets of Bahá'u'lláh and 'Abdu'l-Bahá, resulting in several volumes in his beautiful script.[24]

In 1910, Mishkín-Qalam went travel-teaching in India at the bidding of 'Abdu'l-Bahá. As he was departing, the Master told him that 'You will return [to the Holy Land]'.[25] Mishkín-Qalam travelled with Sydney Sprague, who was on his way to spend a year travel-teaching through India and Burma. Though 83 years of age, Mishkín-Qalam 'seemed always brimming over with fun and good spirits, and told many amusing stories which convulsed everyone with laughter'.[26]

But after a time in India,

> he became ill to the point that the believers had lost hope for him to live through it. They even had prepared the burial shroud and other necessities for his interment. When he was at the door of death, the friends closed their shops and came to prepare for his burial.
>
> At that time, the physician, out of desire for testing, suggested that he be placed in a pool of hot water and massaged. In short, he regained his health, and in perfect condition returned to the Holy Land. The point is since Abdul-Bahá had said to him, You will return, then it was fulfilled.[27]

Mishkín-Qalam arrived back in Haifa in 1911 while 'Abdu'l-Bahá was away in the West and passed away that same year in the Khán-i-Avámíd caravanserai. 'Abdu'l-Bahá wrote an obituary:

> He wielded a musk-black pen, and his brows shone with faith. He was among the most noted of mystics, and had a witty and subtle mind. The fame of this spiritual wayfarer reached out to every land. He was the leading calligrapher of Persia and well known to all the great; he enjoyed a special position among the court ministers of Tihrán, and with them he was solidly established. He was famed throughout Asia Minor; his pen was the wonder of all calligraphers, for he was adept at every calligraphic style. He was besides, for human virtues, a bright star . . .

He was at all times my close companion. He had amazing verve, intense love. He was a compendium of perfections: believing, confident, serene, detached from the world, a peerless companion, a wit and his character like a garden in full bloom. For the love of God, he left all good things behind; he closed his eyes to success, he wanted neither comfort nor rest, he sought no wealth, he wished only to be free from the defilement of the world. He had no ties to this life, but spent his days and nights supplicating and communing with God. He was always smiling, effervescing; he was spirit personified, love embodied. For sincerity and loyalty he had no match, nor for patience and inner calm. He was selflessness itself, living on the breaths of the spirit.

If he had not been in love with the Blessed Beauty, if he had not set his heart on the Realm of Glory, every worldly pleasure could have been his. Wherever he went, his many calligraphic styles were a substantial capital, and his great accomplishment brought him attention and respect from rich and poor alike. But he was hopelessly enamored of man's one true Love, and thus he was free of all those other bonds, and could float and soar in the spirit's endless sky.

Finally, when I was absent, he left this darksome, narrow world and hastened away to the land of lights. There in the haven of God's boundless mercy, he found infinite rewards. Upon him be praise and salutations, and the Supreme Companion's tender grace'.[28]

16

MÍRZÁ ḤASAN-I-ADÍB – ADÍBU'L-'ULAMÁY-I-ṬÁLIQÁNÍ – ADÍB

(1848–1919)

Mírzá Ḥasan-i-Adíb, also known as Adíbu'l-'Ulamáy-i-Ṭáliqání and who was given the title of Adíb by Bahá'u'lláh, had only been a Bahá'í for three years when the Blessed Beauty named him a Hand of the Cause of God. Adíb was born in the hamlet of Karkabud in Taliqán, Persia, east of Qazvín, in September 1848. He was the son of an eminent cleric, Mírzá Muḥammad-Taqí, who had been a teacher to the daughter of Fatḥ-'Alí Sháh.[1]

Adíb was 11 when his father died and 'the turban of the father was put upon the head of the son'. A week later, his uncle, the illustrious religious scholar Múlla 'Abdu'l-Ghání Ḥishání arrived in Taliqán to oversee his nephew's education. The múlla had studied under Shaykh Murtidá-i-Ansárí, who was favourably mentioned in Tablets by both Bahá'u'lláh and 'Abdu'l-Bahá. After four years, Adíb went to study in Tehran. Because his father was well known, Adíb was given much attention and encouragement. He later transferred to the Khán-i-Marvi Madrissih, and studied mathematics, literature, religious jurisprudence, interpretation, diction, oration, philosophy, and metaphysics with the highest religious educators of that time. In 1868–1869, he moved to Iṣfahán for further studies.[2]

When he returned to Tehran, Adíb became a highly respected and learned man in his own right for his achievements in both literature and theology, gaining the title of Adíbu'l-'Ulamá (litterateur of the clerics, a person very knowledgeable in literature) for the books he wrote.[3] Adíb had been financially supported by his father's estate during this time, but in 1874, those funds were gone and he set out to find work. A friend introduced him to Prince 'Alí-Qulí Mírzá, the Minister of

Education, who hired him and with whom he co-authored a number of important books. Adíb also worked with another prince, Prince Farhad Mírzá, Náṣir'id-Dín Sháh's paternal uncle and a respected scholar.[4] The Princes published his writing under their own names in works such as the encyclopaedic *Námiy-i-Dánishvarán*. Adíb was also a teacher at the Dáru'l-Funún, a school organised on modern Western educational principles. During this time, Adíb mixed with influential people in government and society, as well as with religious scholars from all groups. His open mind searched for truth amongst the traditions.[5]

One of Adíb's close friends, Shaykh Hádí Najmábádí, first pointed out to him the similarity of his beliefs with those of the Bahá'ís:

> Adíb was hurt by this remark but it also interested him, and he asked Shaykh Hádí if the Bábís had anything worthwhile to say, and if it was worthy of investigation. The Shaykh gave him an affirmative answer. Before this time Adíb did not consider the new faith to be legitimate or grounded in reality.
>
> Upon return to Tihran, Adíb urgently visited a Bahá'í acquaintance [Siyyid Muhammad] and insistently requested to borrow some books on the Baha'i Faith. When Adíb was preoccupied with his intense spiritual search and investigation his demeanor would become strange and intimidating. Therefore, with some trepidation and misgiving, his Baha'i acquaintance lent him a book of Baha'i Writings. Following his studies of the Baha'i writings and conversations with Baha'i scholars and teachers, and finally studying with Fadil-i-Qa'ini [Nabil-i-Akbar] he became convinced of the truth of the Bahá'í Faith and the Revelation of Bahá'u'lláh.[6]

The book he was given by Siyyid Muḥammad was the *Kitáb-i-Íqán*.

Nabíl-i-Akbar (see Chapter 9) helped Adíb to understand the Revelation of Bahá'u'lláh and in 1889, Adíb acknowledged Bahá'u'lláh as the Manifestation of God for this day.[7] Shortly before His passing, Bahá'u'lláh designated Adíb a Hand of the Cause. He was one of the few Apostles of Bahá'u'lláh who never met the Blessed Beauty.[8] Adib Taherzadeh wrote that

> All his learning and erudition were now harnessed to the new powers which the Faith of Bahá'u'lláh had conferred upon him. Soon his heart

> became a wellspring of divine melodies. The soul-stirring poems he wrote proclaim the advent of the Day of God and, in offering up his all in the path of his Lord, serve as ample testimony to the intensity of his faith and the exultation of his rank. No wonder that soon after his entering under the shadow of the Cause, Bahá'u'lláh designated this great spiritual being as one of the Hands of His Cause.[9]

In 1895, 'Abdu'l-Bahá directed Adíb to arrange a wedding for Ibn-i-Abhar (see Chapter 11) and Munírih Khánum, the daughter of Hand of the Cause Mullá 'Alí-Akbar, upon Ibn-i-Abhar's return from pilgrimage.[10]

In that same year, the Russian Consul in Tehran, Georgiy Dmitrievich Batyushkov, asked Adíb to write an article on the history of the lives of the Báb and Bahá'u'lláh. Adíb delivered his history on 28 April 1896. When Náṣiri'd-Dín Sháh was assassinated two days later, Batyushkov was able, because of Adíb's history, to protect some of the Bahá'ís during the crackdown that followed.[11]

In 1897 and 1898, Adíb worked with the other three Hands of the Cause, Ḥájí Ákhund (see Chapter 8), Ibn-i-Aṣdaq (see Chapter 19) and Ibn-i-Abhar on forming the Central Spiritual Assembly of Tehran, which ultimately evolved into the National Spiritual Assembly of Iran. Adíb was the chairman during these consultations. He was also instrumental in founding the Tarbíyat School for girls in Tehran in 1899.[12] In a Tablet to Adíb, 'Abdu'l-Bahá emphasised the importance of the school and that it would become a model for other schools.[13]

'Abdu'l-Bahá sent Adíb numerous Tablets, many in His own hand. He commonly addressed Adíb as 'The Eminent Literary Man of the Primary School of God'. Adíb wrote many books, including a history of the Bahá'í Faith, a treatise on Bahá'í proofs and an autobiography. Regarding his treatise on Bahá'í proofs, 'Abdu'l-Bahá said that his work brought Him joy because one of the duties of the Hands of the Cause was to write informative books and articles to prove the truth and unity of the Prophets of God. He stressed that Adíb should use historical and factual evidence with logical explanations to prove the existence of God. When Adíb sent the Master some of his poems, 'Abdu'l-Bahá replied that each was a brilliant pearl and reflected the utmost effulgence, tenderness and radiance of spirit. One of Adíb's poems is about his discovery of Bahá'u'lláh's Revelation:

Last night, surrounded by books, busy with lesson plans and lecture notes;
I was consumed by arguments and points and counterpoints;

When a voice spoke to me, calling from deep within;
intimating mystic questions, clarifying lifelong mysteries.

I heard the voice of wisdom speaking to my heart,
saying, O Adíb! O master of every literary art.

How long will you spend life in vain pursuits?
How long will you waste time with talk and retort?

How long will you be seeking and longing?
How long will you be thinking idle thoughts?

If you seek the Best Beloved, open your inner eye!
Lose your head if you seek true Love!

Give up life and drink from the Fountain of Life;
Give away your heart to the Possessor of Hearts.

Hearing the call and this mystical counsel,
I cleared my head of idle thoughts and notions.

My inner eye opened to see reality;
my gaze fell on the beauty of the mystic Friend.

Mind and thought and sense all escaped,
as did confusion, ushering in enlightenment.

I offered my life as a token of love, and gave my spirit to the Eternal Spirit;
The body can still move even when its head is removed.

When life is given in the path of the Loved One;
does it matter if the body is wrapped in silk or brambles?

If seated on a golden throne or a bench of rough-hewn boards?
If fed raw scavenged fare or a scrumptious spread of delights?

Bitter and sweet are the same to the truly famished;
for the body responds to what the spirit commands.

I embraced a new life,
once I subdued my willful self.

How sweet, this bounty and grace!
Receiving such favors in this physical plane![14]

Though he had suffered persecution before, the year 1903 was Adíb's true baptism by fire. 'Abdu'l-Bahá instructed him to make a teaching trip to Iṣfahán. He arrived on 20 May, just as tensions were about to explode from the machinations of Shaykh Muḥammad-Taqí, known as Áqá Najafí, and designated as the Son of the Wolf by Bahá'u'lláh:

> Adíb and his son [Mírzá 'Alí] had arrived at the house of one of the Baha'is in Iṣfahán. The members of the household were unable to get any sleep that night because of their fear and concern that the enemies would break into the house at any moment if they knew about Adíb's presence. In consideration for their comfort, the guests left the house at dawn and started to walk through the city. They did not know the city well and just walked aimlessly all day. They would pass through large raucous crowds who were armed and prepared to apprehend the Bahá'í teacher who had arrived from Tehran, making derogatory and inflammatory comments among themselves. They would look at the strangers with suspicion, but did not recognize them. Adíb and Mírzá 'Alí walked until their feet blistered and, having no other option, they returned to their host's house.
>
> After a brief rest, Adíb wrote a letter to Mírzá Assad'u'lláh Khán-i-Vazír [a government minister and well-known Bahá'í], explaining the terror and fear gripping the members of the household, and making it clear that staying at the house was not advisable because of the danger it posed for the household. The Vazír immediately vacated a garden cottage . . . which was under his care. Even the gardener was ordered to leave the property. He then moved to the

> property with his own household. He designated one of his trusted agents to take Adíb and his son, with extreme caution and using byways, to this property.
>
> Upon arrival Adíb realized that the Vazír and his family had not left the property in two days, and the household had stayed hidden in the inner part of the house, fearful, and exercising extreme caution and wisdom so that their presence would not be detected from the outside . . . Adíb and his son, Mírzá 'Alí, stayed for six days and nights.[15]

While Adíb was hidden, a notable banker in Iṣfahán, who was a Bábí, died of natural causes and a funeral was organised for him. Áqá Najafí sent a group of 'theological students and ruffians' to break into the funeral. They arrested one Bahá'í, beat him and dragged him in front of Áqá Najafí in the mosque. The charge was not that he was a Bahá'í, but that he drank wine. The man was stripped of his clothes and given 80 lashes.[16]

Adíb and the Bahá'ís had expected these actions and consulted about what to do, with the decision being made to seek refuge in the Russian Consulate. Initially, only two families went and the Consul, M. Boronovski, told them to bring in all the Bahá'ís. Soon, 4,000 Bahá'ís thronged the Consulate. Prince Ẓillu's-Ṣultán, one of Náṣiri'd-Dín Sháh's sons, took over negotiations. To the Bahá'ís and Boronovski, he said that no one would question their religion if they left the Consulate. Realising that the Bahá'ís were about to be given freedom, Áqá Najafí forged a telegram from the Prime Minister that gave him the authority to destroy the Russian Consulate and kill all the Bahá'ís. During the night, a large crowd surrounded the consulate.

The crowd slowly dispersed as the night drew on, and the Bahá'ís began to leave in groups of two or three. Some of the mob, however, were still waiting and four Bahá'ís were killed and many severely beaten. Finally, a large group of Bahá'ís were allowed to leave the area.[17]

After seven days in hiding, Adíb and his son left for Ábádih. Adíb wrote that

> We had to wear clothing that would disguise our identity, and travel cautiously through Isfahan to get to the city gate. The gatekeeper was asleep when we got there and the gate was locked. The Vazír's

> man woke the gatekeeper and told him to open the gate for the Chief so he can inspect his properties. Someone said hurry up so that you can receive a handout from the Chief. The gatekeeper woke up and wearing his undergarments and still groggy bowed to me and opened the gate. I gave him two coins for his trouble. The Vazír's man returned and the three of us rode all night until we got to Margh. In Margh we changed horses and waited for the arrival of Prince Ghulam-Ḥusayn Mirza and Mirza Baqir-Khan who were supposed to join us. They arrived before dawn and we rode through the wilderness. Although agents of the Governor and the religious authorities were in hiding and looking for us on the main thoroughfares, we managed to ride night and day without being apprehended until they reached Qumshih. The superintendent of the stables in Qumshih was a Baha'i and we spent the night reciting prayers and Baha'i writings at Abbasiyyih, which was a garden owned by one of the Baha'is.[18]

The party reached Ábádih very early the next day, and one of the believers hid them in his house. But the other Bahá'ís soon learned that the Hand of the Cause was there. Even the mayor, Midhat'ul-Mulk who was friendly with the Bahá'ís, went to meet Adíb and learn more about the Bahá'í Faith. When Áqá Najafí learned of the mayor's visits, he sent a group of Muslim clergy to prove to him that Islam was the true Faith. Upon hearing their arguments, the mayor invited them to meet with the Bahá'ís where they could demonstrate the falsity of the Bahá'í beliefs. The group agreed, and a few days later met with Adíb, and the civic, governmental and religious leaders of Ábádih. When they were ready,

> The leader of the group of clergy started by recounting the prophesies of the Quran regarding the coming of the Promised One, all of which are logically and scientifically impossible to prove without doubt because they use the language of symbolic and mystical meanings instead of irrefutable, observable ones. He was arguing that prophesies such as the coming of Dajjal, the Anti-Christ of Islam, and the monstrous donkey on which he rides; . . . the cry of the sun at midday; and the like, had not been observed, therefore the Baha'i claims could not be true since they are not consistent with prophesy.

> However, before he could get to . . . the Traditions about the return of the Qa'im, Adíb made fundamental comments about the manner of search for spiritual truth. He said that suspicion is not an adequate measure for investigating spiritual truth; certitude and clarity are necessary so the result is expanded knowledge and arrival at true conviction . . .
>
> Adíb . . . used logical, scientific reasoning and scriptural quotes to establish and prove the validity and authenticity of the Bahá'í Faith. The priest listened to all of these explanations and agreed with their authenticity, had to agree with their origin in the Holy Scriptures, and did not object to any of them. After dinner, the priest asked some questions to get clarity on some questions he had based on what he had heard about Baha'is. He asked if they believed in life after death. Adíb responded that the manner in which Bahá'ís have behaved should be an adequate answer to this question. He stated that the events in Isfahan alone should make it clear that despite all the injustice and cruel and vicious treatment that they had suffered in the hands of their attackers, the Bahá'ís had shown resignation and reliance on God and the willingness to tread a martyr's path to God. Similarly in Yazd and other places innocent Bahá'ís were set on fire and butchered to pieces and killed in various ways, and they had embraced all of this with submission and acquiescence to the Will of God. They had not given up their belief in the religion of God to protect anything of property or money or even their families and children . . . The priest was embarrassed for his line of questioning. After that he expressed his appreciation for having had the opportunity to hear the explanations that Adib had provided, and took his leave.[19]

During the six months Adíb was in Ábádih, he helped the believers to elect their first Local Spiritual Assembly.[20]

After that time, Adíb wrote:

> I left Ábádih for Shíráz joyfully and was surprised at every stop to find villages and hamlets on the brink of unrest and upheaval. Every traveller was questioned and scrutinized at every stop and treated with suspicion. The resident Bahá'ís desired to visit me but would not approach me openly, but would rather convey their love and

affection secretly. In Zarqan . . . , I stayed for four days and sent a messenger to Shíráz to establish and confirm my accommodations. Even in Zarqan it was not possible to send my attendants out because they could be recognized, and the friends could only visit me four and five hours after dark. They had even concealed my belongings so it would not appear that anyone was staying at my place of accommodation. On the fourth night they removed my belongings surreptitiously piece by piece, and I walked away from the city and mounted my horse outside the city. When I arrived in Shíráz I discovered that the well-known Bahá'ís had been removed from the city by the government to protect them from the violence incited against them by the religious leaders and the unrest among the residents who were eager to direct their violence against the Bahá'ís. The rest of the Bahá'í community was in constant danger and fear of violence to such an extent that even if two of the friends happened to meet one another on the street, they would not show familiarity or acknowledge one another.[21]

While in Shiraz, Adíb received a Tablet from 'Abdu'l-Bahá directing him to travel to Bombay (Mumbai), India, with his son Mírzá 'Alí and Mírzá Maḥmúd Zarqání. Following that journey, Adíb went to 'Akká to be with the Master.

Sydney Sprague, an American Bahá'í, arrived in 'Akká while Adíb was there. Sydney was on his way to spend a year travel-teaching through India and Burma, and 'Abdu'l-Bahá directed Adíb to accompany him. Mishkín-Qalam (see Chapter 15) also travelled with them. Though 83 years old, Mishkín-Qalam 'seemed always brimming over with fun and good spirits, and told many amusing stories which convulsed everyone with laughter'. Sprague noted that

There is one thing I have always remarked about the Persian Bahais, that notwithstanding the earnestness of their faith, their truly deep spiritual natures, their readiness to become martyrs for the Cause, that they always seem happy and enjoy a good hearty laugh; they do not take their religion, as did our ancestors the Puritans, with long faces and acid countenances. Religion is a thing of joy to them, and they rejoice in the spirit and are glad.[22]

The group sailed on a heavily laden steamer from Port Said to Bombay, where Adíb left Sydney and visited Bombay, Calcutta, Rangoon, and Mandalay.[23] When Sydney later reached Calcutta, he found Adíb there ahead of him.[24]

Adíb returned to Tehran then continued his service to the Faith until his death on 2 September 1919.[25]

17

SHAYKH MUḤAMMAD-'ALÍ-QÁ'ÍNÍ

(1860–1924)

Shaykh Muḥammad-'Alí-Qá'íní was born in 1860 in the village of Naw-Firist, near Birjand in central Iran. His father, Mullá Muḥammad Ḥusayn, was Nabíl-i-Akbar's brother (see Chapter 9). Shaykh Muḥammad-'Alí was described as:

> First, physically he was tall, handsome, and well proportioned, with a head full of hair. Second, he had a good voice. Upon hearing Shaykh Muhammad-'Alí's voice, 'Abdu'l-Bahá told him that if God gave Abu Musa Ash'ari, one of the companions of Muhammad the Prophet of God, the gift of singing one of the Psalms of David, then God has given you the ability to sing the hymns in the entire book of Psalms. Third, he had beautiful penmanship. Fourth, he had a natural grace and pleasant demeanor combined with eloquent speech and impeccable reasoning which attracted and influenced the listener. Fifth, he was from a family known for erudition as well as wealth and status. Sixth, he was very good at reading people's character. Seventh, he was the recipient of many tablets from Baha'u'llah and Abdu'l-Baha, and they both showered their love and favor on him. Eighth, He was trusted by Abdu'l-Baha. Ninth, he was a tireless defender of the Baha'i Faith and the Center of the Covenant against covenant-breakers.[1]

Shaykh Muḥammad-'Alí's parents died within a week of each other when he was 12 years old, so his uncle, Mullá Áqá 'Alí, took responsibility for him. A year later, Mullá Áqá 'Alí sent his son and Shaykh Muḥammad-'Alí to Mashhad for higher religious training. The cousins studied there for five years. In addition to his religious education, Shaykh Muḥammad-'Alí also studied traditional medicine in his spare time.[2]

Shaykh Muḥammad-'Alí did not know that his uncles were Bahá'ís and he became very 'distressed and puzzled' when the religious and civil authorities tried to arrest Nabíl-i-Akbar. When he later learned about the Faith from Mullá 'Alí Bajistání, he understood why his uncle had been attacked, and that drove him to go and find him. Thinking that his uncle was in 'Ishqábád, he first went there. It was some time before Shaykh Muḥammad-'Alí encountered his first Bahá'í, Ḥájí Muḥammad Káẓim-i-Iṣfaháni. But when he visited the Ḥájí, looking like a 'turbaned preacher', Ḥájí Muḥammad tried to send him away, saying that he had no need for a preacher. When he learned that his visitor was the nephew of Nabíl-i-Akbar, he became respectful and explained that his uncle was not there.[3]

Returning to Mashhad, Shaykh Muḥammad-'Alí found Nabíl-i-Akbar there and begged to be allowed to accompany him on his travels. Though his uncle tried to dissuade him by explaining how dangerous his travels were, Shaykh Muḥammad-'Alí insisted that he was ready to face any dangers his uncle faced. Relenting, the two went to Tehran. The reality was that Nabíl-i-Akbar was always in danger and was constantly forced to move from place to place. Things got so bad that, at the advice of the Hands of the Cause of God in Tehran, Nabíl left by himself for Khurásán, riding an emaciated donkey. When Shaykh Muḥammad-'Alí discovered that his uncle had left, he immediately procured a camel and followed, catching up with him near the city of Sabzivár. The two men arrived in 'Ishqábád in the late summer or early autumn of 1891.[4]

Shaykh Muḥammad-'Alí wrote that 'Fadl [Nabíl-i-Akbar] and I were approaching Sabzivár . . . , when we decided not to enter the city in order to avoid recognition. Therefore we went to a caravanserai and lodged in a room. Our disguise in civilian clothing had worked so far. However, at midnight an agent came and told my uncle, "you are Fadl, and I am ordered to take you to the governor"'. At first the governor was very antagonistic, but when Nabíl-i-Akbar answered him, he was so impressed that he said that he would pretend that he had never seen him and told him to leave the city. Nabíl-i-Akbar and Shaykh Muḥammad-'Alí wasted no time leaving and headed for the Russian border.[5]

Sometime later, Nabíl-i-Akbar travelled with Mírzá 'Abu'l-Faḍl to Bukhárá, where he passed away on 6 July 1892. When Shaykh Muḥammad-'Alí heard the news, he immediately went to Bukhárá and arranged for his uncle's burial.[6]

Following the funeral, Shaykh Muḥammad-‘Alí travelled to Naw-Firist to deal with the sale of his uncle's properties and ended up spending the next two years there. After that time, he traveled with his uncle's family to Mashhad and Tehran. The difficulties that had followed his uncle, Nabíl-i-Akbar, now followed him. He hired a cameleer who turned out to be hostile, intolerant, and fanatical with a deep prejudice against Shaykh Muḥammad-‘Alí. When they reached Mashhad,

> the cameleer stopped at a caravanserai . . . to make it easier to potentially harm the Shaykh Having noticed this situation, the Shaykh told his aunt and cousin that he would leave town through the Nishapur gate with the excuse of collecting some debt, and [for] them to leave with the caravan and join him along the way to the city of Sabzivár towards Tihran. He then told the cameleer that he had debts to collect in villages around Mashhad and planned to return . . . In this manner he managed to get away from the cameleer and left Mashhad. Nabil's wife and daughter left with the caravan the next day and eventually caught up with Shaykh Muhammad Ali and arrived at the city of Sabzivár and found lodging at a caravanserai. The Shaykh had gone to the bazaar to buy supplies when a man . . . ran out of a carpenter's shop and greeted him. The Shaykh responded and started conversing with him but did not recognize him. The man had been a carpenter in ‘Ishqábád and had worked on the grounds of the Bahá'í House of Worship in that city and had recognized Shaykh Muhammad Ali. He introduced himself, told him about slowness of business and of the financial difficulties he was experiencing in Sabzivár, and asked for some help. The Shaykh gave him a draft for a few Tumans, and went on to get supplies for the trip. An hour later this carpenter came to the caravanserai with a few constables with a summons for the Shaykh to present himself at the Governor's court. At the Governor's court, the Shaykh was informed that the carpenter had claimed that he owed him 80 Tumans. The Shaykh explained the events to the Governor and it became clear very quickly that the carpenter had lied. Seeing this turn of events the carpenter tried to create a spectacle by yelling that the Shaykh was a Bábí who had come from ‘Ishqábád to cause unrest. The Governor and his companions ruled him out of order and stated that a claim of debt has nothing to do with religion. They

> quietly told Shaykh Muhammad-'Alí that these types of schemers were everywhere preying on travellers. They suggested . . . that he be given some money to send him on his way
>
> The next morning Shaykh Muhammad-'Alí saw the carpenter entering the caravanserai with a number of religious students looking for him. The Shaykh quickly removed his turban and put on his nightcap and picked a water pitcher, acting like he was going to the washroom. On his way out of the living quarters he told his companions that he was leaving, and to catch up with him down the road. He kept his head down and hurried out of the caravanserai and the city on foot towards the city of Shahrud on the way to Tihran. He walked fast for some distance until he got to a coffeehouse, fatigued and discomforted. He sat down and asked for tea. The shop ownergot suspicious of the stranger and asked him where he was coming from and where was he headed. In his confusion, Shaykh Muhammad-'Alí responded that he was heading to the Holy shrine in Mashhad. He immediately recognized his error and upon drinking his tea headed back towards Mashhad to calm the suspicion of the locals. After some distance, he turned around and took a path far from the coffeehouse, trying to evade detection. However, one of the locals saw the Shaykh and alerted the rest of the crowd in the coffeehouse. They chased him for a while but were unable to capture him, got tired and returned. The Shaykh thus managed to evade his pursuers and arrived at the city of Shahrud after walking all night and another day. He waited in Shahrud for his aunt and cousin to arrive, and they eventually made their way together to Tihran.[7]

Nabíl-i-Akbar had written in his will that he wished for Shaykh Muḥammad-'Alí to marry his daughter, Ḍía'íyyih Khánum, and this he did in 1896 or 1897. The couple stayed in Tehran for two years and then, at the request of 'Abdu'l-Bahá, went to Yazd, where they lived with Ḥájí Mírzá Muḥammad-Taqí-i-Afnán (see Chapter 10) and assisted him for several months. Shaykh Muḥammad-'Alí also travelled to Iṣfahán, Káshán and Qúm. After seven months, they returned to Tehran.[8]

In May 1903, 'Abdu'l-Bahá asked Mírzá Ḥasan-i-Adíb (see Chapter 16) to go to India to help the community there better understand the

Covenant and His station as the Centre of the Covenant. When the Covenant-breakers learned of his mission

> they informed their compatriots in Iṣfahán so that some unrest and mischief could be created to keep Adib in that city and prevent his departure. Shaykh Muhammad-'Alí was therefore instructed to provide assistance and accompany Adib to India. This coincided with the third year of the Shaykh's stay in Tihran. The mission was communicated to the Shaykh through a tablet from 'Abdu'l-Bahá . . .
>
> Shaykh Muhammad-'Alí followed Adib to Iṣfahán and got there three days after his arrival. As the Shaykh was approaching the city gate, he saw one of the Bahá'ís of Iṣfahán from some distance. This man was motioning the Shaykh to follow him. He informed the Shaykh that a cloud of persecution and repression had descended upon the Baha'is of Iṣfahán. At about two hours after sunset, he took the Shaykh to the house of Mirza Assadu'llah Khán-i-Vazir, the minister to the Ẓillu's-Sulṭán the Governor.[9]

Shaykh Ḥaydar-i-Mu'allem recorded the events as told to him by Shaykh Muḥammad-'Alí:

> Once the ruffians got a hold of him [the Shaykh] in Iṣfahán, one took off his turban, the other took off his robe, another his tunic, shirt, shoes, and socks until he was only in his undergarment, and all his belongings had been taken from him. They beat him and yelled profanities at him, and then dragged him in that condition through the bazaar where the beatings and the hurling of insults continued. A baker ran out of his shop in the bazaar and landed a hard blow on the Shaykh's back with his hot metal bread rod. This resulted in immediate and profuse bleeding out of the wound. His body was black and blue from the beatings. They took him and some other Bahá'ís to the house of Shaykh Muhammad Taqi-i-Najafi [the Son of the Wolf] and locked them up in a large room with no floor covering. The crowd of ruffians didn't give up and crowded outside the locked doors all night trying to enter, but were pushed back by Shaykh Najafi's men. Shaykh Muhammad-'Alí recalled that the Bahá'ís were so badly beaten and their faces so disfigured that they did not recognize one another. He overheard two of the believers

whispering to one another in the middle of the night, wondering about the fate of poor Shaykh Muhammad-'Alí and whether the crowd of ruffians had killed him. Shaykh Muhammad-'Alí slowly moved towards them and recognized them as Áqá Siyyid Mustafa and Áqá Mirza Aghay-i-Sahhaf, and all three finally recognized one another.

The following morning a group of religious students surrounded the room, shouting profanities and insults at the prisoners, and confronted Shaykh Najafi's men and eventually got them to open one of the doors. One of the students who was known to be particularly aggressive, named Mulla Haydar, pulled a knife out of his waist and asked the prisoners for the mulla amongst them. He then noticed Shaykh Muhammad-'Alí and rushed towards him, saying: 'it must be this one; I will kill him right here.' They all intervened and stated that there was no mulla in their midst, and that they were all shopkeepers and traders. The other students intervened as well and asserted that until Shaykh Najafi issues his judgment no one should kill any of these people. Mulla Haydar tried to attack Shaykh Muhammad-'Alí several more times, and the crowd of ruffians had by this time filled the room causing a chaotic scene. Meanwhile Shaykh Najafi's men spirited the prisoners out through another door that led to a courtyard, and hid them in a stable in another part of the estate. The ruffians found their whereabouts a couple of hours later, got on the roof of the stable and hurled insults, rocks and dirt at the prisoners through skylights on the roof. This went on all day.

After nightfall, the Lieutenant Governor's agents arrived to interrogate the prisoners . . . They asked Shaykh Muhammad-'Alí where he resided, and he responded that he was a merchant from Tihran and on his way to Shiraz when, unaware of the unrest, he was caught up in it . . . Late that night, when Shaykh Muhammad-'Alí was sleeping, the Lieutenant Governor's men woke him up and secretly took him far out of the city. He was taken to a half-ruined house with only one habitable room in which a few elderly women were living and taking care of a sick person. The Shaykh was housed in the ruined part of the house in a roofless room used for the disposal of garbage . . . The Shaykh had no clothes; therefore he clothed himself with some dirty clothes that had belonged to the sick man. He stayed there for a week [then] two of the agents visited to inform

> Shaykh Muhammad-'Alí that he needed to leave . . . He was taken to the Lieutenant Governor who showed him kindness and told him that in a day or two he should return to Tihran with the governmental postal carriage.[10]

Shaykh Muḥammad-'Alí spent the next six months recovering in Tehran and then left for India, arriving in Bombay two months later. After spending a year and half there providing 'numerous services', in 1904 'Abdu'l-Bahá invited him to the Holy Land. Shaykh Muḥammad-'Alí travelled from India with a group of Zoroastrians, then in Beirut he boarded a ship carrying a group of Persian Bahá'ís that included Ibn-i-Aṣdaq (see Chapter 19). While in Haifa, 'Abdu'l-Bahá 'showered him with love and affection'.[11]

When Shaykh Muḥammad-'Alí left Haifa, 'Abdu'l-Bahá told him to go to 'Ishqábád to help establish a Bahá'í school there. A year later, the Master sent him a Tablet instructing him to move his family to 'Ishqábád and also to bring an 'experienced and wise' teacher. Shaykh Muḥammad-'Alí and his family arrived in 'Ishqábád in 1906 along with the new teacher, Shaykh Ḥaydar-i-Mu'allem. During this time, Shaykh Muḥammad-'Alí wrote the book *Durus'ul-Diyana*, which was used in his classes. He also wrote an article in Arabic in response to the Covenant-breakers, titled *Su'al Va Javab* (Questions and Answers), which was an exposition on Bahá'í subjects and was used in his classes as well.[12]

'Ishqabád at that time was an exciting place to be. The Mashriqu'l-Adhkár was being constructed and the city was a centre of learning and intellectual pursuits, due to a series of high-quality visiting teachers like Mírzá Abu'l-Faḍl, his nephew Siyyid Mahdi and Shaykh Muḥammad-'Alí himself.[13] 'Ishqábád would be his home for the rest of his life, though 'Abdu'l-Bahá sent him on a number of assignments to the surrounding provinces.

His next mission from 'Abdu'l-Bahá was to go to Khussif, to counter the activities of Covenant-breakers. Completing his task, he returned home via Naw-Firist. There, a priest immediately began to stir up trouble. He issued an order to exile Shaykh Muḥammad-'Alí and had all the clergy in the area sign it. The Governor, however, thought highly of Shaykh Muḥammad-'Alí and showed him the letter so that he could leave of his own accord, which he did. Back in 'Ishqábád, Shaykh Muḥammad-'Alí wrote the priest a powerful letter:

Some time has passed since my trip to Qa'in, and I have finally found some time to write to you. I am writing to explain that the purpose for my journey to that province was to achieve the honor of visiting the enlightened court of the Governor, of whose compassion, justice, equity, integrity and morality I had heard. I also intended to visit my relatives and friends whom I had not seen in twelve years. I had no intention of staying, and had no other purpose. Is it fair and seemly that even before I arrived and without ever meeting me, you would hasten, with no due cause and based purely on your personal passion and baseness, to leave the bounds of humanity and make me the target of your animosity and cruelty? Is it fair that using the excuse that I am deluded and perverted in my beliefs and conscience you would raise a hue and cry in concert with other corrupt clergy to petition the government to exile me? You should have at least investigated to find out if my intent was to stay or just visit and return to 'Ishqábád. I swear by your life that I was more eager and impatient to leave Qa'in and return to 'Ishqábád than you could ever know. Thus you needlessly sullied the integrity of the government by forcing its agents to agree to my unjustifiable exile.

O Shaykh, let's agree for the sake of argument that this servant is deluded and perverted in his belief and conscience, and deserving of exile. What then of the holy and divine beings whose greatness and magnanimity has enveloped all the visible and invisible realms? Why were they persecuted and rejected? Why were they the targets of the arrows, spears and swords from their enemies and detractors? Look with sincere eyes to see the lessons of history. Forever, servants of God and those who sought nearness to his Holy precincts have been persecuted and hated by the ignorant and wayward people. They have been forever victims of the edicts of evil rulers and clergy or the vile actions of dark hearted criminals. They have been refugees in deserts and hills or hidden in caves in mountains, locked in chains and yokes or imprisoned in dark dungeons or crucified . . .

Who were the sources of all this animosity and opposition to the Prophet of God? Ponder! Were they merchants and traders? Were they carpenters and masons? Were they cotton ginners? Were they grocers and grain sellers? No! They were leaders and chiefs of the tribes; they were the nobles amongst their people, and religious authorities of their time . . .

> Recall the command of the Clement God in the Quran, and the stories of the difficult lives of the blessed Imams; reflect on the histories of past religions and the pain and suffering in the lives of past prophets. Admonition of the prideful and arrogant is akin to pounding a wooden nail into stone, and is usually futile. Nonetheless, I appeal to your conscience; whenever base motives take control of you and passions fill your being causing your heart to drown in darkness, and you desire to speak of someone's fault or error, immediately think of yourself and your own actions and motives. Look at your own self and try to understand the motives behind your own actions. Then focus on correcting and improving yourself by focusing on God's grace . . .
>
> Do not join in with the religious clerics who are stars of darkness and seek their bearing from imaginary sun and moon. These clerics are branches of the tree of hell, and embers of fire driven by toxic winds. They are leaders of ignorance and its manifestations; they are armies of ego and its dawning place; they are opposed to knowledge and certitude, and are enemies of enlightenment and true faith. Their behavior is satanic and they live in that world. They are masters of pride and conceit, and are dependent on compulsion and force. They are full of envy and animosity, and are embodiments of transgression, rebellion, and perfidy against the will of God. They seek status and rank, and are habituated to greed, lust and desire . . .
>
> O' Shaykh! Do you know what benefits man . . . ? Man benefits if he is characterized by both inward and outward perfections; he must possess a good character, and enlightened nature, a pure intent, as well as intellectual power, brilliance and discernment, intuition, discretion and foresight, temperance, reverence, and heart-felt fear of God. For an unlit candle, however great in diameter and tall, is no better than a barren palm tree or a pile of dead wood.[14]

In 1914, Mírzá Abu'l-Faḍl (see Chapter 5) died in Egypt and all his papers and documents were sent to 'Abdu'l-Bahá. One of Mírzá Abu'l-Faḍl's books was unfinished at the time of his death and he had wanted a relative, Siyyid Mihdí Gulpaygání, to finish it. With a young family, Siyyid Mihdí didn't have time, so 'Abdu'l-Bahá called Shaykh Muḥammad-'Alí to Haifa. He gave him all of Mírzá Abu'l-Faḍl's papers, telling him that they 'were God's trust and needed to be protected'. 'Abdu'l-Bahá told him to take the papers to 'Ishqábád and then go to Tehran with Siyyid Mihdí and consult with the Hands of the Cause about how to complete the book. The work was organised so that Shaykh Muḥammad-'Alí and the Hands of the Cause would gather the needed materials and Siyyid Mihdí would do the writing. The project took ten months to complete.

In 1915, after completing the book, Shaykh Muḥammad-'Alí returned to 'Ishqábád and remained there until 1918. In that year he went with his eldest son, Bahá'u'ddin, to Sabzivár, where they stayed for a month. While there, Shaykh Muḥammad-'Alí received another invitation from 'Abdu'l-Bahá to visit Haifa. On the way, Bahá'u'ddin fell ill with typhoid fever, forcing them to spend three months in Birjand. Unlike his previous visit to that city, this time, 'all the nobles and clergy of Birjand visited Shaykh Muhammad-'Alí and honored him. Shawkat'ul-Mulk, the governor of Qa'in, also welcomed him warmly'.[15]

When Bahá'u'ddin was well, they left Birjand and travelled to Bombay. Since the First World War had only recently ended, the British were refusing visas to anyone, but since they knew that Bahá'ís did not participate in politics, they did issue visas to Shaykh Muḥammad-'Alí and his son, who then sailed to Port Said, then under British control. When they arrived, an Egyptian Bahá'í, Maḥmud Effendi Alneshoqati

> saw Shaykh Muhammad-'Alí and Bahá'u'ddin disembark, and ran up to them and enquired if they were Bahá'ís. They responded, so he immediately picked up their belongings and took them to his own guesthouse, and showed them warm hospitality and affection. Nonetheless, they experienced difficulties in Port Said because a man, named Shaykh Jamal, had animosity toward Bahá'ís and was causing intrigue to arouse the townspeople against Bahá'ís. He had been so effective in spreading hate that port laborers, who carried coal to ships and were employees of Mahmud Effendi, encircled the guesthouse and would yell obscenities at Shaykh Muhammad-'Alí and his son. Their ship to Haifa was not ready yet and they had to wait five or six days. However the animosity was getting so heightened that they did not feel safe, and went to Aḥmad-i Yazdi to consult on what to do. The Consul thought it wise for them to go to [Cairo] until their ship was ready. Shaykh Muhammad-'Alí and a number of other [Egyptian] Baha'is who had also been attacked by the ruffians [went to Cairo].[16]

After a week, they returned to Port Said and sailed to Haifa. When they disembarked from the ship, they were met by 15 Bahá'ís who 'Abdu'l-Bahá had sent to welcome them. When S͟hayk͟h Muḥammad-'Alí met 'Abdu'l-Bahá, the Master quoted a poem by Rumi: 'Are the waves of the sea more delightful or the mead? Is the Beloved's sword more endearing or His shield?' According to Kamran Mesbah, who translated the poem, these lines suggest that for the true lover who seeks the Beloved (God), there is no difference between tribulations on land and sea, or to being attacked for the Beloved (sword) or experiencing the loving protection of the Beloved (shield). Shortly after his arrival, the Master sent S͟hayk͟h Muḥammad-'Alí to Alexandria to confront the problems caused by Covenant-breakers. Upon his return, he stayed in Haifa for a year and a half until 'Abdu'l-Bahá told him it was time to leave and return to 'Is͟hqábád.[17]

S͟hayk͟h Muḥammad-'Alí sailed first to India in the middle of November 1921, where he gave a talk on brotherhood in Surat:

> This gathering is motivated by a vision of brotherhood. When I ponder brotherhood, I reflect on the unity that exists between siblings who share one lineage and bloodline. They share in hard times and pleasant times, so that grief and pain, joy and happiness are all shared equally. Spiritual brotherhood should be even stronger because it has a greater influence on the society and creates a more powerful example. I can imagine that if spiritual unity is firmly established, a person in distress in the remotest part of the world can call 'O my brother!' without addressing anyone in particular, and all of his spiritual brothers around the world will intuitively feel his pain and respond from the depth of their soul to come to his aid. If someone in the east has a reason to be happy or sad, his spiritual brothers in the west will feel this in their heart and likewise be happy or sad. I have seen this kind of unity in the Bahá'í community with my own eyes, where spiritual unity results not only in the sacrifice of material things for one another but sacrificing one's life for another. For example, in the city of Tabriz in Ad͟harbayjan, the clergy had sentenced one of the Bahá'ís to death because of his religion. This Baha'i was from Nis͟hapur and his name was S͟hayk͟h Aḥmad. When they were taking him to the gallows, one of his friends ran up to the executioner and begged to take his friend's

place on the gallows. When the executioner refused this request, this friend asked to be killed for the same crime as his friend, and to be killed before Shaykh Aḥmad's execution, because he could not bear to see his friend dead. The authorities finally had to accept his request.

These stories should adequately show the nature and power of spiritual brotherhood and true unity. My purpose in retelling these events is to show that treading this path requires casting off blind attachment to rejected traditions and distancing oneself from the attractions of the material world. The necessary provisions for this journey are divine attributes and spiritual virtues. The intent of the traveller on this path should be to show kindness and favor to all humanity, and to serve each one as would a caring father, and to prefer others to oneself. The welfare of others should be seen just as important as one's own welfare. This needs to be manifested in action not just in words; there is a tremendous difference between words and deeds.

The key to this great concept among Bahá'ís is that their love for one another is a reflection of the love of God, and influenced by the word of God. Therefore, this love is completely realized and thoroughly present in their hearts and souls in such wise as to have transformed their world. This is the true meaning of the promise that God will create new heavens and a new earth signifying the advent of the spirit of God, and this is the meaning of being born again.[18]

Shaykh Muḥammad-'Alí was still travelling when 'Abdu'l-Bahá passed away. He wrote that

> the passing of 'Abdu'l-Bahá so completely upended the foundation of my existence that the body cannot muster any strength, the soul is unable to receive grace, and the spirit is bereft of enthusiasm. This has left me unable to function at a level that is worthy of the station of a human being; there is no intellectual faculty left for me and everything is out of control. I spend my days wandering and weary. The effect of this great calamity, and the depression that is always present, has resulted in the erosion of my health, and by the early summer the signs of disease became visible. Day by day my strength and stamina diminished, to the point where death appeared imminent.[19]

Another reason for his debilitation was that he had stomach cancer. By January 1923, the physicians gave up hope because he was too weak for surgery. Shaykh Muḥammad-'Alí wrote to a friend and asked him to write to the Greatest Holy Leaf. In the letter, which his friend forwarded to the Greatest Holy Leaf, Shaykh Muḥammad-'Alí 'begged her for prayers that if my services are no longer needed in this blessed Faith, to shorten my suffering and the suffering of the Baha'i community and my family'. Then Shaykh Muḥammad-'Alí had a dream in which he said that:

> 'Abdu'l-Bahá entered my room carrying a dish of warm milk in one hand and some sugar in the other hand. He told me that he had brought these for me, and he put the milk and sugar before me. I awoke from the joy of seeing my beloved Master, the time was two hours before dawn. From that day I have been taking milk and sugar even though the doctors have told me to specifically stay away from milk. Thanks to God the symptoms of the disease have diminished daily and the swelling of the stomach has been reduced.[20]

Shaykh Muḥammad-'Alí recovered enough to travel to Tashkent, where he underwent surgery to remove the cancer. Unfortunately, the cancer soon returned and he passed into the Abhá Kingdom in April 1924. Upon hearing of his passing, Shoghi Effendi wrote:

> The noteworthy services of that illustrious personage rendered at the threshold of God are all accepted and eternally memorialized. Not a jot of the pure and sacrificial deeds of the followers of the Greatest Name will be forgotten or lost. These deeds will grow continually like a tree and their fruits and effects will become clear and apparent in the contingent world. He took his flight to the Beloved and is enjoying divine blessings in the midmost center of Paradise. Be assured that prayers will be said at the Holy Shrines for the elevation of his soul.[21]

18

MULLÁ ZAYNU'L-'ÁBIDÍN NAJAFÁBÁDÍ – ZAYNU'L-MUQARRABÍN

(1818–1903)

Zaynu'l-'Ábidín Najafábádí, to whom Bahá'u'lláh gave the title Zaynu'l-Muqarrabín, meaning 'Ornament of Them that Are Nigh unto God', so lived up to his title that 'Abdu'l-Bahá described him as 'one of the greatest of all the Báb's companions and all the loved ones of Bahá'u'lláh'.[1]

Zaynu'l-Muqarrabín was born in Najafábád, a village near Iṣfahán, in May 1818. His father, Áqá Muḥammad, was one of the learned of the village and the Mullá of the local mosque which he built himself and which exists to this day. Zaynu'l-Muqarrabín was raised in the traditional way, to accept whatever he was taught about Islam. Upon turning 15, however, he started to feel that the religious instruction he received from the clergy was not satisfactory, so he began to carefully read the Qur'án and reflect on its meaning. He soon realised that a person's faith had to result from study and meditation, not blind acceptance. Zaynu'l-Muqarrabín reread the Qur'án several times until he found a passage that said, 'those who are in doubt about the validity of the Qur'an, let them bring forth another Surah like it.' He realised that this meant that no one except a Manifestation of God could produce verses like those in the Qur'án.[2]

Zaynu'l-Muqarrabín's father died while on pilgrimage to Mecca in about 1837, and Zaynu'l-Muqarrabín inherited the duties of the mullá of his father's mosque. He travelled to Karbilá in January 1845, meeting a Mullá Momen on the way. Mullá Momen was a disciple of Siyyid Káẓim and he said that he hoped his new acquaintance would have the bounty of meeting the Báb in Karbilá, where the Bábís expected the Báb to pass through on His return from pilgrimage to Mecca. He did not reveal the station of the Báb at that point. Later, when the Báb took a different route, Zaynu'l-Muqarrabín went home to Najafábád, not giving this new information any further thought.

Zaynu'l-Muqarrabín had a policy of allowing visiting mullás to give sermons in his mosque, so when a Mullá Muḥammad asked to give a sermon in 1850, he agreed. The young mullá's sermon was a breath of fresh air to Zaynu'l-Muqarrabín and he asked him to pray for him:

> This youth . . . responded with 'the best prayer is to inform you of a big event that you are unaware of.' Jináb-i-Zayn said, 'please go ahead'. Mullah Muhammad continued: 'That person whom I know to be good, you do not know'. Jináb-i-Zayn responded: 'I have no issues with anyone. Any matter that I hear, I will put it to my consideration. If I deem it to be true, I will accept it. If not, I will reject it without protesting'.
>
> Mullah Muhammad then told Jináb-i-Zayn that the One Whose advent all are waiting for has come. At that moment Jináb-i-Zayn became shocked as if he had been shaken to the core of his being. He became confused as if he had lost his mental balance and his mind overflowed with superstitious thoughts from traditional Shia doctrine.[3]

Shi'a doctrine stipulated that before the Qa'im could be revealed, the antichrist had to appear, so Zaynu'l-Muqarrabín questioned where he was and continued to contest the explanations until Mullá Muḥammad exclaimed: 'how long will you be blinded by the veil? Forty Mujtahids have sacrificed their lives in the path of the Báb and you have not awakened still'.[4] Zaynu'l-Muqarrabín was bewildered and confused, until he realised that some things in the Qur'án must be symbolic and not literal. He had many questions, but at that time it was too dangerous to seek out the Bábís. So he began to pray:

> God, you know I am looking for the truth but do not know where to go or from whom to ask. Open a door and show me the way. Turn my anxiety to tranquillity and my doubt to certitude because I have abandoned two things. One is to look at the peoples and what they say. If there are a hundred Mujtahids who unanimously deny, I cannot follow them, and if they unanimously accept, I cannot follow them either because I know my personal responsibility. I

> will be questioned in the end, not them. Another thing is that if I hear that the rules and ordinances of Islam have changed or been renewed, I see no reason to deny it. If He is right, then change is right and if he is not from you [God], then we will not follow him, even if he says what the Quran says.
>
> Then I fell asleep. I dreamt I was sitting in a room and a lamp was lit on the right side. Suddenly His eminence the Báb entered the room and sat near the lamp. I was seated a few steps from Him I asked meekly about the claim that was put forth. What was the proof of that claim? I did not see or understand. With His blessed finger, He pointed to the lamp and said; 'This light being light, what reason should it present except its effulgence? This same light is its proof'.[5]

More than one year passed after his dream. Sometime during the early part of 1852, a Bábí teacher named Mírzá Sulaymán Quli-Turk passed through Najafábád and went to the Midán mosque, where he gave a sermon and announced, in a discreet manner, the appearance of the Báb. One of the learned of the village, Mullá 'Aḥmad, was impressed by the sermon and desired to meet Mírzá Sulaymán. After a discussion of over one hour, Mullá 'Aḥmad found that he needed help and so he invited Zaynu'l-Muqarrabín, who by then was considered amongst the most learned of the village and renowned for his piety and humbleness, to the meeting. There followed three days of discussion and reading, during which Mullá 'Aḥmad, with love and patience, convinced Zaynu'l-'Ábidín of the truth. At some point Zaynu'l-'Ábidín remembered the dream he had had, and the Youth who had pointed to the lamp.[6]

Then he was given the *Qayyúmul-Asmá* to read. After just a couple paragraphs, 'He said to himself that the verse he just heard was from the same source as that of the Quran. If this verse is not a holy verse, then he would have to deny the Quran. If he accepts the Quran, he has to accept this. He found himself having no recourse except accepting this new faith'.[7]

Zaynu'l-Muqarrabín lost no time in proclaiming the good news of the new Manifestation to some of his close friends. Rapidly it became known that he was a Bábí, and many came to him for guidance and advice. This aroused the jealousy and hatred of his enemies, who complained to the Governor of Iṣfahán, Tsherágh 'Alí Khán. The Governor sent some of his men to look into the matter and then asked to see Zaynu'l-Muqarrabín. He came to Iṣfahán and met with the Governor, and a fruitful conversation ensued. The Governor appreciated Zaynu'l-Muqarrabín's frank and reasonable thinking and attitude, commended him and gave him a cloak as a gift.[8]

Suddenly, although Zaynu'l-Muqarrabín had been venerated for his knowledge and piety, 'the people, "the mass, as a snake in the grass," who had worshipped him before, now rose up to do him harmHe endured it all and went on teaching with great eloquence'. He remained staunch, unmoved, as their wrath increased.[9]

Mírzá Ḥaydar-'Alí, one of Zaynu'l-Muqarrabín's friends, told a story about how Zaynu'l-Muqarrabín taught the Faith:

> In Isfahan, I spent most of my time in the presence of Zaynul-Muqarrabin. We used to go to distant and desolate places far from the tumult of the towns and villages, just to be together, study the Writings, chant prayers, and discuss the Cause of God. These moments of joy kept us alive, but we longed to teach and make His Name known in any way we could. We tried different methods of approach. We went to an Indian who claimed to have some medical knowledge, and Jináb-i-Zayn opened the discussion by saying,
>
> 'I feel a painful sensation in my heart. I know of no physician who can help me.'
>
> 'What is the cause?' asked the physician.
>
> Jináb-i-Zayn replied, 'A few days ago, I was walking down the street when suddenly I beheld a strange sight. Some people, held captive and helpless in the hands of a savage mob, were being tortured and mercilessly persecuted. I was so disturbed and alarmed that, ever since then, I have felt this pain in my heart.' Then Jináb-i-Zayn went on to tell the Indian doctor about the Revelation of the Bab, His tragic history, and His Writings.[10]

In August 1852, two misguided Bábís attempted to assassinate the Sháh, beginning a period of intense attacks on Bábís across Iran. Remaining in Najafábád would endanger the local Bábís, so Zaynu'l-Muqarrabín left and went to Baghdad in the hope of meeting Mírzá Yaḥyá, who he had been told was the designated successor of the Báb. But Mírzá

Yaḥyá was in hiding, and it was at this time that Bahá'u'lláh was in the mountains of Sulaymaniyyih. Zaynu'l-Muqarrabín searched for the Bábís and encountered Mírzá Músá (see Chapter 1), but since the Bábís were extremely cautious about contact with anyone, he learned little. Zaynu'l-Muqarrabín travelled to Karbilá and spent some time there copying out the Writings of the Báb.[11]

While he was in Iraq, the Muslim clergy back home in Najafábád ransacked and destroyed Zaynu'l-Muqarrabín's house and threw some of the Bábís into prison. They wanted to put the Bábís to death, but were stymied by the mayor who, after interviewing the Bábís, released them. Hearing of these events as he travelled home, Zaynu'l-Muqarrabín knew that his return to Najafábád would cause greater difficulties for the Bábís, so he went back to Baghdad.[12]

When Zaynu'l-Muqarrabín arrived in Baghdad, Bahá'u'lláh had returned from His time of seclusion and Zaynu'l-Muqarrabín enjoyed a two-hour meeting with Him. Though very impressed with Bahá'u'lláh, he did not perceive His station and continued to search for the successor to the Báb. Then Zaynu'l-Muqarrabín received his first Tablet from Bahá'u'lláh and was very moved by its content. He wrote back to Bahá'u'lláh with some questions and when He responded, His answer caused Zaynu'l-Muqarrabín to recognise His true station.[13]

Zaynu'l-Muqarrabín then returned to Najafábád and all seemed to be quiet at first. A land dispute in Iṣfahán, however, quickly escalated when the matter was taken to Shaykh Muḥammad-Báqir, who Bahá'u'lláh named the 'Wolf' and whose son was the recipient of the *Epistle to the Son of the Wolf.* The clerics involved in the case claimed that the Bábís in Najafábád were led by Zaynu'l-Muqarrabín and that they had 'betrayed Islam by becoming Bahá'ís'. The result was that some of the Najafábádí Bábís were imprisoned. One was executed and others were tortured.[14]

At that time, probably in 1864, Zaynu'l-Muqarrabín and a friend were hiding in a house in Iṣfahán. When the Wolf began a house-to-house search for him, they were forced to stay for a time in some ruins on the edge of the city. Realising that they could not get back into the city, Zaynu'l-Muqarrabín and his friend went to the village of Dolatábád, where Mírzá Ḥasan (see Chapter 3) and his brother Mírzá Ḥusayn, who later became known as the King of the Martyrs and the Beloved of Martyrs, lived. Mírzá Ḥasan helped them to escape to Baghdad. They were never to return to Iran. The Wolf and his fellow clerics never forgot Zaynu'l-Muqarrabín and each day, someone would stand in the market square of Iṣfahán and curse 'Abu-Bakr, Omar, Uthman (the first three Caliphs who are considered to have gone against the last Will of Prophet Muḥammad by Shi'a Muslims), Yazid and Shemr (they were responsible for the martyrdom of Imam Ḥusayn). At the end, he would add, "upon Mulla Zaynu'l-Muqarrabín, Babi-i-Najafábád, also be a curse."'[15]

When Zaynu'l-Muqarrabín arrived in Baghdad, Bahá'u'lláh had been exiled to Adrianople, so he made a pilgrimage to the House of Bahá'u'lláh. This pleased Bahá'u'lláh, Who responded in a Tablet saying that Zaynu'l-Muqarrabín radiated as brightly as the sun. It was while in Baghdad that Zaynu'l-Muqarrabín introduced Mis͟hkín-Qalam (see Chapter 15) to the Faith.

In 1868, all the Bahá'ís in Baghdad were arrested and exiled to Mosul. This was to be Zaynu'l-Muqarrabín's home for the next 20 years. Mosul was not a hospitable city to the Bahá'ís:

> These refugees were subjected to severe hardships in Mosul. When they arrived, some of the inhabitants crowded onto the rooftops and threw stones at them. The shopkeepers refused to sell them food and no one would give them shelter. It took a long time for them to settle in Mosul. After much privation and difficulties most of them managed to engage in some work, sharing their modest income with each other.[16]

Fortunately, pilgrims passing through brought gifts of goods and clothing from Bahá'u'lláh, and the King and Beloved of the Martyrs gave them financial assistance. It fell to Zaynu'l-Muqarrabín to keep the Bahá'í community united. He set up a 'charity fund', the first local Bahá'í fund in the world, and mediated all disputes among the Bahá'ís. Bahá'u'lláh sent him a series of Tablets charging him to 'gather the friends together, exhort them to unity and love, encourage them to deepen in the Faith, and help them to attain heavenly qualities'. Taherzadeh wrote that 'His knowledge and learning, his understanding of the Faith, his intelligent and well-balanced personality, together with a delightful sense of humour, endeared him to the believers and made him the focal point of the community'.

When Mírzá Ḥaydar-'Alí visited Mosul, he wrote that

> The friends in Mosul, together with the person of Zaynul-Muqarrabín, made one remember the days spent in Bahá'u'lláh's holy presence in the holy city of 'Akká. These believers were living in the utmost unity and harmony. They vied with each other in their efforts and their services. They had no desire except to gain the good pleasure of the Blessed Beauty, and secondly, to attain His presence.[17]

In one of the Tablets sent to Zaynu'l-Muqarrabín during this time, Bahá'u'lláh wrote 'blessings be upon him and upon he who loved him and he who loves him and listens to his words . . .'[18]

In the September or October of 1885, Zaynu'l-Muqarrabín received another Tablet from Bahá'u'lláh that said: 'Your longing to attain the Presence of the Sacred Threshold hath been mentioned. God Willing, He will draw you close to Him and grant you the best of both worlds'. The call came in 1886 and Zaynu'l-Muqarrabín journeyed to 'Akká to spend the rest of his life there until his passing in 1903.[19] 'Abdu'l-Bahá described his arrival and stay in 'Akká:

> He . . . was received in His holy presence and occupied himself with the transcription of the Writings and encouraging the spirit of service amongst the friends and harmony amongst the refugees. He enflamed the hearts of everyone with the fire of love and lost no moment in rendering service. He was the recipient of special favours and worked night and day in transcribing the Books and Tablets meticulously and without error.[20]

Zaynu'l-Muqarrabín moved into a two-room apartment on the upper floor of the Khán-i-'Avámíd caravanserai. He left to posterity many volumes of his transcriptions and these were later used to authenticate modern publications in Persian and Arabic. He transcribed a number of Bahá'u'lláh's Tablets, put them together and gave them to the Blessed Beauty as a gift. Bahá'u'lláh kept the volume near where He sat and would on occasion recite from them to visitors. Zaynu'l-Muqarrabín also transcribed 'Abdu'l-Bahá's *A Traveller's Narrative*, and one of his copies was given to E.G. Browne when he visited Bahá'u'lláh in 1890.[21]

When Bahá'u'lláh revealed the *Kitáb-i-Aqdas*, He gave Zaynu'l-Muqarrabín permission to ask any questions he had about the laws revealed in the Book. In a provisional transcription of a Tablet given to

Zaynu'l-Muqarrabín, Bahá'u'lláh told him that 'God Willing, you will be embraced by the Bounty of God in all the worlds of God. Your questions in My presence are acceptable because mankind will benefit from them. We have especially commanded you to ask questions about the laws and verses of God. We have made you a source of good for the peoples of the world'. Bahá'u'lláh's answers to Zaynu'l-Muqarrabín's questions form the chapter in the *Aqdas* called 'Questions and Answers'.[22]

Zaynu'l-Muqarrabín was favoured with a number of Tablets from Bahá'u'lláh. One begins with 'O Zayn, upon thee by My Glory'[23]:

> Say: the essence of all power is God's, the highest and the last End of all creation. The source of all majesty is God's, the Object of the adoration of all that is in the heavens and all that is on the earth. Such forces as have their origin in this world of dust are, by their very nature, unworthy of consideration.
>
> Say: The springs that sustain the life of these birds are not of this world. Their source is far above the reach and ken of human apprehension. Who is there that can put out the light which the snow-white Hand of God hath lit? Where is he to be found that hath the power to quench the fire which hath been kindled through the might of thy Lord, the All-Powerful, the All-Compelling, the Almighty? It is the Hand of Divine might that hath extinguished the flames of dissension. Powerful is He to do that which He pleaseth. He saith: Be; and it is. Say: The fierce gales and whirlwinds of the world and its peoples can never shake the foundation upon which the rocklike stability of My chosen ones is based. Gracious God! What could have prompted these people to enslave and imprison the loved ones of Him Who is the Eternal Truth? . . . The day, however, is approaching when the faithful will behold the Daystar of justice shining in its full splendor from the Dayspring of glory.[24]

> Concerning thy question whether human souls continue to be conscious one of another after their separation from the body. Know thou that the souls of the people of Bahá, who have entered and been established within the Crimson Ark, shall associate and commune intimately one with another, and shall be so closely associated in their lives, their aspirations, their aims and strivings as to be even as one soul . . .

> The people of Bahá, who are the inmates of the Ark of God, are, one and all, well aware of one another's state and condition, and are united in the bonds of intimacy and fellowship. Such a state, however, must depend upon their faith and their conduct. They that are of the same grade and station are fully aware of one another's capacity, character, accomplishments and merits. They that are of a lower grade, however, are incapable of comprehending adequately the station, or of estimating the merits, of those that rank above them . . .
>
> The souls of the infidels, however, shall—and to this I bear witness—when breathing their last be made aware of the good things that have escaped them, and shall bemoan their plight, and shall humble themselves before God. They shall continue doing so after the separation of their souls from their bodies.
>
> It is clear and evident that all men shall, after their physical death, estimate the worth of their deeds, and realize all that their hands have wrought. I swear by the Daystar that shineth above the horizon of Divine power! They that are the followers of the one true God shall, the moment they depart out of this life, experience such joy and gladness as would be impossible to describe, while they that live in error shall be seized with such fear and trembling, and shall be filled with such consternation, as nothing can exceed.[25]

One day in 1891, Bahá'u'lláh and some of the Bahá'ís went to Nahariyya for a picnic from morning until late afternoon. Zaynu'l-Muqarrabín and Mishkín-Qalam were privileged to attend. Zaynu'l-Muqarrabín's son recounted that

> A sheep had previously been slaughtered, but all were worried about how they were going to cook and feed those gathered there. Eventually, they gave the responsibility for organizing the cooking and preparing the food to my father (Jináb-i-Zayn). He called for cooking utensils to be brought from the nearby village and he began to prepare two sorts of kebab. One was the sort known as Ḥusayni, but which from that day on became known as Kabab Zayni, the other Kabab Barg. All of this was done in a spirit of joy and happiness. When it came to eating, a portion of the food was taken to Bahá'u'lláh and it was said to Him: 'This is what Zayn has cooked'.

He replied: 'Although it has been some time that I have not partaken of meat because Zayn has put himself to a lot of trouble, I will take a small portion to eat'.[26]

Bahá'u'lláh also began to reveal the *Epistle to the Son of the Wolf* at the picnic, aimed at the son of the man who so hated Zaynu'l-Muqarrabín in Iṣfahán.

The story of the life of Zaynu'l-Muqarrabín would not be complete without referring to his great sense of humour which always cheered the believers. At times, he used to make amusing remarks in the presence of Bahá'u'lláh (like 'Abdu'l-Bahá's relationship with Fujita). On one occasion, Ḥájí Mírzá Ḥaydar-'Alí, Zaynu'l-Muqarrabín and Mishkín-Qalam were all in the presence of the Blessed Beauty when He asked them,

'Do you want Me to send you to the Abhá Kingdom?'

Mírzá Haydar-'Alí's response was in line with his life philosophy that, 'I surrender to whatever is Thy holy will'.

Mishkín-Qalam then said, 'No, my Beloved; I want to be here in Thy presence'. Jináb-i-Zayn, not really wishing to think of death and such matters, turned to Ḥájí Mírzá Haydar-'Alí and said: 'Tell the Blessed Beauty that I am hard of hearing and can't hear Him'.[27]

Following the passing of Bahá'u'lláh in 1892, Zaynu'l-Muqarrabín remained steadfast in the Cause and gave his full devotion to 'Abdu'l-Bahá. 'Abdu'l-Bahá organised classes for the children in which Zaynu'l-Muqarrabín taught Arabic and study of the Bahá'í Writings, and Mishkín-Qalam taught calligraphy.[28]

In September 1898, Mírzá Ḥabíbu'lláh Afnán made his fourth pilgrimage and was in 'Abdu'l-Bahá's presence with Ḥájí Mírzá Ḥaydar-'Alí and Zaynu'l-Muqarrabín when 'Abdu'l-Bahá revealed a secret:

One day, when a number of the elder residents and the pilgrims were with the Master, He told them that 'Certain [good] news has been received from Iran. If divulged, the old would dance in joy. But the time for its announcement has not yet arrived'. Zaynu'l-Muqarrabín and the honored Mírzá Haydar-'Alí asked, 'Is the time for proclaiming this good news near?' 'Abdul-Bahá responded with: 'God willing'.

The next week, 'Abdu'l-Bahá ended their speculation, saying 'The good news that I had promised is this: the sacred remains of the Exalted Báb have safely left the soil of Iran and just arrived in the Ottoman land. They are now completely out of danger. After 50 years, what the Blessed Beauty promised has come to pass'.[29] The holy remains of the Báb arrived in the Holy Land on 31 January 1899.[30]

After the historic pilgrimage of Phoebe Hearst in 1898, Western pilgrims began to flood into 'Akká. Youness Afroukhteh wrote that

> The pilgrim house [the rooms rented for this purpose in Khán-i-'Avámíd] was now in a buzz: loyal and steadfast friends were appearing from every direction. The atmosphere of love and unity infused a spirit of joy and elation into the hearts of all the believers, washing away the bitter anguish of the renewal of incarceration. Signs of happiness and gaiety were evident in every face. At times the pilgrims from the West and the East openly associated with each other. The letters from the West brought many happy tidings; some of them were read aloud in the pilgrim house. At times the Master visited the pilgrims. Mírzá Haydar-'Alí, the anchor of the pilgrim house, shared loving and fatherly counsel with the newcomers, helping them to orient themselves in this happy paradise. Zaynu'l-Muqarrabin was the soul of the pilgrim house, while the wonderful Mishkin-Qalam brought delight and cheer to the hearts.[31]

Upon the death of Zaynu'l-Muqarrabín in 1903, 'Abdu'l-Bahá wrote:

> From his early years till his last breath, this eminent man never failed in service to the Manifestation. After the ascension, he was consumed with such grieving, such constant tears, and anguish, that as the days passed by, he wasted away. He remained faithful to the Covenant and was a close companion to this servant of the Light of the World, but he longed to rise out of this life and awaited his departure from day to day. At last, serene and happy, rejoicing in the tidings of the Kingdom, he soared away to that mysterious land. There he was loosed from every sorrow, and in the gathering-place of splendors he was immersed in light.[32]

19

MÍRZÁ 'ALÍ-MUḤAMMAD – IBN-I-AṢDAQ

(c 1851–1928)

Mírzá 'Alí Muḥammad, better known as Ibn-i-Aṣdaq and also as S͟hahíd Ibn-i-S͟hahíd (Martyr and Son of Martyr)¹, was one of the four Apostles who were also named as Hands of the Cause by Bahá'u'lláh.

Ibn-i-Aṣdaq was born in Mas͟hhad in about 1851.² His title, Ibn-i-Aṣdaq, means 'son of Aṣdaq' and was given to him by Bahá'u'lláh because his father, Mullá Ṣádiq-i-K͟hurásání, formerly known as Muqaddas and who was a follower of Siyyid Kázim, was an illustrious Muslim divine who became a devout Bábí in 1844. He recognised the Báb after meeting Mullá Ḥusayn, the first person to believe in the Báb, who told him that the promised Manifestation had arrived, but would not divulge His identity. Mullá Ṣádiq retired to meditate and suddenly saw the face of the Báb. He was with Quddús in Shiraz and fought at S͟hayk͟h Ṭabarsí.³ Bahá'u'lláh gave him the name Ismu'lláhu'l-Aṣdaq, meaning 'The Name of God the Most Truthful'.⁴

In 1860, father and son went to Baghdad to meet Bahá'u'lláh and they spent 14 months in His presence. For the young Ibn-i-Aṣdaq, meeting the Manifestation of God face to face was life-changing and set him on a path of service and dedication to the Faith. Bahá'u'lláh revealed a prayer for him: 'I ask Thee, O my God! To give him to drink of the milk of Thy bounty so that he may raise the standards of victory through Me, – a victory which is Thine – and arise to serve Thy Cause, when he groweth up, just as, when a youth, he hath arisen at Thy Command'.⁵

Soon after their return to Persia in 1862, both father and 13-year-old son were arrested by order of the Governor of K͟hurásán at the behest of 18 Muslim divines. They were put in chains and thrown into prison in Tehran for their belief in Bahá'u'lláh. At first, they were ordered to be executed, but instead were chained together in the notorious Síyáh-Chál, the same prison where their Beloved had experienced His Revelation. They were imprisoned for two years and four months.

Conditions in the prison caused Ibn-i-Aṣdaq to fall seriously ill. The chief jailer, being a benevolent man, sent for a doctor, but no Muslim doctor could be found who would treat a Bahá'í youth. A desperate search found Ḥakím Masíh, a Jewish doctor who agreed to treat him. Ḥakím Masíh had been the physician to the court of Muḥammad Sháh and had gone with him to Baghdad soon after the declaration of the Báb. While there, he had heard Ṭáhirih speak before a group of Muslim divines, all of whose arguments she had refuted with powerful answers. Now he was attending a Bábí child in a prison in Tehran.[6]

For two months Ḥakím Masíh took care of Ibn-i-Aṣdaq. He also sat at Mullá Ṣádiq's feet, learning about the Faith. Not long afterwards, he became the first person from a Jewish background in Persia to believe in Bahá'u'lláh. He taught the Faith to his family, and his youngest grandson, Lotfullah Hakim, became a member of the first Universal House of Justice.[7]

When they were finally released from prison, father and son returned to Mashhad and Ibn-i-Aṣdaq accompanied his father as he travelled around Persia teaching the Faith. Ibn-i-Aṣdaq married a niece of Mullá Ḥusayn, but she soon died. He later married a Qajar princess, Udhrá Khánum Ḍiyá'u'l-Ḥájjiyyih, called Áqá Ján by her family. She was the great-granddaughter of Fatḥ-'Alí Sháh, who had been the Persian Emperor from 1797 until 1834. Ibn-i-Aṣdaq's new wife was already a Bahá'í and was educated, talented and well versed in Persian poetry and literature. Together they had four daughters.[8]

In about 1875, Ibn-i-Aṣdaq was invited by a Turkman chief to the fortress of Karim-Virdi Ishan in Turkmenistan. Twelve members of this community became Bahá'ís because of his visit.[9]

In 1878, Ibn-i-Aṣdaq travelled to Hamadan where he met the believers and was successful in teaching the Faith. He shared the Faith with a number of individuals of Jewish origin, amongst whom was the all-respected Ḥakím Áqá Ján Hamadání. Afterwards, Bahá'u'lláh sent Ibn-i-Aṣdaq a Tablet saying that 'We beheld ye in the land of H and M', meaning Hamadan.

A year later, Ibn-i-Aṣdaq was able to return to 'Akká and meet

Bahá'u'lláh. During his two weeks there, he received multiple favours and kindnesses. Returning to Iran, he pursued his travel teaching to Hamadan again, then to Tehran and Iṣfahán. In Iṣfahán, he was able to visit the families of the King of Martyrs and the Beloved of Martyrs and obtain two photographs of them which he sent to the Holy Land.[10]

When Ibn-i-Aṣdaq was about 30, he wrote to Bahá'u'lláh asking to be detached from 'life and death', 'body and soul', 'existence and nothingness', 'reputation and honour', and to be given the station of 'utter self-sacrifice'.[11] In January 1880, he received Bahá'u'lláh's response:

> Thou didst beg the Supreme Lord to bestow upon thee a station whereat in the path of His love thou wouldst give up everything: thy life, thy spirit, thy reputation, thine existence, all in all. All of these behests were submitted in the most sanctified, most exalted Presence of the Abhá Beauty. Thus did the Tongue of the Merciful speak in the Kingdom of Utterance: God willing, he shall be seen in utmost purity and saintliness, as befitteth the Day of God, and attain the station of the most great martyrdom. Today, the greatest of all deeds is service to the Cause. Souls that are well assured should with utmost discretion teach the Faith, so that the sweet fragrances of the Divine Garment will waft from all directions. This martyrdom is not confined to the destruction of life and the shedding of blood. A person enjoying the bounty of life may yet be recorded a martyr in the Book of the Sovereign Lord. Well is it with thee that thou hast wished to offer whatsoever is thine, and all that is of thee and with thee in My path.[12]

Ibn-i-Aṣdaq knew then that martyrdom did not necessarily mean physically dying for the Faith. Two years later, he again wrote to Bahá'u'lláh asking for martyrdom. This time, Bahá'u'lláh reassured him that he had been given the station of a martyr, but without the need for death. Bahá'u'lláh wrote: 'We, verily, have ordained for him this exalted station, this high designation. Well it is with him that he attained this station prior to its appearance, and We accepted from him that which he intended in the path of God, the One, the Single, the All-Knowing, the All-Informed'.[13] Some sources state that Bahá'u'lláh gave Ibn-i-Aṣdaq the title of 'Shahíd Ibn-i-Shahíd' (Martyr, Son of the Martyr), but the Research Department of the World Centre did not find any reference to this title in the Writings of Bahá'u'lláh, although Bahá'u'lláh did address Ibn-i-Aṣdaq with the title of 'Shahíd' meaning 'Martyr'. 'Abdu'l-Bahá, however, used the title of 'Shahíd Ibn-i-Shahíd' in a number of Tablets.[14]

Bahá'u'lláh's answer set Ibn-i-Aṣdaq on the path of a travelling teacher, journeying to every part of Persia to teach the Faith. He and Áqá Ján moved from Mashhad to Tehran. His marriage to royalty brought Ibn-i-Aṣdaq into contact with many wealthy people in high positions. This allowed him to teach individuals who could use their influence to help the persecuted Bahá'í community.[15] His constant moving from one place to another solely for the sake of the Cause brought another Tablet from Bahá'u'lláh, which read in part: 'The movement itself from place to place, when undertaken for the sake of God, hath always exerted, and can now exert, its influence in the world'.[16]

Bahá'u'lláh had directed Ibn-i-Aṣdaq as early as 1881 to consult with Ḥájí Ákhund (see Chapter 8) and another Bahá'í about appointing a resident Bahá'í teacher in every locality in Persia, placing great emphasis on this.[17]

In 1882, Ibn-i-Aṣdaq sent two letters to Bahá'u'lláh requesting clarification on various questions. Accompanying these two letters were a number of letters from other friends. The response to Ibn-i-Aṣdaq came in a Tablet dated 17 August 1882, over ten pages long, answering the many questions and referring to the grave situation of the world, the war in Alexandria of July 1882, and exhorting the friends to teach the Faith with wisdom and eloquence, advising: '. . . this day is the day of pure action and service to the Faith, haply the light of good character may envelop the world . . .'[18]

In 1886, Ibn-i-Aṣdaq went back to 'Akká and was blessed with attaining the presence of Bahá'u'lláh a number of times during his month there. Following his return to Tehran, he received a number of Tablets from Bahá'u'lláh in which he was addressed as 'Beloved of my heart' and 'Son of My Name'. They also included many blessing upon him.[19]

On 13 April 1887, Bahá'u'lláh sent Ibn-i-Aṣdaq a Tablet in which He gave him the station of a Hand of the Cause. This is the first time Bahá'u'lláh introduced the institution of the Hands of the Cause. In the Tablet, He called on Mírzá Aqá Ján, in whose name the Tablet was sent, to 'beseech the All-Abiding Lord to confirm the chosen ones, that is those souls who are Hands of the Cause, who are adorned with the robe of teaching, and have arisen to serve the Cause, to be enabled to exalt the Word of God'.

In 1890, Ibn-i-Aṣdaq visited 'Akká for the fourth time and was blessed with meeting Bahá'u'lláh for the last time. He received, upon his return to Tehran, a number of Tablets that bestowed bountiful favours upon him.

During the final years before His ascension, Bahá'u'lláh appointed four Hands of the Cause: Ḥájí Á<u>kh</u>und (see Chapter 8), Ibn-i-Abhar (see Chapter 11), Adíb (see Chapter 16) and Ibn-i-Aṣdaq. Each one received a special Tablet from Bahá'u'lláh in which he was informed of his appointment to the station of Hand of the Cause.[20]

From that time on, Bahá'u'lláh would send Ibn-i-Aṣdaq many Tablets destined for Bahá'ís all over Persia. In one case, Ibn-i-Aṣdaq received nine Tablets intended for nine different people, none of which had the recipient's name on it. A separate list was included with the names of those nine souls, but with no reference as to who was to receive which Tablet. This was to protect the individual Bahá'ís from the enemies of the Faith. Bahá'u'lláh told Ibn-i-Aṣdaq to 'Carry out certain devotions, then to position the Tablets in a high place, and while turning his heart to Bahá'u'lláh to reach for one, write on it whichever of the nine names came to mind, and deliver it to him'.[21]

At one time, after Bahá'u'lláh had been informed that the Bahá'ís of Tehran had gathered for prayer, He sent a reply to Ibn-i-Aṣdaq that included the well-known prayer 'Blessed is the Spot'.[22]

After the ascension of Bahá'u'lláh, 'Abdu'l-Bahá exhorted Ibn-i-Aṣdaq to continue his travel-teaching and he did so, journeying to all corners of Persia as well as to India, Burma and Russian Turkistan. When the Covenant-breaking activities of Mírzá Muḥammad-'Alí in 'Akká and his sympathisers in Persia began, 'Abdu'l-Bahá directed the Hands of the Cause to counteract their activities in Persia, so all four Hands criss-crossed the country explaining the nature and power of the Covenant.[23] Ibn-i-Aṣdaq also initiated teacher training classes for women in Tehran.[24]

Ibn-i-Aṣdaq's travels outside Persia took him to the ancient city of Marv (also called Merv and today called Mary), about 300 kilometres east of 'I<u>sh</u>qábád. At that time, it had an active Bahá'í community and Ibn-i-Aṣdaq spent a number of years there, helping them found a hospice and a junior school. When the Merv Bahá'ís heard about the construction of the Mas͟hriqu'l-Ad͟hkár in 'Is͟hqábád, they asked permission to build their own. When 'Abdu'l-Bahá gave them permission, they constructed a much smaller Mas͟hriqu'l-Ad͟hkár.[25]

In India, Ibn-i-Aṣdaq visited Bombay, Lahore (now in Pakistan) and Delhi. Going on to Burma, he went to Rangoon and Mandalay.[26]

Ibn-i-Aṣdaq made a number of pilgrimages to see 'Abdu'l-Bahá. One in 1904 was particularly noteworthy simply for all the trouble they endured trying to get there. Ibn-i-Aṣdaq, along with Azízu'lláh Azízí, Siyyid Ḥasan Hás͟himí-Zádih, Ústád Maḥmud K͟habiri and two others, left for pilgrimage early in the year during the time when cholera was epidemic in Persia. Azízu'lláh called it an eventful journey:

> While in Anzali, a town on the Iranian coast of the Caspian Sea near Rasht, they had been quarantined in a wooden building when a fire broke. They only survived because of the efforts of Khabiri. Then, when they reached the Russian town of Badkubih, they again were put into quarantine. When finally released, they travelled to the Black Sea, planning to sail to Beirut. The captain of their ship refused to allow them to board for some undisclosed reason. Then, an Italian ship had pity on them and greed for money prompted the captain to accept to take them to Beirut. But he failed to keep his promise and left them stranded in Istanbul, where they were again quarantined. This time, their baggage were disinfected with steam. The steam ruined all their leather items, including their shoes.[27]

Ibn-i-Aṣdaq and a large number of his family travelled to Haifa in late 1913, arriving in November, disappointingly while 'Abdu'l-Bahá was still in Egypt. They travelled through Qazvín, Ras͟ht, Bákú, Tiflis, Istanbul, finally reaching Beirut on 11 November. Their ship anchored offshore. Soon a boat approached and its occupant asked if there were any 'followers of Abbás Effendi'. The man, a Bahá'í named Tarbash, carried the pilgrims to the dock and the group spent three days in Beirut with the local Bahá'ís. After they returned to the ship, but before sailing, another rowing boat approached with 16-year-old Shoghi Effendi and a group of students.[28]

The ship arrived in Haifa the next day, but because of the stormy conditions, the captain decided to return to Beirut. Ibn-i-Aṣdaq , however, insisted on going ashore and finally two boats were lowered over the side and part of the party disembarked. It was a rough trip and as Ibn-i-Aṣdaq, who had stayed aboard to wait for the second trip, watched the two struggling boats disappear between the swells, he feared they would be lost. However, all made it to shore safely and were quickly taken to the house of the Master where the Greatest Holy Leaf welcomed them.[29]

At some point, Ibn-i-Aṣdaq had to go to Alexandria and the Greatest Holy Leaf spent a mysterious hour in conversation with him before he left. The Hand of the Cause reached 'Abdu'l-Bahá's presence on 25 November.[30] It isn't known what happened in Alexandria, but two days later, 'Abdu'l-Bahá suddenly announced that he would soon sail for Haifa.

The day after He arrived in Haifa, 'Abdu'l-Bahá appeared out of the pouring rain and told the gathered friends that He had returned to Haifa because Ibn-i-Aṣdaq had begged him. Then He spoke about Ismu'lláhu'l-Aṣdaq, Ibn-i-Aṣdaq's father, and the great services rendered by both father and son. The family remained in Haifa for 72 days.[31]

Sometime during the First World War, the Iranian Government was struggling to get its Parliament functioning because of strong internal disagreements. One day, two representatives of that body visited Ibn-i-Aṣdaq to ask a question: 'At present there are two main opposing parties in the [Parliament], Constitutionalist and Absolutist. Both say that the Bahá'ís side with them. We have been sent to investigate to which party you really belong'. Ibn-i-Aṣdaq's answer was: 'In case you ask any reasonable person whether if a man becomes sick, a doctor should be consulted, undoubtedly he will reply yes. It would be foolish, however, to rely on a doctor who does not know his business. The foundation of our Cause is justice, equity, service and harmony. We do not consider the present delegates to be real physicians'. A while later, they returned, saying that they had presented his answer to the Parliament and that 'Some smiled and seemed to like it'. As the conversation continued, Ibn-i-Aṣdaq gave them a copy of 'Abdu'l-Bahá's *The Secret of Divine Civilization*, and read about a third of it to them. Over time, both of the delegates became Bahá'ís, one attaining martyrdom two years later.[32]

Ibn-i-Aṣdaq's last pilgrimage began in 1918 and lasted for 30 months. In November 1919, while Ibn-i-Aṣdaq was in Haifa, 'Abdu'l-Bahá asked him and Aḥmad Yazdání to deliver the *Tablet to The Hague*, written by 'Abdu'l-Bahá, to the Central Organisation for Durable Peace in The Hague.[33] This organisation had published its constitution a few years earlier, which Aḥmad Yazdání had read. He and Ibn-i-Aṣdaq had written to the group, informing them of the Bahá'í principles and suggesting they seek guidance from 'Abdu'l-Bahá if they wished to establish world peace. Their response, written in February 1916 and delayed by the war, had been passed on to 'Abdu'l-Bahá. In the *Tablet to the Hague*, 'Abdu'l-Bahá wrote that

> For example, the question of universal peace, about which Bahá'u'lláh says that the Supreme Tribunal must be established: although the League of Nations has been brought into existence, yet it is incapable of establishing universal peace. But the Supreme Tribunal which Bahá'u'lláh has described will fulfil this sacred task with the utmost might and power.[34]

Also in November 1919, John Esslemont was in Haifa collecting information for a chapter in his book, *Bahá'u'lláh and the New Era,* that was to be called 'Progress of the Bahá'í Movement'. Though the chapter ultimately did not appear in the book, he collected a large amount of information about the development of the Faith in Persia, much of it from interviews he had with Ibn-i-Aṣdaq.[35]

In yet another effort in 1919, Ibn-i-Aṣdaq, with the assistance of the other Hands of the Cause, wrote a rebuttal to the misguided and false accusation written by Prof E. G. Browne, the only Westerner to have met Bahá'u'lláh, in some of his books.[36]

Ibn-i-Aṣdaq outlived his fellow Hands and was one of the three Apostles of Bahá'u'lláh who passed away in 1928, in Tehran.

1. Mírzá Músá-i-Núrí – Áqáy-i-Kalím: the only true brother of Bahá'u'lláh, surnamed Kalím

2. Mírzá Buzurg-Khurásání: youthful martyr, bearer of Bahá'u'lláh's Tablet to Náṣiri'd-Dín Sháh, surnamed Badí'

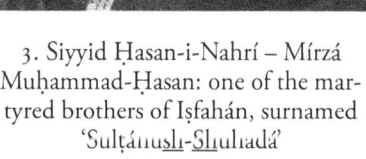

3. Siyyid Ḥasan-i-Nahrí – Mírzá Muḥammad-Ḥasan: one of the martyred brothers of Iṣfahán, surnamed 'Sulṭánush-Shuhadá'

4. Mullá Abu'l-Ḥasan-i-Ardikání – Ḥájí Amín: faithful steward of Bahá'u'lláh and 'Abdu'l-Bahá, surnamed 'Amín'

5. Mírzá Abu'l-Faḍl: foremost and authoritative expounder of the Bahá'í Revelation

6. Mírzá 'Alí-Muḥammad: poet, teacher, and martyr of the Faith, surnamed 'Varqá'

7. Mírzá Maḥmúd-i-Furúg͟hí: an indomitable spirit and jealous defender of the Faith

8. Mullá ʻAlí-Akbar-i-S͟hahmírzádí – Ḥájí Ák͟hund: a flame of zeal and devotion

9. Mullá Muḥammad: learned and steadfast exponent of the Bahá'í Revelation, surnamed 'Nabíl-i-Akbar'

10. Ḥájí Mírzá Muḥammad-Taqí-i-Afnán – Vakílu'd-Dawlih – Vakílu'd-Haqq (*centre*): cousin of the Báb and chief builder of the Mas͟hriqul-Ad͟hkár of 'Ishqábád, surnamed 'Kabír-i-Afnán'

11. Ḥájí Mírzá Muḥammad-Taqí-i-Abhar – Ibn-i-Abhar: prominent teacher

12. Mullá Muḥammad-i-Zarandí, poet, historian, and teacher of the Faith, surnamed ‘Nabíl-i-A‘ẓam’

13. Shaykh Muḥammad Káẓim-i-Qazvíní: a flame of the love of God, favoured of Bahá'u'lláh, surnamed 'Samandar'

14. Muḥammad Muṣṭafáy-i-Baghdádí: brave and vigilant custodian and bearer of the remains of the Báb

15. Mírzá Ḥusayn-i-Iṣfahání: distinguished calligraphist, and companion-in-exile of Bahá'u'lláh, surnamed 'Mis<u>h</u>kín Qalam'

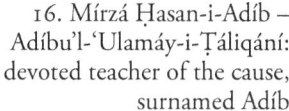

16. Mírzá Ḥasan-i-Adíb – Adíbu'l-'Ulamáy-i-Ṭáliqání: devoted teacher of the cause, surnamed Adíb

17. Shaykh Muḥammad-ʻAlí-Qá'iní: eloquent and learned champion of the Faith in Russian Turkestan

18. Mullá Zaynu'l-ʻÁbidín Najafabádí: noted scribe, chief figure among the exiles of Mosul, surnamed 'Zaynu'l-Muqarrabín'

19. Mírzá ʻAlí-Muḥammad – Ibn-i-Aṣdaq: zealous advocate in the early days of the proclamation of the covenant of Bahá'u'lláh, surnamed 'Shahíd-ibn-i-Shahíd'

BIBLIOGRAPHY

'Abdu'l-Bahá. *Light of the World: Selected Tablets* of 'Abdu'l-Bahá. Wilmette, IL: Bahá'í Publishing Trust, 2021.

— *Memorials of the Faithful.* Wilmette, IL: Bahá'í Publishing Trust, 1971.

— *Selections from the Writings of 'Abdu'l-Bahá.* Wilmette, IL: Bahá'í Publishing Trust, 2010.

— *Tablets of the Divine Plan.* Wilmette, IL: Bahá'í Publishing Trust, 1993.

— *Tablet to the Hague.* 1919. http://bahai-library.com/abdulbaha_lawh_hague_bwc.

— *Tablet on the Passing of Mírzá 'Abu'l-Faḍl-i-Gulpáygání.* https://bahai-library.com/abdulbaha_passing_abu-fadl_gulpaygani.

Abu'l-Faḍl, Mírzá. *Miracles and Metaphors.* Los Angeles, CA: Kalimát Press, 1981.

Afnán, Mírzá Ḥabíbu'lláh. *Memories of the Báb, Bahá'u'lláh, and 'Abdu'l-Bahá.* Los Angeles, CA: Kalimát Press, 2005.

— The Genesis of the Bábí-Bahá'í Faiths in Shíráz and Fárs. Leiden: Brill, 2008.

Afroukhteh, Dr Youness. *Memories of Nine Years in 'Akká.* Oxford: George Ronald, 2003.

Akhtarhavari, Nesreen. *Personal communication with her own translation of the poem*, 28 Mar 2025.

Asdaq, Rúhá. *One Life, One Memory.* Oxford: George Ronald, 1999.

Ashchi, Aqa Husayn. 'A Lifetime with Bahá'u'lláh: Events in Baghdad, Istanbul, Edirne and 'Akká while in the Company of Bahá'u'lláh', trans. Rabbani, *Witnesses to Bábí and Bahá'í History*, vol. 14, 2007. bahai-library.com/ashchi_rabbani_lifetime_bahaullah.

Atkinson, Anne Gordon, Robert Atkinson, Rosanne Buzzell, Richard Grover, Diane Iverson, Robert Stockman, and Burton WF Trafton Jr. *Green Acre on the Piscataqua.* Eliot: Green Acre Bahá'í School Council, 1991.

Azizi, Jinab-i-Azizullah. *Crown of Glory.* Teheran: Bahai Publishing Trust of Iran, English translation, 1991.

Baha'i Heroes and Heroines, http://bahaiheoresheroines.blogspot.com/2013/12/mirza-ali-muhammad-ibn-i-asdaq-apostle.html

Bahá'í News. Periodical. National Spiritual Assembly of the Bahá'ís of the United States.

Bahá'í World Centre Research Department. *Bahíyyih Khánum.* Haifa: World Centre Publications, 1982.

— Memorandum to the Universal House of Justice, 'Tablet of the Báb Lawh-i-Vasaya, "Will and Testament"; Titles of Mírzá Yaḥyá', 28 May 2004, bahai-library.com/uhj_vasaya_mirza_yahya.

Bahá'u'lláh. *Gleanings from the Writings of Bahá'u'lláh.* Wilmette: Bahá'í Publishing Trust, 1983.

Balyuzi, H. M. *'Abdu'l-Bahá.* Oxford: George Ronald, 1971.
— *Bahá'u'lláh, King of Glory.* Oxford: George Ronald, 1980.
— *Eminent Bahá'ís in the Time of Bahá'u'lláh.* Oxford: George Ronald, 1985.
— *The Báb.* Oxford: George Ronald, 1973.

Blomfield, Lady Sarah. *The Chosen Highway.* Wilmette: Bahá'í Publishing Trust, 1967.

Cameron, Glenn. *A Basic Bahá'í Chronology.* Oxford: George Ronald, 1996.

Chehabi, Houchang. *Distant Relations: Iran and Lebanon in the Last 500 Years.* New York, London: I.B. Publishers, 2006.

Day, Michael. *Journey to a Mountain: The Story of the Shrine of the Báb. Vol. 1: 1850–1921.* Oxford: George Ronald, 2017.

Dhuká'íy-i-Bayḍá'í, Mírzá Ni'matu'lláh. Dar Sharh-i-Ahvál va Áthár-i-Jináb-i-Áqá Mírzá Hasan-i-Adíbu'l-'Ulamay-i-Taliqani (Ṭihran): Mu'assisiy-i-Milliy-i-Maṭbu'at -i-Amri, 129 B.E. (1972–3), translated by Kamran Mesbah, May 2020. *Encyclopaedia Iranica.* New York: Columbia University, 1982 to present. http://www.iranicaonline.org

Fadil-i-Mazandarani, Asad'u'llah. *Tarikhi Zuhur'u'l-Haqq.* Tehran: Baha'i Publishing Trust, c. 1974.

Fikri, 'Abdu'l-Hussayn. *Hawariyyu Haḍrat-i-Baha'u'llah* (Apostles of Bahá'u'lláh), Kuwait: unidentified publisher, in Arabic, 2017.

Gail, Marzieh. *Arches of the Years.* Oxford: George Ronald, 1991.

Haddad, Anton. *Message from 'Akká.* 1900 (http://bahai-library.com/haddad_message_acca).

Harper, Barron. *Lights of Fortitude.* Oxford: George Ronald, 1997.

Hofman, David. *Bahá'u'lláh.* Oxford: George Ronald, 1992.

Masumian, Adib. 'Bahá'u'lláh's Tablet of Visitation for His Brother, Mírzá Músá (Áqáy-i-Kalím)', provisional translation, https://adibmasumian.com/translations/bh02247/

Momen, Moojan. *Amin, Haji Abu'l-Hasan.* http://bahai-library.com/momen_encyclopedia_amin_haji, 1995
— *The Bábí and Bahá'í Religions, 1844–1944.* Oxford: George Ronald, 1981.
— *Bahá'u'lláh, A Short Biography.* Oxford: OneWorld, 2007.
— *Dr J E Esslemont.* London: Bahá'í Publishing Trust, 1975
— 'Gulpáygání, Mirza Abu'l-Faḍl', 1995 (http://bahai-library.com/momen_encyclopedia_abul-Fadl _gulpaygani).
— 'The Baha'i Community Of Ashkhabad; Its Social Basis and Importance in Baha'i History'. 1987 (http://www.momen.org/relstud/ishqabad.htm)

— Religious Studies and Baha'i Studies. https://www.momen.org/relstud/turkmnst.html

Mú'ayyad, Dr Ḥabíb. *Eight Years Near 'Abdu'l-Bahá*. Translated by Ahang Rabbani in Witnesses to Bábí and Bahá'í History Vol. 3, 2007.

Nabíl-i-A'ẓam – *An Apostle of Baha'u'llah and the author of Dawn-Breakers*. http://bahaisworldwide.blogspot.com/2012/07/nabil-i-azam-author-of-dawn-breakers.html, 2012.

Nabíl. *The Dawn-Breakers: Nabíl's Narrative of the Early Days of the Bahá'í Revelation*. Trans. and ed. Shoghi Effendi. Wilmette, IL: Bahá'í Publishing Trust, 1932.

Nakhjavání, Bahíyyih. *Four on an Island*. Oxford: George Ronald, 1983.

Nakhjavani, Violette. 'Notes from the Archives Building in Haifa'. United States: National Bahá'í Archives, 1965.

New York Herald. Periodical published between 1835 and 1924.

Rabbani, Ahang. 'The Conversion of the Great-Uncle of the Báb' in *World Order*, Spring 1999.

Rafati, Vahid. 'Tablets of Bahá'u'lláh Revealed in Honor of Hand of the Cause Jináb-i-Ibn-i-Abhar'. Irfan Collquia Session #111, 2012. (http://irfancolloquia.org/111/rafati_abhar).

Rahmani, Mitra, translation. Interview of Mahmoud Foroughi with Mozaffaredin Shah, 2023.

Redman, Earl. *'Abdu'l-Bahá in Their Midst*. Oxford: George Ronald, 2011.
— *Visiting 'Abdu'l-Bahá*, Vol. 1. Oxford: George Ronald, 2019.

Rohani, Aziz. *Sweet and Enchanting Stories*. Hong Kong: Juxta Publishing, 2005.

Rowshan, Mustafa. Email to the author dated Oct 2018.
— Email to the author dated 19 Jan 2019.

Ruhe-Shoen, Janet. *Rejoice in my Gladness: The Life of Tahirih*. Wilmette: Bahá'í Publishing, 2011.

Ruhe, David. *Door of Hope*. Oxford: George Ronald, 2nd Edition, 2001.

Rúḥíyyih Khánum. *The Priceless Pearl*. Haifa: Bahá'í World Centre, 2000.

Salmání, Muḥammad-'Alí. *My Memories of Bahá'u'lláh*. Los Angeles: Kalimat Press, 1982.

Shahídí, Khalíl. *With 'Abdu'l-Bahá: Reminiscences of Kahlíl Shahidi*. 2008. (https://bahai-library.com/pdf/r/rabbani_reminiscences_khalil_shahidi.pdf)

Shahrokh, Darius. *Windows to the Past*. http://bahai-library.com/windows_to_the_past, 1992.

Shoghi Effendi. *Bahá'í Administraion: Selected Messages 1922–1932*. Wilmette: Bahá'í Publishing Trust, 1998.
— *Citadel of Faith*. Wilmette: Bahá'í Publishing Trust, 1965.

— *God Passes By.* Wilmette: Bahá'í Publishing Trust, 1974.
— *The World Order of Bahá'u'lláh.* Wilmette: Bahá'í Publishing Trust, 1991.

Smith, Peter. *A Concise Encyclopedia of the Bahá'í Faith.* Oxford: Oneworld, 2000.
— Bahá'ís in the West. Los Angles: Kalimát, 2004.

Sohrab, Ahmad. *'Abdu'l-Bahá in Egypt.* New Histories Foundation, 1929. Available at: http://bahai-library.com/Sohrab_abdulbaha_egypt, 1929.

Sohrab, Ahmad. *Ahmad Sohrab's Diary.* The Heritage Project of the National Spiritual Assembly of the United States.

Sohrab, Ahmad. Letter to Harriet Magee, dated 26 Jan 1913.

Star of the West, Vol 1. Chicago: Bahá'í News Service, 1910–1911.
— Vol. 3. Chicago: Bahá'í Publishing Society, 1912.
— Vol. 9. Chicago: Bahá'í News Service, 1918–1919.
— Vol. 13, Chicago: Bahá'í News Service, 1922–1923.
— Vol. 14. Chicago: Bahá'í News Service, 1923–1924.

Sulaymani, Azizullah. *Massabih-i-Hidayat.* Tehran: Bahá'í Publishing Trust, 9 volumes written between 1950–1975. (available at UK: Afnan Library, 2018 or https://www.h-net.org/~bahai/areprint/authors/sulayman/sulaymani.htm). Translation by Mesbah, Kamran, emailed to author 20 Jan 2020.
— 'The Story of Zaynul-Muqarrabin'. 2016. (https://bahaiwritings.files.wordpress.com/2016/12/the-story-of-jinab-i-zayn.pdf)

Taherzadeh, Adib. *The Child of the Covenant.* Oxford: George Ronald, 2000.
— *The Covenant of Bahá'u'lláh.* Oxford: George Ronald, 1992.
— *The Revelation of Bahá'u'lláh*, Vol. 1. Oxford: George Ronald, 1976.
— *The Revelation of Bahá'u'lláh*, Vol. 2. Oxford: George Ronald, 1977.
— *The Revelation of Bahá'u'lláh*, Vol. 3. Oxford: George Ronald, 1983.
— *The Revelation of Bahá'u'lláh*, Vol. 4. Oxford: George Ronald, 1987.

Thomas, Michael W. 'Glossary of Arabic and Persian Transcription', bahai-library.com/glossary_arabic_persian_transcription.

The Bahá'í World, Vol. III. New York: Bahá'í Publishing Committee, 1930.

The Bahá'í World, Vol. IV. Wilmette: Bahá'í Publishing Trust, 1933.

The Bahá'í World, Vol. XVIII. Haifa: Bahá'í World Centre, 1986.
The Universal House of Justice. Letter dated 30 July 2002, Revised – Development of the Institution of Ḥuqúqu'lláh. (http://bahai-storytelling.blogspot.com)

Walbridge, John. *The Bahá'í Faith in Iran.* 2002.

Wetzel, David. The Vanishing Messiah: The Life and Resurrections of Francis Schlatter. Iowa City: University of Iowa Press, 2016.

Whitmore, Bruce. 'The City of Love: 'Ishqábád and the Institution of the Mashriqu'l-Adhkár'. *Bahá'í News*, 1975.

'The Journey of Abdu'l-Baha's Tablet to the Hague', https://www.bahaigeschiedenis.nl/abdul-baha-tablet-to-the-hague/

REFERENCES

Introduction

1 *The Bahá'í World*, vol. III, pp. 80–81.
2 ibid. pp 84–85.
3 *The Bahá'í World*, vol. IV, pp. 108–109, 118–119.
4 'Abdu'l-Bahá, *Selections from the Writings of 'Abdu'l-Bahá*, pp. 329–330.
5 Shoghi Effendi, *Citadel of Faith*, pp. 69–70.
6 *Bahá'í News*, no. 48, p. 9.
7 Universal House of Justice, letter to an individual believer dated 17 Sept 1991.
8 Research Department, Bahá'í World Centre, letter to the author dated 6 Feb 2019.
9 'Abdu'l-Bahá, *Tablets of the Divine Plan*, pp. 49–50.
10 Shoghi Effendi, *Citadel of Faith*, p. 7.
11 Shoghi Effendi, *The World Order of Bahá'u'lláh*, p. 21.
12 Shoghi Effendi, *Bahá'í Administration*, p. 112.
13 Shoghi Effendi, *God Passes By*, p. 7.
14 *The Bahá'í World*, vol. III, pp 84–85.
15 ibid. pp 84–85.

1. Mírzá Músá-i-Núrí – Áqáy-i-Kalím

1 Shoghi Effendi, *God Passes By*, p. 108.
2 Thomas, *Glossary of Arabic and Persian Transcription.*
3 Bahá'í World Centre Research Department, *Bahíyyih, Khánum*, p. 37.
4 Fikri, *Ḥawariyyu Ḥaḍrat-i-Baha'u'llah*, p. 13.
5 'Abdu'l-Bahá, *Memorials of the Faithful*, pp. 86–87.
6 Taherzadeh, *The Covenant of Bahá'u'lláh*, p. 35.
7 'Abdu'l-Bahá, *Memorials of the Faithful*, p. 87.
8 *The Dawn-Breakers*, p. 255.
9 ibid. p. 286–288.
10 Momen, *Bahá'u'lláh, A Short Biography*, pp. 22–23; Taherzadeh, *The Covenant of Bahá'u'lláh*, p. 61.
11 Memorandum from the Research Department to the Universal House of Justice, 'Tablet of the Báb Lawh-i-Vasaya, "Will and Testament"; Titles of Mírzá Yahyá', 28 May 2004, bahai-library.com/uhj_vasaya_mirza_yahya.
12 *The Dawn-Breakers*, pp. 432–433.
13 ibid. pp. 520–521.
14 Hofman, *Bahá'u'lláh*, p. 51.
15 Ashchi, 'A Lifetime with Bahá'u'lláh,' ch. 1.

16 Momen, *Bahá'u'lláh, A Short Biography*, pp. 33–34.
17 Taherzadeh, *The Covenant of Bahá'u'lláh*, pp. 62–63.
18 Hofman, *Bahá'u'lláh*, p. 63.
19 'Abdu'l-Bahá, *Memorials of the Faithful*, pp. 87–88.
20 Balyuzi, *Bahá'u'lláh*, pp. 121–122.
21 Momen, *Bahá'u'lláh, A Short Biography*, p. 41–42.
22 Nabíl, *The Dawn-Breakers*, p. 189.
23 Blomfield, *The Chosen Highway*, p. 47.
24 Balyuzi, *Bahá'u'lláh, King of Glory*, p. 137.
25 Momen, *Bahá'u'lláh, A Short Biography*, pp. 52–53.
26 ibid. pp. 53–54.
27 Balyuzi, *Bahá'u'lláh, King of Glory*, pp. 149–150.
28 Nabil, quoted in Shoghi Effendi, *God Passes By*, p. 147; see also Taherzadeh, *The Revelation of Bahá'u'lláh*, vol 1, p. 228; Momen, *Bahá'u'lláh, A Short Biography*, p. 59.
29 Momen, *Bahá'u'lláh, A Short Biography*, p. 59.
30 Taherzadeh, *The Revelation of Bahá'u'lláh*, vol. 1, p. 284.
31 'Abdu'l-Bahá, *Light of the World*, p. 36.
32 Taherzadeh, *The Revelation of Bahá'u'lláh*, vol. 2, pp. 154, 160.
33 Shoghi Effendi, *God Passes By*, p. 164.
34 Salmání, *My Memories of Bahá'u'lláh*, p. 48.
35 'Abdu'l-Bahá, *Memorials of the Faithful*, pp. 88–89.
36 Taherzadeh, *The Revelation of Bahá'u'lláh*, vol. 2, pp. 162–164.
37 Balyuzi, *Bahá'u'lláh, King of Glory*, pp. 277–279, 283.
38 Balyuzi, *Bahá'u'lláh, King of Glory*, pp. 347–348; Smith, *A Concise Encyclopedia of the Bahá'í Faith*, p. 255.
39 http:/bahaisworldwide.blogspot.com/2012/07/nabil-i-azam-author-of-dawn-breakers.html
40 'Abdu'l-Bahá, *Memorials of the Faithful*, p. 90.
41 Fikri, *Ḥawáríyyú Ḥaḍrat-i-Bahá'u'lláh*, p. 14.
42 Masumian, *provisional translation.*

2. Mírzá Buzurg-Khurásání – Badí'

1 Balyuzi, *Bahá'u'lláh, King of Glory*, p. 294; Cameron, *A Basic Bahá'í Chronology*, p. 54.
2 Taherzadeh, *The Revelation of Bahá'u'lláh*, vol. 3, p. 176.
3 Balyuzi, *Bahá'u'lláh, King of Glory*, pp. 294, 296.
4 ibid. pp. 296–97.
5 Akhtarhavari, Nesreen, personal communication with her own translation of the poem.
6 Taherzadeh, *The Revelation of Bahá'u'lláh*, vol. 3, p. 179.
7 ibid. p. 179–180.
8 Taherzadeh, *The Revelation of Bahá'u'lláh*, vol. 3, p. 182; Balyuzi, *Bahá'u'lláh*, p. 297.
9 Taherzadeh, *The Revelation of Bahá'u'lláh*, vol. 3, p. 183.
10 ibid. pp. 183–84.
11 *Ahmad Sohrab's Diary*, 25 March 1913, pp. 7–19.
12 Balyuzi, *Bahá'u'lláh, King of Glory*, p. 309.

13 Taherzadeh, *The Revelation of Bahá'u'lláh*, vol. 3, pp. 201–202.
14 Balyuzi, *Bahá'u'lláh, King of Glory*, p. 455.
15 Taherzadeh, *The Revelation of Bahá'u'lláh*, vol. 3, p. 200.

3. Siyyid Ḥasan-i-Nahrí – Mírzá Muḥammad-Ḥasan – King of the Martyrs

1 Taherzadeh, *The Revelation of Bahá'u'lláh*, vol. 4, p. 73; Balyuzi, *Eminent Bahá'ís in the Time of Bahá'u'lláh*, p. 33.
2 Taherzadeh, *The Revelation of Bahá'u'lláh*, vol. 4, pp. 73–74.
3 Momen, *The Bábí and Bahá'í Religions, 1844–1944*, p. 274.
4 Taherzadeh, *The Revelation of Bahá'u'lláh*, vol. 4, p. 87.
5 ibid. p. 75.
6 Momen, *The Bábí and Bahá'í Religions, 1844–1944*, p. 275.
7 Balyuzi, *Eminent Bahá'ís in the Time of Bahá'u'lláh*, p. 35; Taherzadeh, *The Revelation of Bahá'u'lláh*, vol. 4, p. 75.
8 Balyuzi, *Eminent Bahá'ís in the Time of Bahá'u'lláh*, pp. 35–36.
9 ibid. pp. 36–37.
10 Balyuzi, *Eminent Bahá'ís in the Time of Bahá'u'lláh*, p. 37; Momen, *The Bábí and Bahá'í Religions, 1844–1944*, p. 275.
11 Momen, *The Bábí and Bahá'í Religions, 1844–1944*, p. 276.
12 ibid. p. 275.
13 Balyuzi, *Eminent Bahá'ís in the Time of Bahá'u'lláh*, p. 37.
14 ibid. p. 38.
15 Taherzadeh, *The Revelation of Bahá'u'lláh*, vol. 4, p. 79–80.
16 ibid. pp. 82, 88–89.
17 Walbridge, *The Bahá'í Faith in Iran.*
18 Taherzadeh, *The Revelation of Bahá'u'lláh*, vol. 4, p. 91.
19 Shoghi Effendi, *God Passes By*, p. 201.
20 Taherzadeh, *The Revelation of Bahá'u'lláh*, vol. 4, p. 100.
21 ibid. p. 100–101.
22 ibid. p. 101.
23 ibid. p. 89.

4. Mullá Abu'l-Ḥasan-i-Ardikání – Ḥájí Amín

1 Taherzadeh, *The Revelation of Bahá'u'lláh*, vol. 3, p. 76; Harper, *Lights of Fortitude*, p. 53; Momen, *Amin, Ḥájí Abu'l-Hasan.*
2 Harper, *Lights of Fortitude*, p. 54; Taherzadeh, *The Revelation of Bahá'u'lláh*, vol. 3, p. 79.
3 Taherzadeh, *The Revelation of Bahá'u'lláh*, vol. 3, p. 84.
4 Taherzadeh, *The Child of the Covenant*, p. 398.
5 Taherzadeh, *The Revelation of Bahá'u'lláh*, vol. 3, p. 74.
6 Momen, *Amin, Ḥájí Abu'l-Hasan.*
7 Taherzadeh, *The Revelation of Bahá'u'lláh*, vol. 3, p. 74–75.
8 Ruhe, *Door of Hope*, p. 30.
9 Momen, *Amin, Ḥájí Abu'l-Hasan.*
10 Taherzadeh, *The Revelation of Bahá'u'lláh*, vol. 4, pp. 252–253.
11 ibid. pp. 253.
12 ibid. pp. 394–396.
13 ibid. p. 337.

14 Momen, *The Bábí and Bahá'í Religions, 1844–1944*, p. 357.
15 Taherzadeh, *The Revelation of Bahá'u'lláh*, vol. 3, p. 85.
16 The Universal House of Justice, *letter dated 30 July 2002*, Revised - Development of the Institution of Ḥuqúqu'lláh.
17 Momen, *Amin, Ḥájí Abu'l-Hasan.*
18 Balyuzi, *'Abdu'l-Bahá*, p. 347.
19 *Ahmad Sohrab's Diary*, dated 19 Dec 1912, p. 1.
20 *Star of the West*, vol. 3, no. 19 (2 March 1913), p. 5.
21 *Ahmad Sohrab's Diary*, dated 24 Jan 1913, p. 11.
22 ibid. pp. 14–15
23 Gail, *Arches of the Years*, p. 225.
24 The Universal House of Justice, letter dated 30 July 2002, Revised - Development of the Institution of Ḥuqúqu'lláh.

5. Mírzá Abu'l-Faḍl

1 Mírzá Abu'l-Faḍl, *Miracles and Metaphors*, p. ix.
2 Shahrokh, *Windows to the Past: Abu'l-Faḍl*, pp. 22–23.
3 Mírzá Abu'l-Faḍl, *Miracles and Metaphors*, pp. ix–x.
4 ibid. pp. x–xi.
5 Taherzadeh, *The Revelation of Bahá'u'lláh*, vol. 3, pp. 93–94.
6 ibid. pp. 96–97.
7 ibid. p. 97–98.
8 Taherzadeh, *The Revelation of Bahá'u'lláh*, vol. 2, pp. 219–220.
9 Taherzadeh, *The Revelation of Bahá'u'lláh*, vol. 3, pp. 99–100.
10 ibid. pp. 100–103.
11 Shahrokh, *Windows to the Past: Abu'l-Faḍl*, p. 9.
12 Momen, *Gulpáygání, Mirza Abu'l-Faḍl.*
13 Shahrokh, *Windows to the Past: Abu'l-Faḍḷ*, pp. 9–10.
14 ibid. p. 10–11.
15 Taherzadeh, *The Revelation of Bahá'u'lláh*, vol. 4, pp. 263–265.
16 Mírzá Abu'l-Faḍl, *Miracles and Metaphors*, pp. xi–xii.
17 Taherzadeh, *The Revelation of Bahá'u'lláh*, vol. 4, pp. 344–345.
18 Shahrokh, *Windows to the Past: Abu'l-Faḍl*, p. 14.
19 Taherzadeh, *The Revelation of Bahá'u'lláh*, vol 3, p. 106.
20 Shahrokh, Darius, *Windows to the Past: Abu'l-Faḍḷ*, p. 15.
21 Taherzadeh, *The Revelation of Bahá'u'lláh*, vol. 3, pp. 437–438.
22 Shahrokh, *Windows to the Past: Abu'l-Faḍḷ*, pp. 15–16.
23 Shahrokh, *Windows to the Past: Abu'l-Faḍḷ*, pp. 16–17; Momen, *Gulpáygání, Mirza Abu'l-Faḍl.*
24 Shahrokh, *Windows to the Past: Abu'l-Faḍḷ*, p. 17.
25 ibid. pp. 17–18.
26 Shadhídí, *With 'Abdu'l-Bahá*, p. 70.
27 Redman, *Visiting 'Abdu'l-Bahá*, vol. 1, p. 207.
28 ibid. p. 48.
29 ibid. p. 143.
30 Redman, *'Abdu'l-Bahá in Their Midst*, pp. 329–330.
31 Shahrokh, *Windows to the Past: Abu'l-Fadl*, p. 20.
32 *Star of the West*, vol. 9, no. 3 (28 April 1913), p. 26.

33 Balyuzi, *'Abdu'l-Bahá*, p. 150.
34 Mú'ayyad, *Eight Years Near 'Abdu'l-Bahá*, pp. 101–102.
35 Sohrab, Ahmad, letter to Harriet Magee, dated 26 Jan 1913, p. 12.
36 Shahrokh, *Windows to the Past: Abu'l-Faḍl*, p. 22.
37 ibid. pp. 22–23.
38 'Abdu'l-Bahá, *Tablet on the Passing of Mírzá 'Abu'l-Faḍl-i-Gulpáygání.*

6. Mírzá 'Alí-Muḥammad – Varqá

1 Shahrokh, *Windows to the Past: Varqá and Son, The Heavenly Doves*, pp. 2–3.
2 ibid. pp. 3–4.
3 Taherzadeh, *The Revelation of Bahá'u'lláh*, vol. 4, p. 53.
4 Shahrokh, *Windows to the Past: Varqá and Son, The Heavenly Doves*, p. 4.
5 ibid. p. 4.
6 ibid. p. 5.
7 Taherzadeh, *The Revelation of Bahá'u'lláh*, vol. 4, pp. 51–52.
8 Shahrokh, *Windows to the Past: Varqá and Son, The Heavenly Doves*, p. 5.
9 Taherzadeh, *The Revelation of Bahá'u'lláh*, vol. 4, p. 54.
10 Shahrokh, *Windows to the Past: Varqá and Son, The Heavenly Doves*, p. 6.
11 ibid. pp. 6–7.
12 ibid. pp. 7–8.
13 ibid. p. 9.
14 ibid. p. 10.
15 ibid. pp. 12–13.
16 ibid. p. 9
17 ibid. p. 15.
18 Balyuzi, *Eminent Bahá'ís in the Time of Bahá'u'lláh*, p. 83.
19 Balyuzi, *Eminent Bahá'ís in the Time of Bahá'u'lláh*, p. 84; Shahrokh, *Windows to the Past: Varqá and Son, The Heavenly Doves*, p. 16.
20 Shahrokh, *Windows to the Past: Varqá and Son, The Heavenly Doves*, pp. 16–17.
21 Taherzadeh, *The Revelation of Bahá'u'lláh*, vol. 4, p. 63.
22 Shahrokh, *Windows to the Past: Varqá and Son, the Heavenly Doves*, pp. 17–18.
23 ibid. pp. 19–20.
24 Balyuzi, *Eminent Bahá'ís in the Time of Bahá'u'lláh*, p. 90.
25 Shahrokh, *Windows to the Past: Varqá and Son, the Heavenly Doves*, pp. 22–23.
26 ibid. p. 26 (page 25 is missing in manuscript).
27 ibid. pp. 26–28.
28 ibid. p. 28.
29 ibid. pp. 28–29.
30 Shahrokh, *Windows to the Past: Varqá and son, the Heavenly Doves*, p. 27; Balyuzi, *Eminent Bahá'ís in the Time of Bahá'u'lláh*, p. 156.

7. Mírzá Maḥmúd-i-Furúghí

1 Balyuzi, *Eminent Bahá'ís in the Time of Bahá'u'lláh*, pp. 157–158.
2 Taherzadeh, *The Revelation of Bahá'u'lláh*, vol. 2, pp. 114–115.
3 Balyuzi, *Eminent Bahá'ís in the Time of Bahá'u'lláh*, p. 159.
4 ibid. p. 160.
5 Sulaymani, *Massabih-i-Hidayat*, translation by Mesbah, emailed 20 Jan 2020.

6 *The Bahá'í World,* vol. XVIII, p. 384; Balyuzi, *Eminent Bahá'ís in the Time of Bahá'u'lláh*, pp. 160–161.
7 Balyuzi, *Eminent Bahá'ís in the Time of Bahá'u'lláh*, p. 169.
8 ibid. pp. 167–168.
9 ibid. p. 163.
10 ibid. pp. 163–164.
11 Shahídí, *With 'Abdu'l-Bahá: Reminiscences of Kahlíl Shahídi,* p 125–126.
12 Balyuzi, *Eminent Bahá'ís in the Time of Bahá'u'lláh*, p. 169.
13 Afnán, *The Genesis of the Bábí-Bahá'í Faiths in Shíráz and Fárs*, pp. 135–136.
14 ibid. pp. 137–140.
15 ibid. p. 148.
16 Fikri, *Ḥawáríyyu Ḥaḍrat-i-Bahá'u'lláh.*
17 Balyuzi, *Eminent Bahá'ís in the Time of Bahá'u'lláh*, pp. 164–165.
18 ibid. p. 165.
19 ibid. pp. 165–166.
20 ibid. p. 167.
21 Interview of Mahmoud Foroughi with Mozaffaredin Shah translated from Persian by Mitra Rahmani, p. 2.
22 ibid. pp. 2–3.
23 ibid. p. 3.
24 Balyuzi, *Eminent Bahá'ís in the Time of Bahá'u'lláh*, pp. 156–157.
25 Balyuzi, *Eminent Bahá'ís in the Time of Bahá'u'lláh*, p. 169; *Star of the West*, vol. 14, no. 4, pp. 120–121; Fikri, *Ḥawáríyyú Ḥaḍrat-i-Bahá'u'lláh.*
26 Balyuzi, *Eminent Bahá'ís in the Time of Bahá'u'lláh*, pp. 169–170.
27 Rohani, *Sweet and Enchanting Stories*, p. 131.
28 *Star of the West*, vol. 14, no. 7, p. 213.
29 *Star of the West*, vol. 14, no. 11, p. 345.
30 Balyuzi, *Eminent Bahá'ís in the Time of Bahá'u'lláh*, p. 170; Fikri, *Ḥawáríyyú Ḥaḍrat-i-Bahá'u'lláh.*

8. Mullá 'Alí-Akbar-i-Shahmírzádí – Ḥájí Ákhund

1 Harper, *Lights of Fortitude*, p. 3.
2 'Abdu'l-Bahá, *Memorials of the Faithful*, pp. 9–10.
3 Harper, *Lights of Fortitude*, p. 3; 'Abdu'l-Bahá, *Memorials of the Faithful*, p. 10.
4 'Abdu'l-Bahá, *Memorials of the Faithful*, pp. 10–11.
5 Taherzadeh, *The Revelation of Bahá'u'lláh*, vol. 4, pp. 296–297; Harper, *Lights of Fortitude*, p. 4.
6 Day, *Journey to a Mountain*, p. 10.
7 ibid. p. 11.
8 Nakhjavani, *Notes from the Archives Building, in Haifa*, United States National Bahá'í Archives, pp. 4–5.
9 Day, *Journey to a Mountain*, pp. 11–12.
10 Day, *Journey to a Mountain*, p. 15.
11 Taherzadeh, *The Revelation of Bahá'u'lláh*, vol. 4, p. 297.
12 Harper, *Lights of Fortitude*, p. 5.
13 Taherzadeh, *The Revelation of Bahá'u'lláh*, vol. 3, p. 200–201.
14 The date is uncertain. Harper in *Lights of Fortitude* cites 1870 (p. 5) while Taherzadeh has 1873 in *Revelation of Bahá'u'lláh*, vol. 4 (p. 298) and Momen cites 1870–71.

15 Harper, *Lights of Fortitude*, p. 5; Taherzadeh, *The Revelation of Bahá'u'lláh*, vol. 4, p. 297.
16 Taherzadeh, *The Revelation of Bahá'u'lláh*, vol. 4, pp. 297–298.
17 ibid. pp. 379–380.
18 ibid. p. 380.
19 ibid. pp. 297, 299.
20 ibid. pp. 322–323.
21 ibid. p. 298.
22 'Abdu'l-Bahá, *Memorials of the Faithful*, p. 11.
23 Taherzadeh, *The Revelation of Bahá'u'lláh*, vol. 4, p. 299.
24 Harper, *Lights of Fortitude*, p. 6.
25 Taherzadeh, *The Revelation of Bahá'u'lláh*, vol. 4, p. 300.
26 ibid. p. 338.
27 ibid. p. 337.
28 Taherzadeh, *The Revelation of Bahá'u'lláh*, vol. 3, p. 85.
29 Harper, *Lights of Fortitude*, p. 7.
30 ibid. p. 7.
31 'Abdu'l-Bahá, *Memorials of the Faithful*, p. 12.

9. Mullá Muḥammad – Nabíl-i-Akbar – Faḍl-i-Qá'iní

1 Shahrokh, *Windows to the Past: Faḍl-i-Qáiní*, pp. 1–2.
2 ibid. p. 4.
3 ibid. p. 4–5.
4 ibid. pp. 5–6.
5 ibid. p. 7.
6 ibid. pp. 8–10.
7 ibid. pp. 11–12.
8 Taherzadeh, *The Revelation of Bahá'u'lláh*, vol. 1, pp. 92–94.
9 ibid. p. 95.
10 Shahrokh, *Windows to the Past: Faḍl-i-Qáiní*, pp. 16–17.
11 ibid. p. 17.
12 ibid. p. 18.
13 ibid. p. 19.
14 'Abdu'l-Bahá, *Memorials of the Faithful*, p. 3.
15 Shahrokh, *Windows to the Past: Faḍl-i-Qáiní*, pp. 19–20.
16 ibid. pp. 19, 23.
17 ibid. pp. 19–20.
18 ibid. pp. 20–21.
19 ibid. pp. 21–22.
20 'Abdu'l-Bahá, *Memorials of the Faithful*, pp. 4–5.

10. Ḥájí Mírzá Muḥammad-Taqí-i-Afnán – Vakílu'd-Dawlih – Vakílu'd-Haqq

1 Mustapha, email to the author dated 19 Jan 2019.
2 Whitmore, *The City of Love, 'Ishqábád and the Institution of the Mashriqul-Adhkár*, p. 7.
3 Rabbani, *The Conversion of the Great-Uncle of the Báb* in *World Order*, p. 26.
4 Balyuzi, *Eminent Bahá'ís in the Time of Bahá'u'lláh*, p. 266.
5 Momen, *The Bábí and Bahá'í Religions, 1844–1944*, p. 514.

6 Rabbani, *The Conversion of the Great-Uncle of the Báb* in *World Order*, pp. 34–35.
7 'Abdu'l-Bahá, *Memorials of the Faithful*, p. 126.
8 Taherzadeh, *The Revelation of Bahá'u'lláh*, vol. 1, p. 198.
9 Taherzadeh, *The Revelation of Bahá'u'lláh*, vol. 4, pp. 347, 349.
10 Momen, *The Bábí and Bahá'í Religions, 1844–1944*, pp. 301–302.
11 ibid. p. 514.
12 'Abdu'l-Bahá, *Memorials of the Faithful*, pp. 127–128.
13 Taherzadeh, *The Revelation of Bahá'u'lláh*, vol. 1, p. 199.
14 Afroukhteh, *Memories of Nine Years in 'Akká*, p. 223.
15 ibid. p. 226.
16 Whitmore, 'The City of Love: 'Ishqábád and the Institution of the Mashriqu'l-Adhkár', *Bahá'í News*, vol. 52, no. 7, p. 8.
17 ibid. pp. 8–9.
18 Taherzadeh, *The Revelation of Bahá'u'lláh*, vol. 1, pp. 199–201.
19 Redman, *Visiting 'Abdu'l-Bahá*, vol. 1, p. 198.
20 Balyuzi, *Eminent Bahá'ís in the Time of Bahá'u'lláh*, p. 268.
21 'Abdu'l-Bahá, *Memorials of the Faithful*, pp. 128–129.

11. Ḥájí Mírzá Muḥammad-Taqí-i-Abhar – Ibn-i-Abhar

1 Balyuzi, *Eminent Bahá'ís in the Time of Bahá'u'lláh*, p. 268.
2 Taherzadeh, *The Revelation of Bahá'u'lláh*, vol. 4, p. 305.
3 *The Bahá'í World*, vol. XVIII, p. 383.
4 Taherzadeh, *The Revelation of Bahá'u'lláh*, vol. 4, pp. 305–306.
5 *Star of the West*, vol. 13, no. 12, p. 333.
6 ibid. pp. 333, 335.
7 ibid. p. 335.
8 ibid. p. 336.
9 ibid. p. 336.
10 ibid. p. 335.
11 ibid. pp. 336–338.
12 ibid. p. 339.
13 Taherzadeh, *The Revelation of Bahá'u'lláh*, vol. 4, pp. 306–307.
14 ibid. p. 310.
15 ibid. p. 307.
16 ibid. p. 306.
17 ibid. pp. 310–311.
18 Harper, *Lights of Fortitude*, p. 7.
19 Hogenson, *Lighting the Western Sky*, p. 192.
20 Balyuzi, *Eminent Bahá'ís in the Time of Bahá'u'lláh*, p. 268.
21 *Star of the West*, vol. 13, no. 12, p. 333.
22 Rafati, *Tablets of Bahá'u'lláh Revealed in Honor of Hand of the Cause Jináb-i-Ibn-i-Abhar.*
23 Haddad, *Message from 'Akká*, p. 5.

12. Mullá Muḥammad-i-Zarandí – Nabíl-i-A'ẓam

1 Nabíl, *The Dawn-Breakers*, p. 434.
2 ibid. 435–436.
3 Balyuzi, *Eminent Bahá'ís in the Time of Bahá'u'lláh*, p. 269.

4 ibid. p. 269.
5 Nabíl, *The Dawn-Breakers*, p. 587.
6 Balyuzi, *Bahá'u'lláh, The King of Glory*, pp. 64–65.
7 Nabíl, *The Dawn-Breakers*, pp. 591–592.
8 Balyuzi, *Eminent Bahá'ís in the Time of Bahá'u'lláh*, p. 269.
9 Taherzadeh, *The Revelation of Bahá'u'lláh*, vol. 1, p. 202.
10 Balyuzi, *Bahá'u'lláh, The King of Glory*, pp. 128–129.
11 Taherzadeh, *The Revelation of Bahá'u'lláh*, vol. 1, pp. 202–203.
12 Balyuzi, *Bahá'u'lláh, The King of Glory*, pp. 131–132.
13 ibid. p. 132.
14 Taherzadeh, *The Revelation of Bahá'u'lláh*, vol. 1, p. 69.
15 Balyuzi, *Bahá'u'lláh, The King of Glory*, pp. 145, 150.
16 Taherzadeh, *The Revelation of Bahá'u'lláh*, vol. 1, p. 203.
17 Balyuzi, *Bahá'u'lláh, The King of Glory*, p. 204; Taherzadeh, *The Revelation of Bahá'u'lláh*, vol. 2, p. 59.
18 Taherzadeh, *The Revelation of Bahá'u'lláh*, vol. 4, pp. 329–330.
19 Taherzadeh, *The Revelation of Bahá'u'lláh*, vol. 2, p. 236.
20 Encyclopaedia Iranica, *Nabil-e A'ẓam Zarandi, Mollā Moḥammad.*
21 Balyuzi, *Bahá'u'lláh, The King of Glory*, p. 250.
22 Taherzadeh, *The Revelation of Bahá'u'lláh*, vol. 1, pp. 203–204.
23 Balyuzi, *Bahá'u'lláh, The King of Glory*, pp. 265–267.
24 Taherzadeh, *The Revelation of Bahá'u'lláh*, vol. 3, p. 5.
25 ibid. pp. 6–7.
26 Taherzadeh, *The Revelation of Bahá'u'lláh*, vol. 3, pp. 56–57.
27 Taherzadeh, *The Revelation of Bahá'u'lláh*, vol. 1, p. 204.
28 ibid. pp. 116–117.
29 Balyuzi, *Bahá'u'lláh, The King of Glory*, p. 331.
30 Taherzadeh, *The Revelation of Bahá'u'lláh*, vol. 4, pp. 106–108.
31 ibid. pp. 243–244.
32 Nabíl, *The Dawn-Breakers*, p. xxxvii.
33 Taherzadeh, *The Revelation of Bahá'u'lláh*, vol. 4, p. 419.
34 Ruhe, *Door of Hope*, p. 80.

13. Shaykh Muḥammad Káẓim-i-Qazvíní – Samandar

1 Qurán 24 v. 37.
2 Fikri, *Ḥawáríyyu Ḥaḍrat-i-Bahá'u'llá'h*, p. 255.
3 Balyuzi, *Eminent Bahá'ís in the Time of Bahá'u'lláh*, pp. 191–192.
4 ibid. p. 194.
5 ibid. p. 198.
6 Balyuzi, *Eminent Bahá'ís in the Time of Bahá'u'lláh*, p. 200.
7 Fikri, *Ḥawáríyyu Ḥaḍrat-i-Bahá'u'lláh*, pp. 258–259.
8 Taherzadeh, *The Revelation of Bahá'u'lláh*, vol. 2, pp. 72–74.
9 Balyuzi, *Eminent Bahá'ís in the Time of Bahá'u'lláh*, pp. 200–201.
10 Taherzadeh, *The Revelation of Bahá'u'lláh*, vol. 3, p. 89.
11 Balyuzi, *Eminent Bahá'ís in the Time of Bahá'u'lláh*, p. 201.
12 ibid. pp. 206–207.
13 ibid. pp. 207–208.
14 ibid. pp. 201–202.

15 Taherzadeh, *The Revelation of Bahá'u'lláh*, vol. 3, p. 91.
16 Balyuzi, *Eminent Bahá'ís in the Time of Bahá'u'lláh*, pp. 208–209.
17 ibid. pp. 203–205.
18 ibid. pp. 209–211.
19 ibid. pp. 211–213.
20 ibid. pp. 213–214.
21 ibid. p. 215.

14. Muḥammad Muṣṭafáy-i-Baghdádí

1 Nabíl, *The Dawn-Breakers*, p. 271; Encyclopaedia Iranica, *The Baghdadi Family.*
2 Balyuzi, *The Báb*, p. 60.
3 Encyclopaedia Iranica, *The Baghdadi Family.*
4 'Abdu'l-Bahá, *Memorials of the Faithful*, p. 131.
5 Encyclopaedia Iranica, *The Baghdadi Family.*
6 Encyclopaedia Iranica, *The Baghdadi Family*; Balyuzi, *The Báb*, p. 166.
7 Encyclopaedia Iranica, *The Baghdadi Family.*
8 'Abdu'l-Bahá, *Memorials of the Faithful*, pp. 131–132.
9 Muḥammad-'Alíy-i Salmání, Ustád, *My Memories of Bahá'u'lláh*, p. 85.
10 Encyclopaedia Iranica, *The Baghdadi Family.*
11 Balyuzi, *Eminent Bahá'ís in the Time of Bahá'u'lláh*, p. 270.
12 Chehabi, *Distant Relations: Iran and Lebanon in the Last 500 Years*, p. 97.
13 Redman, *Visiting 'Abdu'l-Bahá*, v 1, pp 58–59.
14 Mustafa, email to author dated 1 Oct 2018.
15 Bahá'u'lláh, *Gleanings from the Writings of Bahá'u'lláh, CXLVI*, pp. 315–316.
16 Encyclopaedia Iranica, *The Baghdadi Family.*
17 Day, *Journey to a Mountain*, pp. 35–36.
18 Afroukhteh, *Memories of Nine Years in 'Akká*, p. 378.
19 Smith, *Bahá'ís in the West*, p. 99.
20 *Star of the West*, vol. 1, no. 17, 19 Jan 1911, p. 10.
21 Encyclopaedia Iranica, *The Baghdadi Family.*
22 'Abdu'l-Bahá, *Memorials of the Faithful*, pp. 133–134.

15. Mírzá Ḥusayn-i-Iṣfahání – Mishkín-Qalam

1 Cameron, *A Basic Bahá'í Chronology*, p. 6.
2 Nakhjavání, *Four on an Island*, p. 21.
3 Fikri, *Ḥawáríyyú Ḥaḍrat-i-Bahá'u'lláh*, p. 314.
4 'Abdu'l-Bahá, *Memorials of the Faithful*, p. 98.
5 Fikri, *Ḥawáríyyú Ḥaḍrat-i-Bahá'u'lláh*, p. 314.
6 'Abdu'l-Bahá, *Memorials of the Faithful*, p. 98.
7 Balyuzi, *Bahá'u'lláh*, p. 240.
8 Balyuzi, *Bahá'u'lláh*, p. 247; Ustád Muḥammad-'Alíy-Salmání, *My Memories of Bahá'u'lláh*, p. 58; 'Abdu'l-Bahá, *Memorials of the Faithful*, p. 99.
9 Fikri, *Ḥawáríyyu Ḥaḍrat-i-Bahá'u'lláh*, pp. 315–316.
10 Balyuzi, *Bahá'u'lláh*, p. 248; 'Abdu'l-Bahá, *Memorials of the Faithful*, p. 99.
11 'Abdu'l-Bahá, *Memorials of the Faithful*, p. 99.
12 Salmání, *My Memories of Bahá'u'lláh*, p. 63.
13 Balyuzi, *Bahá'u'lláh*, p. 260.
14 Nakhjavání, *Four on an Island*, p. vii.

15 ibid. p. 24.
16 ibid. p. 24.
17 Afnán, *Memories of the Báb, Bahá'u'lláh, and 'Abdu'l-Bahá*, pp. 217–218.
18 Nakhjavání, *Four on an Island*, p. 33.
19 ibid. p. 51, provisional translation.
20 Afnán, *Memories of the Báb, Bahá'u'lláh, and 'Abdu'l-Bahá*, pp. 154–156.
21 ibid. p. 217.
22 Azízí, *Crown of Glory*, p. 96.
23 ibid. p. 99.
24 Taherzadeh, *The Revelation of Bahá'u'lláh*, vol. 1, pp. 27–28.
25 Shahídí, *With 'Abdu'l-Bahá* in *Witness to Babi and Bahá'í History*, vol. 9, p. 49.
26 Sprague, A Year with the Bahá'ís in India and Burma, pp. 13–14.
27 Shahídí, *With 'Abdu'l-Bahá* in *Witness to Babi and Bahá'í History*, vol. 9, p. 49.
28 'Abdu'l-Bahá, *Memorials of the Faithful*, pp. 98, 101.

16. Mírzá Ḥasan-i-Adíb – Adíbu'l-'Ulamáy-i-Ṭáliqání – Adíb

1 Dhuká'íy-i-Bayḍá'í, *Dar Sharh-i-Ahvál va Áthár-i-Jináb-i-Áqá Mírzá Hasan-i-Adíbu'l-'Ulamáy-i-Táliqání*, p. 1 (Mesbah).
2 ibid. pp. 1–2.
3 Balyuzi, *Eminent Bahá'ís in the Time of Bahá'u'lláh*, p. 272; Harper, *Lights of Fortitude*, p. 17.
4 Dhuká'íy-i-Bayḍá'í, *Dar Sharh-i-Ahvál va Áthár-i-Jináb-i-Áqá Mírzá Hasan-i-Adíbu'l-'Ulamáy-i-Táliqání*, pp. 1–2.
5 Dhuká'íy-i-Bayḍá'í, *Dar Sharh-i-Ahvál va Áthár-i-Jináb-i-Áqá Mírzá Hasan-i-Adíbu'l-'Ulamáy-i-Táliqání*, pp. 1–2.
6 ibid. p. 3.
7 Balyuzi, *Eminent Bahá'ís in the Time of Bahá'u'lláh*, p. 272.
8 Harper, *Lights of Fortitude*, p. 17.
9 Taherzadeh, *The Revelation of Bahá'u'lláh*, vol. 4, p. 313.
10 ibid. p. 311.
11 Fadil–i-Mazandaran, *Tarikh-i-Zuhur'ul-Haqq*, pp. 464–466. (pp. 10–11 in Mesbah translation)
12 Balyuzi, *Eminent Bahá'ís in the Time of Bahá'u'lláh*, p. 272.
13 Dhuká'íy-i-Bayḍá'í, *Dar Sharh-i-Ahvál va Áthár-i-Jináb-i-Áqá Mírzá Hasan-i-Adíbu'l-'Ulamáy-i-Táliqání*, p. 4 (Mesbah).
14 ibid. pp. 4–7.
15 Fadil-i-Mazandaran, *Tarikh-i-Zuhur'ul-Haqq*, pp. 11–12 in Mesbah translation.
16 Momen, *The Bábí and Bahá'í Religions, 1844–1944*, pp. 382–383.
17 ibid. pp. 383–384.
18 Fadil-i-Mazandaran, *Tarikh-i-Zuhur'ul-Haqq*, pp. 13–14 in Mesbah translation.
19 ibid. p. 14.
20 ibid. p. 15.
21 ibid. p. 18.
22 Sprague, *A Year with the Bahá'ís of India and Burma*, p. 14.
23 Fadil-i-Mazandaran, *Tarikh-i-Zuhur'ul-Haqq*, p. 17 in Mesbah translation.
24 Sprague, *A Year with the Bahá'ís of India and Burma*, pp. 19–20.
25 Harper, *Lights of Fortitude*, p. 18.

17. Shaykh Muḥammad-'Alí-Qá'íní

1 Sulaymani, *Massabih-i-Hidayat*, pp. 3–4 (page numbers in translated doc).
2 ibid. p. 3.
3 ibid. pp. 3–4.
4 ibid. p. 4.
5 Shahrokh, *Windows to the Past: Faḍl-i-Qáiní*, pp. 20–21.
6 Sulaymani, *Massabih-i-Hidayat*, p. 4.
7 ibid. pp. 4–6.
8 ibid. p. 6.
9 ibid. pp. 6–7.
10 ibid. pp. 7–8.
11 Sulaymani, *Massabih-i-Hidayat*, p. 9; Azízí, *Crown of Glory*, p. 69.
12 Sulaymani, *Massabih-i-Hidayat*, pp. 9, 21.
13 Momen, *The Bahá'í Community of Ashkabad: Its Social Basis and Importance in Bahá'í History* in *Cultural Change and Continuity in Central Asia.*
14 Sulaymani, *Massabih-i-Hidayat*, pp. 10–13.
15 ibid. pp. 14–15.
16 ibid. p. 15.
17 ibid. pp. 15–16.
18 ibid. pp. 17–19.
19 ibid. p. 19.
20 ibid. p. 20.
21 ibid. p. 22.

18. Mullá Zaynu'l-'Ábidín Najafábádí – Zaynu'l-Muqarrabín

1 Sulaymani, *The Story of Zaynul-Muqarrabín*, p. 1.
2 ibid. pp. 1–2.
3 ibid. pp. 2–3.
4 ibid. p. 4.
5 ibid. p. 5.
6 Fikri, *Ḥawáríyyu Ḥaḍrat-i-Bahá'u'lláh*, p. 342.
7 Sulaymani, *The Story of Zaynul-Muqarrabín*, p. 5.
8 Fikri, *Ḥawáríyyú Ḥaḍrat-i-Bahá'u'lláh*, p. 342.
9 'Abdu'l-Bahá, *Memorials of the Faithful*, p. 151.
10 Sulaymani, *The Story of Zaynul-Muqarrabín*, p. 10.
11 Sulaymani, *The Story of Zaynul-Muqarrabín*, p. 6; 'Abdu'l-Bahá, *Memorials of the Faithful*, p. 151.
12 Sulaymani, *The Story of Zaynul-Muqarrabín*, p. 9.
13 ibid. p. 9–10.
14 ibid. p. 11.
15 ibid. pp. 12–13.
16 Taherzadeh, *The Revelation of Bahá'u'lláh*, vol. 2, p. 334.
17 ibid. pp. 334–336.
18 Fikri, *Ḥawáríyyú Ḥaḍrat-i-Bahá'u'lláh*, p. 348.
19 Sulaymani, *The Story of Zaynul-Muqarrabín*, p. 16.
20 Fikri, *Ḥawáríyyú Ḥaḍrat-i-Bahá'u'lláh*, p. 356.
21 Sulaymani, *The Story of Zaynul-Muqarrabín*, p. 17.
22 Taherzadeh, *The Revelation of Bahá'u'lláh*, vol. 1, p. 26; Sulaymani, *The Story of*

Zaynul-Muqarrabín, p. 18.
23 Fikri, *Ḥawáríyyu Ḥaḍrat-i-Bahá'u'lláh*, p. 353.
24 Bahá'u'lláh, *Gleanings*, pp. 387–388.
25 Bahá'u'lláh, *Gleanings*, pp. 192–94.
26 Sulaymani, *The Story of Zaynul-Muqarrabín*, pp. 18–19.
27 ibid. p. 19.
28 ibid. p. 20.
29 Afnán, *Memories of the Báb, Bahá'u'lláh, and 'Abdu'l-Bahá*, p. 135.
30 Shoghi Effendi, *God Passes By*, p. 274.
31 Afroukhteh, *Memories of Nine Years in 'Akká*, p. 150.
32 Sulaymani, *The Story of Zaynul-Muqarrabín*, p. 20.

19. Mírzá 'Alí-Muḥammad – Ibn-i-Aṣdaq

1 Taherzadeh, *The Revelation of Bahá'u'lláh*, vol. 4, p. 303.
2 http://bahaiheoresheroines.blogspot.com/2013/12/mirza-ali-muhammad-ibn-i-asdaq-apostle.html
3 Nabíl, *The Dawn-Breakers*, p. 100.
4 Balyuzi, *Eminent Bahá'ís in the Time of Bahá'u'lláh*, p. 7, 171.
5 Harper, *Lights of Fortitude*, p. 9.
6 Taherzadeh, *The Revelation of Bahá'u'lláh*, vol. 3, pp. 266–267.
7 ibid. pp. 266–268.
8 http://bahaiheoresheroines.blogspot.com/2013/12/mirza-ali-muhammad-ibn-i-asdaq-apostle.html
9 Momen, http://www.momen.org/relstud/turkmnst.html
10 Fikri, *Ḥawáríyyu Ḥaḍrat-i-Bahá'u'lláh*, p. 363.
11 Taherzadeh, *The Revelation of Bahá'u'lláh*, vol. 4, p. 302.
12 Balyuzi, *Eminent Bahá'ís in the Time of Bahá'u'lláh*, p. 172.
13 Taherzadeh, *The Revelation of Bahá'u'lláh*, vol. 4, p. 303; http://bahaiheoresheroines.blogspot.com/2013/12/mirza-ali-muhammad-ibn-i-asdaq-apostle.html
14 Fikri, *Ḥawáríyyú Ḥaḍrat-i-Bahá'u'lláh*, p. 377.
15 Harper, *Lights of Fortitude*, p. 11.
16 Taherzadeh, *The Revelation of Bahá'u'lláh*, vol. 4, p. 303.
17 ibid. p. 275.
18 Fikri, *Ḥawáríyyú Ḥaḍrat-i-Bahá'u'lláh*, pp. 378–379.
19 ibid. p. 381.
20 ibid. pp. 381–382.
21 Taherzadeh, *The Revelation of Bahá'u'lláh*, vol. 4, pp. 323–324.
22 Harper, *Lights of Fortitude*, p. 11.
23 http://bahaiheoresheroines.blogspot.com/2013/12/mirza-ali-muhammad-ibn-i-asdaq-apostle.html
24 Harper, *Lights of Fortitude*, p. 12.
25 Momen (http://www.momen.org/relstud/turkmnst.htm); Balyuzi, *Eminent Bahá'ís in the Time of Bahá'u'lláh*, p. 174.
26 Balyuzi, *Eminent Bahá'ís in the Time of Bahá'u'lláh*, p. 174.
27 Redman, *Visiting 'Abdu'l-Bahá*, vol. 1, p. 95.
28 Asdaq, *One Life, One Memory*, pp. 14–21.
29 ibid. pp. 22–23.

30 Sohrab, *Ahmad Sohrab's Diary*, 25 Dec 1913, p. 516.
31 Asdaq, *One Life, One Memory*, pp. 27–28, 40.
32 Momen, *Esslemont's Survey of the Bahá'í World, 1919–1920*, in Smith, *Bahá'ís in the West*, p. 69.
33 *'The Journey of Abdu'l-Baha's Tablet to the Hague, Bahá'í Geschiedenis*, https://www.bahaigeschiedenis.nl/abdul-baha-tablet-to-the-hague/.
34 'Abdu'l-Bahá, *Tablet to the Hague*, http://bahai-library.com/abdulbaha_lawh_hague_bwc.
35 Momen, *Esslemont's Survey of the Bahá'í World, 1919–1920*, in Smith, *Bahá'ís in the West*, p. 65.
36 Taherzadeh, *The Revelation of Bahá'u'lláh*, vol. 4, p. 304.

INDEX

'Ábádih 79-80, 156-8
Abbasiyyih 157
'Abdu'l-Azim, Shrine of 87-8
'Abdu'l-Azíz, Sulṭán 53-5, 132
'Abdu'l-Bahá
  in 'Akká and Haifa 106, 108-9, 134-5, 169-71, 191
  and Apostles of Bahá'u'lláh 6, 8
Abu'l-Faḍl 49, 58-65, 169-70
    Badí' 25, 28
    Ḥájí Ákhund 87, 91-3
    Ḥájí Amín 41, 46-7
    Ḥasan-i-Adíb 153, 155, 159
    Ḥasan-i-Nahrí 39
    Ibn-i-Abhar 115-17
    Ibn-i-Asdaq 189-92
    Maḥmúd-i-Furúghí 78-9, 81
    Mírzá Músá 13-23
    Mishkín-Qalam 142-3, 145-50
    Muḥammad-i-Qá'íní 161, 164-5, 167, 169-71, 172-3
    Muṣṭafáy-i-Baghdádí 136-8, 139-41
    Nabíl-i-A'ẓam 123, 125-6
    Nabíl-i-Akbar 99, 100, 102
    Samandar 133-5
    Vakilu'd-Dawlih 104, 106, 108-9
    Varqá 70
    Zaynu'l-Muqarrabín 174, 180, 183-4
  and Bahá'u'lláh 17, 70, 79, 133
  and Covenant-breakers 78, 116, 124, 189
  Disciples of 1-8
  exile and imprisonment 124, 145
  and Hands of the Cause 116, 189
  humour 46, 62, 147, 148
  kindness 47
  and Mansion of Bahjí 125
  marriage 22
  and Mashriqu'l-Adhkár 106-7, 190
  and Mihdí-i-Yazdí (father of Varqá) 67
  passing 172
  photograph 123
  and remains of the Báb 139-40, 147, 184
  and Rúḥu'lláh (son of Varqá) 71
  station 15, 70, 79
  Tablets to:
    Abu'l-Faḍl (in honour of) 64-5
    Bahá'ís of Zanján 72
    Ḥasan-i-Adíb 153, 159
    Hague, The 191-2
    Ibn-i-Abhar 111, 115, 135
    Maḥmúd-i-Furúghí 81
    Mishkín-Qalam 146-7
    Muḥammad-i-Qá'íní 161, 167
    Muṣṭafáy-i-Baghdádí 140
    Samandar 135
    Vakilu'd-Dawlih 108
  threat to life 108
  titles
    Centre of the Covenant 6, 48, 116, 161, 165
    Master 79
    Most Great Branch 79
    Sarkár-i-Áqá 133
  travels
    Britain 41, 46
    Egypt 83, 90-91
    Paris 28, 63
  and Zilluṣ-Sulṭán 40, 70

Writings 39, 149, 151, 188
A Traveller's Narrative 180
Memorials of the Faithful 2, 13-14, 91, 93, 102, 104, 108-9, 140-41
Secret of Divine Civilization, The 191
Tablets of the Divine Plan 5, 8
see also subhead Tablets to
'Abdu'l-Ghaffár, Áqá 145
'Abdu'l-Ghání Ḥishání 151
'Abdu'l-Ḥusayn (son of Samandar) 129
'Abdu'l-Ḥusayn Ṭihrání, Shaykh 19, 121
'Abdu'l-Jalíl (of Urumiyyih) 129
'Abdu'l-Karím 50-54
'Abdu'l-Karím Qazvíni 15
'Abdu'lláh Khán-i-Núrí 66-7, 68-71
'Abdu'lláh, Áqá 131
'Abdu'l-Majíd, Ḥájí 16
'Abdu'l-Rasúl, Áqá 25
Abhar village 110-11
Abraham 113
Abu-Bakr, Caliph 179
'Abu'l-Azím (uncle of Ibn-i-Abhar) 111
Abu'l-Faḍl-i-Gulpaygání 10, 49-65, 81, 89-90, 94, 102, 162, 167
Abu'l-Ḥasan-i-Ardikání (Ḥájí Amín) 6, 10, 41-8, 91-2
Abu'l-Qásim-i-Názir 17
Abu'l-Talib (of Naw-Firist) 100, 111
Abul Atoof 112
Ádharbáyján *see* Azerbaijan
Adíbu'l-'Ulamáy-i-Ṭaliqání (Ḥasan-i-Adíb) 10, 92, 151-60, 164-5, 189
Adrianople 21, 25, 122, 142
Afnán, Siyyid Aḥmad 45
Afnán, Ḥabíbu'lláh 80, 146-8, 183
Afnán, Muḥammad-Táqí, Vakílu'd-Dawlih (Kabír-i-Afnán) 2, 10, 103-09, 164
Afroukhteh, Youness 138-40, 184
Aghay i Sahhaf 166
'Aḥmad (of Yazd) 76-7
'Aḥmad, Mírzá (amanuensis) 16, 119-20
'Aḥmad, Mullá 176
'Aḥmad, Shaykh (of Nishapur) 171-2
Aḥmad-i-Aḥsá'í, Shaykh 136
'Akká 42-4, 46, 58, 67-8, 79, 91, 92, 101, 106, 108, 115, 116, 123, 146, 159, 180-81, 184
Al-Jazzar bath 43
Al-Jazzar Mosque 25
Khán-i-'Avámíd 131, 149, 180, 184, 186-7, 188-9
Most Great Prison 22, 25-7, 42-3, 147
Mutasarrif of 134-5
Seraye (Government House) 134
Al-Azhar University, Cairo 59
Aleppo, Syria 142-3
Alexander, Agnes 59
Alexandretta 84, 140
Alexandria, Egypt 61-2, 64, 65, 81, 123, 133, 171, 188, 191
'Alí, Mírzá (son of Ḥasan-i-Adíb) 155-6, 159
'Alí, Mullá (tutor) 132-3
'Alí-Akbar-i-Shahmírzádí (Ḥájí Ákhund, Mullá 'Alí-Akbar) 2, 10, 45-6, 78, 86-93, 105, 111, 115, 129, 130, 153, 188-9
'Alí Atabac (Saḍr-i-A'ẓam) 82
'Alí Bastámí, Mullá 136
'Alí Khán, Tsherágh 177
'Alí-Muḥammad, Ibn-i-Aṣdaq (Shahíd-ibn-i-Shahíd) 6, 10, 87, 136, 167, 185-92
'Alí-Muḥammad, Mírzá (Varqá) 10, 56, 66-75, 133
'Alí Páshá, Grand Vizír 53
'Alí-Qulí Mírzá 151-2
'Alíy-i-Arbáb, Áqá 134
'Alíy-i-Kaní, Mullá 88-9
'Alíy-i-Sayyáh 143-5
Alláh'u'Abhá 122
Alláh-u-Akbar 122
Amín, Ḥájí *see* Abu'l-Ḥasan-i-Ardikání
Amír (ruler) of Qá'in 99
Anti-Christ 61
of the Bahá'í Dispensation *see* Muḥammad-i-Iṣfahání
of Islam 157, 175
Anzali 190
Apostles
of Bahá'u'lláh 1-10, 58
of Christ 4-5, 15

Áqá 'Alí, Mullá 161
Áqá Ján (of Káshán, amanuensis of Bahá'ú'lláh) 42, 117, 126, 134, 188
Áqá Mírzá Áqá 122
Áqáy-i-Kalím *see* Músá-i-Núrí
Arabs 137
Ardikan, Yazd 41
Armenians 107
Asadu'lláh-i-Qumí, Siyyid 47
Ash'ari, Abu Musa 161
Azalí(s) 111
Azerbaijan 43-4, 135, 171
Azízí, Azízu'lláh 148, 190
'Azízu'lláh (son of Varqá) 70, 71, 133

Báb, the 21, 60, 66, 103, 108, 118-19, 127-8, 136, 174-6
  and Badí' calendar 124
  claim 176
  companions 174
  Declaration 3, 33, 118, 121, 127
  Dispensation 97
  family 103-5
  House (in Shiraz) 122
  imprisonment 127
  Manifestation of God 87
  martyrdom 20, 83, 88, 131, 137
  Primal Point 18
  recognition 185
  remains 10, 16, 78, 87-8, 139-40, 147, 184
  Revelation 5, 6, 177
  Shrine 84, 109
  station 104, 174
  successor 15, 20, 97, 130, 177-8
  Writings
    Bayán 18, 110
    Qayyúmu'l-Asmá 121, 176
    Tablets to:
      Bahá'u'lláh 14, 120
      Muḥammad Qazvíní 127
Bábá, Ḥájí Mullá 131
Bábís 15-16, 20, 73, 87, 94-5, 120, 123, 129, 130, 152, 175, 177
Bábí communities in:
  Baghdad 17, 20, 97, 120-21, 136, 178
  Iṣfahán 36, 156
  Najafábád 177-8
  Karbilá 174
  Mosul 34
  Nayríz 16
  Persia (generally) 5, 41, 122
  Qazvín 129
  Shiraz 122, 123
  Ṭabarsí 76, 86
  Tehran 14, 94-5, 119, 120, 152
  Yazd 67, 105
  Zanján 72
Bábí Faith 41, 45-6
Badasht, Conference of 15, 35
Badí' (Mírzá Buzurg-i-Khurásání) viii, 2, 10, 24-32, 89, 110
Badí' calendar 124
Badí'u'lláh (son of Bahá'u'lláh) 134
Bádkúbih 131, 190
Baghdad 17-19, 25, 33, 67, 97, 104, 120-21, 122, 136-8, 142, 177-8, 179, 185
Baghdádí, Muḥammad Muṣṭafá 10, 136-41, 147, 166
Bagdadi, Zia 138-9
Bahá'í(s) 81-3, 181-2
  people of Bahá 98, 181-2
  persecution of 4, 5, 15, 34, 56, 79, 80, 87, 95, 97, 106, 110, 131, 155, 165, 168, 177, 181, 188
Bahá'í communities in:
  Ábádih 80, 157-8
  'Akká 124, 182
  Baghdad 179
  Baku 85
  Egypt 58, 170
  Haifa 171
  India 171
  Iṣfahán 69-70, 155-6, 158, 165
  Ishqábád 58, 106-8, 167
  Istanbul 144
  North America 5, 6, 9, 59-60, 116
  Persia (generally) 48, 106, 171, 188
  Russia 47, 10
  Merv (Russia) 189-90
  Mosul 179-80
  Shiraz 79, 159
  Syria 84

Tabríz 68-9, 71, 171
Tehran 47, 48, 49-51, 81, 87-9, 92-3, 100-01, 116, 119-20, 133, 135, 142, 151, 152, 160, 163-4, 165, 188-9, 192
Yazd 158
Zanján 72
Bahá'í Administrative Order 92, 116, 135, 153
Bahá'í law 80
Bahá'í marriage 80
Bahá'í Proofs, The 60
Bahá'í World, The 6-7, 9-10
Bahá'í World Centre 187-8
Bahá'í World Faith 8
Bahá'u'ddin 170
Bahá'u'lláh
and 'Abdu'l-Bahá 17, 70, 79, 133
in Adrianople (Adirne) 21-2, 122, 179
in 'Akká 22, 25, 42-3, 123-4, 130-31, 180, 182, 188-9
Apostles of *see individual entries*
ascension 58, 78, 92, 115, 126, 183, 189
assassination attempts 19, 20, 21
and the Báb 14, 15
remains of 17, 87-8
in Baghdad 17-20, 25, 120, 137, 178, 185
House of 179
at Bahjí 124-5
in Constantinople (Istanbul) 20-21, 121-2
Covenant of *see* Covenant
as Darvish Muḥammad 17
Declaration 33, 110, 121, 122, 129-30, 137
exile and imprisonment 13, 16-17, 20-22, 25, 34, 97, 120, 124-5, 131, 137, 142, 179
in the Síyáh Chál 115, 186
family of 13, 15, 17, 22
Mírzá Músá *see* individual entry
Mírzá Yaḥyá 15, 17, 21-2, 120, 143
Him Whom God shall make manifest 15, 20, 67, 76-7, 120, 121, 130, 137
humour 42, 183
love for 8, 104-5, 150
Revelation of 5, 6, 68, 121, 130, 152
Shrine of 134-5
station 81, 97-9, 101, 104, 137, 178
Supreme Manifestation 68, 152
in Sulaymaniyyih 17, 24, 120, 178
and Ṭáhirih 14
Writings 5, 22, 25-6, 31, 42, 53, 111, 121, 139, 149, 151, 189
Epistle to the Son of the Wolf 178, 183
Gleanings from the Writings of Bahá'u'lláh 139
Hidden Words 67
Kitáb-i-Aqdas 91, 180-81
Kitáb-i-Íqán 52, 87, 103, 104, 123
Lawḥ-i-Burhán (Tablet to the Wolf) 38, 39
Lawḥ-i-Dukhán 58
Lawḥ-i-Dunyá (Tablet of the World) 45, 92, 105
Lawḥ-i-Fu'ád 53-4
Lawḥ-i-Ḥikmat (Tablet of Wisdom)
Lawḥ-i-Ra'ís 55
Lawḥ-i-Siráj 130
Lawḥ-i-Sulṭán (Tablet to Náṣiri'd-Dín Sháh) 2, 26-32, 89, 110
prayers: 'Blessed is the Spot' 189; Obligatory 71, 91
Qazídiy-i-'Izz-i-Varqá'íyyih 24
Súriy-i-Aṣḥáb 130
Súriy-i-Ḥajj 122
Súriy-i-Muluk (Tablet to the Kings) 131-2
Tablets to/of/about/in honour of:
Abu'l-Faḍl 56, 58
Abu'l-Ḥasan-i-Ardikání (Ḥájí Amín) 43, 44
of Aḥmad 76
'Alí-Akbar-i-Shahmírzádí 91, 189
'Alíy-i-Kání 88-9
Badí' 27
Ḥasan-i-Adíb 189
Holy Mariner 20

Ibn-i-Abhar 116-17, 189
Ibn-i-Aṣdaq 185 (prayer for), 186, 188, 189
King and Beloved of Martyrs 33, 34, 38, 40
Maḥmúd-i-Furúghí 77
Mírzá Músá 23
Mihdí-i-Yazdí 68
Muḥammad-'Alí-Qá'íní 161
Muḥammad Muṣṭafáy-i-Baghdádí 139, 140
Nabíl-i-Akbar 99
Nabíl-i-A'ẓam and Fáris 124
Nabíl-i-A'ẓam and Muḥammad-Ṭáhir-i-Málmírí 125
Napoleon III 131-2
Salmán 130
Samandar 129
of Visitation 126
Zaynu'l-Muqarrabín 178-81
Bahá'u'llah and the New Era 192
Bahíyyih Khánum (Greatest Holy Leaf) 18, 71, 116, 173, 190
Bahjí 124-5, 134-5, 146
Bájgírán ('Ishqábád) 78
Bajistání, Mullá 'Alí 161
Baku 84-5
Balyuzi, H.M. 2-3, 143
Banani, Amin 49
Báqir Khán 157
Báqir, Mullá (Letter of the Living) 15, 119
Báqir-i-Sabbagh (of Mashhad) 128
Barney, Laura 59
Bastámí, Mullá 'Álí (Letter of the Living) 136
Bastinado 66, 69
Batyushkov, Georgiy Dmitrievich 153
Bayán 18, 110
Beirut 67, 137, 138-40, 167, 190
Beloved of Martyrs *see* Muḥammad Ḥusayn, Mírzá
Bíbí Túbá 69
Bible 61, 108
Bírjand 94, 99-100, 161, 170
Black Sea 190
Bolles, May 59
Bombay (Mumbai), India 159-60, 167, 170, 190
Boronovski, M. 156
Brauns, Arthur 2, 3
Brilliant Proof, The 49, 63
Britain, British 39, 41, 62, 105, 145, 170
Browne, Edward G. 135, 137, 180, 192
Bruce, Rev. Robert 56-7
Bukhárá 58, 102, 162
Burma 149, 159, 189, 190
Bushihr 103
Buzurg Khán-i-Qazvíni (Persian Consul in Baghdad) 18-19, 121
Buzurg-i-Khurásání, Mírzá (Badí') viii, 2, 10, 24-32, 89, 110

Cairo, Egypt 59, 60, 63, 65, 81, 122-3, 170
Calcutta 160
Calendar (Badí') 124
Caliphs 179
Carmel, Mount 27, 84, 108, 124
Caspian Sea 84-5, 190
Caucasus 44, 59
Central Organisation for a Durable Peace 192
Centre of the Covenant *see* 'Abdu'l-Bahá
Chicago, 59
Chihríq 127
Christ 38, 62, 70, 72, 113
Christians 38, 49, 61-2, 123
Cobham, Mr 146
Commander of the Faithful *see* Imám 'Alí
Concourse on High 38
Constantinople (Istanbul) 20, 43, 44, 84, 121-2, 131, 133, 137, 142-5, 190
Covenant 46, 60, 81, 92, 140, 165, 184, 149
Covenant-breaking 3, 4, 5, 6, 21, 23, 44, 60, 71, 78-9, 88, 92, 111, 126, 134, 139-40, 161, 165, 167, 171, 189
Crimson Ark 181
Cyprus 124, 145-6
Czar of Russia 107

Dajjal, Anti-Christ of Islam 157
Dárábí, Siyyid Yaḥya *see* Vaḥíd

Dáru'l-Funún (school) 152
Darvish Muḥammad *see* Bahá'u'lláh
de Balloy, M. 45-6
Dawn-Breakers, The 20, 23, 118, 126
Delhi, India 190
Disciples of 'Abdu'l-Bahá 1-30, 138
Ḍíyá'u'lláh, Mírzá 134-5
Dízij village 73
Dolatábád village 178
dreams 68, 99-100, 123, 173, 176
Dúghábád village (Furúgh) 76-7, 83, 85
Dunbar, Hooper 1
Durus'ul-Diyana 167
Ḍía'íyyih Khánum 164

Easton, Peter Z. 62-3
Egypt 46, 60-65, 81, 83, 122-3, 190
Elixir, Most Great 70
England, English 62, 146 *see also* Britain
English language 46, 61-2, 63, 139
Esslemont, Dr John 192
Europe, Europeans 36, 40

Fáḍil-i-Mázindarání, Asadu'llah vii
Faḍl-i-Qá'iní *see* Nabíl-i-Akbar
Famagusta, Cyprus 145
Faizi, Abu'l-Qásim 84
Fáizih Khánum 115
Fání, Shaykh 25
Faráid 59
Farhad Mírzá 152
Fáris Effendi 123
Fatḥ-'Alí Sháh 151, 186
Fáṭimih (the Chaste One) 38
Fáṭimih Khánum (wife of Ḥájí Ákhúnd) 89
Fáṭimih Sulṭán (wife of Samandar) 129
Fikri, 'Abdu'l-Ḥusayn viii
Finch, Ida 60
First World War 170, 191
four and twenty elders 108
France, French 45
French language 46, 61
Fraser, Isabel 61
Fujita 183
Furúgh(i) village (Dúghábad) 76-7, 83, 85

Gabriel (angel) 38
Gallipoli 123, 145
Getsinger, Lua 60
Ghulám-'Alí (son of Samandar) 133-5
Ghulám-Ḥusayn 157
Ghulám-Riḍá, Ḥájí 47-8
Gordon, T.E. 105
Greatest Holy Leaf *see* Bahíyyih Khánum
Greatest Name, Most Great Name 143, 147, 173
Green Acre, Maine 59
Guardian, Guardianship *see* Shoghi Effendi
Gulpáygán 49
Gulpaygání, Siyyid Mihdí, 169

Haddad, Anton 61, 117
Hádí, Hájí Mullá 94
Hádí, Mírzá 33
Haifa 26-7, 58, 83-4, 149, 167, 169, 170-71, 190-91
Bahá'í cemetery in 108
Ḥájí 'Alí 27
Ḥájí Ákhúnd *see* 'Alí-Akbar-i-Shahmírzádí
Ḥájí Amín *see* Abu'l-Ḥasan-i-Ardikání
Ḥájíbu'd-Dín 73-4
Ḥakím, Loṭfu'lláh 186
Ḥakím Másih 186
Hamadan 17, 56, 186-7
Hand of the Cause 3-4, 7, 91, 92, 116, 153, 162, 170, 185, 188-9, 192
see also entries for individuals
Harris, Hooper, 39, 74
Ḥasan-i-Adíb (Adíbu'l-'Ulamáy-i-Ṭaliqání) 10, 92, 151-60, 164-5, 189
Ḥasan-i-Nahrí (Mírzá Muhammad Ḥasan), King of Martyrs (Sulṭánu'sh-Shuhadá) 10, 22, 33-40, 178, 179, 187
Háshimi-Zádih, Siyyid Ḥasan 190
Ḥaydar, Mullá (assassin) 166
Ḥaydar-'Alí, Ḥájí Mírzá 51, 63, 122-3, 177, 179-80, 183-4
Ḥaydar-i-Mu'allem, Shaykh 165-7
Ḥazíratu'l-Quds 108
Hearst, Phoebe 184

Hedi, Ḥájí Mírzá 142
Him Whom God shall make manifest 15, 20, 67, 76-7, 120, 121, 130, 137
Ḥi<u>sh</u>mat-Niẓám 80
Hoagg, Emogene 60-61
Hoar, William 138-9
Hosts of God 8
Ḥuqúqu'lláh 26, 41, 42, 44, 46, 47-8, 72, 75
Ḥusayn (brother of Varqá) 66-7
Ḥusayn (son of Varqá) 71
Ḥusayn-i-Bu<u>sh</u>rú'í, Mullá 14, 76, 129, 137, 185, 186
Ḥusayn-i-Iṣfahání see Mi<u>sh</u>kín Qalam
Ḥusayn <u>Kh</u>án (Persian Ambassador in Istanbul)
Ḥusayn-i-<u>Kh</u>artúmí, Mírzá 134
Husayn-i-Nali-Band, Ustád 49-50
Ḥusayn-i-Rúḥí 58
Ḥusayn-i-Zavári'í 119

Ibn-i-Abhar (Muḥammad-Taqí-i-Abhar) 10, 92, 110-17, 135, 153, 189
Ibn-i-Aṣdaq '('Alí-Muḥammad, <u>Sh</u>ahíd-Ibn-i-<u>Sh</u>ahíd) 6, 10, 87, 92, 136, 167, 185-92
Ibráhím, Mírzá 33
Ibráhím-i-Abharí, Mírzá 110
Imáms 73, 80, 103, 169
　'Alí (Commander of the Faithful) 15, 35, 118
　Ḥusayn 19, 73, 97, 113, 127, 179
Imám-Jum'ih *see* Mír Muḥammad-Ḥusayn
Ímán, Ḥájí 73-4
India, Indians 56, 61, 116, 149, 159, 164-5, 167, 171, 177, 189, 190
intellect 132
International Bahá'í Archives 88
Iran (Persia) 31-2, 34, 39-40, 44, 89, 132, 183-4
　Government of 66, 69, 97, 144
　people of 47, 89
Iraq 25, 39, 108-9, 136-8, 178
Iṣfahán 33-8, 49, 56-7, 69-70, 118-19, 142, 151, 155-7, 158, 164-5, 174, 177, 178, 183, 187
'I<u>sh</u>qábád 58, 83, 102, 103, 106-8, 162, 167, 170, 171, 189-90
　Ma<u>sh</u>riqu'l-A<u>dh</u>kár 103, 106-8, 163, 167, 190
Iskandarún, Turkey 138, 140
Islam, Islamic 38, 45, 103, 157, 174, 176, 178
　Caliphs of 179
　law 96
　people of 38
　traditions 73
　see also Muslim(s), Shi'a
Ismá'íl, Mírzá 35-6, 38
Ismá'íl-i-Zavári'í, Siyyid, 121
Ismu'lláhu'l-Aṣdaq (Ṣádiq-i-<u>Kh</u>urásání) 97-8, 131, 185, 191
Istanbul (Constantinople) 20, 42, 44, 84, 121-2, 131, 133, 137, 142-5, 190
Italian language

Jack, Marion 7
Jalíl <u>Kh</u>án 112-14
Jamál-i-Burújirdí 78, 87-8
Jamál, <u>Sh</u>ay<u>kh</u> 170
Jam<u>sh</u>íd-i-Gurjí 143-5
Javád-i-Qazvíní 134
Jews, Jewish 38, 56, 186
Jihad 19
Joseph 113, 121

Kalát-i-Nadírí (town) 78
Kallih-Darri'í 131
Kámrán Mírzá (Governor of Tehran) 45, 81, 89-90, 91
Karbilá 16, 39, 86, 94, 96, 97, 120, 127, 136, 174, 178
Karim-i-Virdi Ishan (fortress) 186
Karkabúd, Taliqán 151
Ká<u>sh</u>án, Iran 164
Káẓim <u>Kh</u>án-i-Warachih-Daghi 28-31
Káẓim-i-Rashtí, Siyyid 127, 136, 174, 185
Káẓim-i-Iṣfahání, Ḥájí Muḥammad 162
<u>Kh</u>abírí, Maḥmúd 190
<u>Kh</u>adíjih-Bagum 122
Khan, Ali Kuli 47, 59-60
Khan, Florence 47

Khán-i-'Avámíd (caravanserai, 'Akká) 131, 149, 180, 184, 186-7, 188-9
Khán-i-Khú'í, Mírzá Ḥasan 123
Khán-i-Vazír, Mírzá Assadu'lláh 155-7, 165
Kheiralla, Ibrahim 3, 6, 59, 116
Khussif, Iran 167
Kirmánsháh 17, 119-20 137
Khurásán 14-15, 27, 39, 46, 76-7, 86, 122, 162, 185
Kínar-Gard village 118
King of Martyrs *see* Ḥasan-i-Nahrí
Kirman, Iran 44
Knights of Bahá'u'lláh 3, 4
Knobloch, Alma 60
Knobloch, Fanny 60
Kurdistan, Kurds 17-18, 19, 43-4, 138

Lahíján, Iran 129
Lahore, Pakistan 190
Larnica, Cyprus 146
Latimer, George 7
League of Nations 192
Letters of the Living 3, 4, 15, 97, 100, 108, 119, 120, 127, 129, 136
Liqá'íyyih Khánum, 71
London, England 46, 47, 61
Lorraine (battleship) 84

Mahdi, Siyyid 167
Maḥmúd (son of Vakilu'd-Dawlih) 105, 108
Maḥmúd-i-al-Álúsí 2
Maḥmúd Effendi (Alneshogati, of Egypt) 170
Maḥmúd-i-Furúghí viii, 2, 6, 10, 75, 76-85, 111
Maḥmúd-i-Káshání 2
Maḥmúd Khán-i-Kalantar (mayor of Tehran) 95
Maḥmúd Mírzá (governor of Yazd) 105
Maḥmúd-i-Qazvíní 2
Maḥmúd-i-Zarqání 2, 74
Mákú 14, 127
Mandalay, Burma 160, 190
Manikji Sahib 56
Manshádí, Sháh Muḥammad 88
Mansúr-i-Uskú'í 131
Manúchihr Khán 118
Margh, Iran 157
martyrdom, martyrs 4, 5, 10, 16, 105, 110, 159, 175, 187-8, 191
of the Báb 20, 83, 88, 131, 137
Marv (Merv), Iran 189-90
Mashhad, Iran 24-5, 77-8, 83, 86-7, 94, 100, 161-4, 186, 188
Mashriqu'l-Adhkár 103, 106-8, 163, 167, 190
Masumian, Adib 23
Maxwell, May 7
Mázindarán, Iran 131
Mazra'ih 67-8
Mecca 42, 174
Mesbah, Kamran 171
Mihdi, Siyyid 142
Mihdí-i-Yazdí, Hájí Mullá 66-7
miracles 52-3
Miracles and Metaphors 49, 59
Mír Muḥammad-Ḥusayn, Imám-Jum'ih (She-Serpent) 33-7, 39, 111-13
Mírzá Músá *see* Músá-i-Núrí (Aqáy-i-Kalím)
Mishkín Qalam (Ḥusayn-i-Iṣfahání) 2, 10, 73, 142-50, 159, 179, 182, 183-4
Miyanduab, Tabríz 44
Momen, Mullá 174
Moses 113
Most Great Name, Greatest Name 143, 147
Most Great Separation 22
Mosul 25, 34, 138, 179-80
Mu'ayyad, Ḥabíb 63
Muḥammad (Prophet) 38, 86, 103, 112-13, 161, 179
Muḥammad, Aqá 174
Muḥammad (Faḍl-i-Qá'iní, Nabíl-i-Akbar) 2, 10, 51, 94-102, 103, 152, 161-4
Muḥammad, Mullá Mírzá 76-7
Muḥammad Sháh 16, 66
Muḥammad-'Alí (father of Munírih Khánum) 33
Muḥammad-'Alí (Ghuṣn-i-Akbar) 60, 78-9, 92, 133-5, 189

Muḥammad-'Alí-Qá'íní, Shaykh 10, 45, 101-2, 132, 161-73
Muḥammad-'Alíy-i-Salmání 21, 138, 143
Muḥammad-Báqir, Shaykh (the Wolf) 33-9, 178-9
Muḥammad-Báqir-i-Mudarrís 35
Muḥammad-Baqír-Qahvih-chí 145
Muḥammad-Ḥasan, Ḥájí 131
Muḥammad-Ḥasan (King of Martyrs) *see* Ḥasan-i-Nahrí
Muḥammad-Ḥusayn, Mírzá (Beloved of Martyrs) 22, 33-40, 178, 179, 187
Muḥammad-Ḥusayn, Mullá (brother of Nabíl-i-Akbar) 161
Muḥammad Ibráhím 123
Muḥammad-i-Iṣfahání, Siyyid 21-2, 120-21, 124
Muḥammad Ismá'íl-i-Dhábiḥ 52-4
Muḥammad Káẓim-i-Qazvíní (Samandar) 10, 127-35
Muḥammad Muṣṭafáy-i-Baghdádí 10, 136-41, 147, 166
Muḥammad-Nasír 130-34
Muḥammad Qazvíní, Shaykh 127-9
Muḥammad-Qulí (half-brother of Bahá'u'lláh) 13, 17, 20, 22
Muḥammad-Riḍáy-i-Iṣfahání 58
Muḥammad-Riḍáy-i-Yazdí, Mullá 41, 89-80
Muḥammad-Ṭáhir-i-Málmírí 124-6
Muḥammad-Taqí, Mírzá 151
Muḥammad-Taqí, Shaykh (Áqá Najafí, Son of the Wolf) 37, 155-6, 157, 165-6, 178, 183
Muḥammad-Taqí-i-Abhar (Ibn-i-Abhar) 10, 92, 110-17, 135, 153, 189
Muḥammad-Taqí-i-Afnán, Vakílu'd-Dawlih (Kabír-i-Afnán) 2, 10, 103-09, 164
Muḥammad-Valí Khán 27-8
Muḥammad-i-Zarandí *see* Nabíl-i-A'ẓam
Muhsin, Siyyid 128
Mullá Ḥusayn *see* Ḥusayn-i-Bushrú'í
Mumbai (Bombay), India 159-60, 167, 170, 190
Munírih Khánum (wife of 'Abdu'l-Bahá) 22, 33
Munírih Khánum (daughter of 'Alí-Akbar Shahmirzádí) 115-16, 153
Murtidá-i-Ansárí, Shaykh 96-7, 151
Músá-i-Núri (Aqáy-i-Kalím) viii, 10, 13-23, 87, 126, 131, 178
Muslims(s) 68
  clergy, divines 66, 68-9, 71, 72-3, 76, 77-8, 88-9, 94, 96, 99, 100, 151, 157-8, 167-8, 174, 178, 185
  see also Islam, Shi'a
Muzaffaru'd-Dín Sháh viii, 66, 68, 71, 74-5, 82-3, 90, 142

Na'ím, Áqá Mírzá 135
Nabíl-i-Akbar (Mullá Muḥammad, Faḍl-i-Qá'iní) 2, 10, 51, 94-102, 103, 152, 161-4
Nabíl-i-A'ẓam (Muḥammad-i-Zarandí) 2, 10, 20, 24, 42, 118-26, 138, 142-3
  The Dawn-Breakers 20, 23, 118, 126
Nahariyya (Naharieh) 182
Najaf 39, 94, 96
Najafábád 174-5
Najafí, Áqá (Shaykh Muḥammad-Taqí, Son of the Wolf) 37, 155-6, 157, 165-6, 178, 183
Najmábádí, Shaykh Hádí 152
Namíq Páshá 20
Napoleon III 131-2
Náṣiri'd-Dín Sháh 16, 24, 27-32, 33, 36-7, 39-40, 46, 69, 77, 81, 91-2, 100-01, 111, 142, 152
  assassination 55, 73-4, 79-80, 82, 89, 94, 120, 132, 153, 177
Navváb (Asíyih Khánum)13, 16
Naw-Firíst village 94, 99, 100, 161, 163, 167
Naw-Rúz 20
Nayríz 16
New York 63
newspapers 17
Nicosia, Cyprus 145
Nishápúr 24-5, 171
Níyávarán 131
Nur'u'lláh Effendi 60-61

Ober, Harlan 61, 116

Obligatory Prayer 71, 79
Omar, Caliph 179
Ottoman Empire 43, 46, 121, 145, 184
see also Turkey

Paris, France 46, 47, 59, 63
persecution 131-2 *see also* Bahá'ís
Persia *see* Iran
Peter, Saint 15
pilgrimage, pilgrims 43, 67, 70-71, 78-9, 84, 89, 91, 110, 116, 122, 125, 130-31, 133, 134, 140, 146, 148, 174, 179, 183, 190-91
Western 60, 116, 184
Pilgrim House 134, 184
Port Said, Egypt 61, 81, 170-71
prison 4, 5, 16, 22, 35-6, 45-6, 53, 56, 64, 69-70, 73-4, 78, 80, 88-92, 100, 110, 113-15, 123, 133, 136, 138, 145-6, 168, 178, 186
chains 73, 114, 115
Most Great ('Akká) 22, 25-7, 42-3, 147
Síyáh-Chál, Tehran 16, 115, 186
prophecy 54
Psalms 161
Puritans 159

Qá'im, return of 158, 175
Qa'in, province 168, 170
Qajar dynasty 186
Qara-Guhar (prison chain) 73
Qazvín, Iran 45-6, 91-2, 101, 105, 110, 120-21, 127-31, 135, 137, 151, 190
Quddús 76, 185
Qumshih, Iran 157
Qur'án (Koran) 14, 60, 61, 68, 73, 113, 115, 118, 121, 127, 140, 157, 169, 174, 175-6

Rajab-Âlí, Mullá 41
Ramadan 20
Rangoon 1147, 160, 190
Rasht 131, 133, 135, 190
Rasúl, Ḥájí 127
Remey, Mason 108
Riḍván, Garden of 20, 129-30
Root, Martha 7, 9
Rosenberg, Ethel 2, 60
Rubát-Karím village 118
Rúḥu'lláh (son of Varqá) 66, 70-74, 133
Ruknu'd-Dawlih 79-80, 111
Rumi 171
Russia, Russian(s) 16, 102, 104-8, 153, 156, 189, 190

Sabzivár 94, 101, 162, 163, 170
Sádiq-i-Khurásání (Ismu'lláhu'l-Aṣdaq) 97-8, 131, 185, 191
Safavid dynasty 89
Salmání, Muḥammad-'Alí 21, 138, 143
Samandar (Muḥammad Káẓim-i-Qazvíní) 10, 127-35
Samandarí, Ṭaráẓu'lláh 133
Samarkand 58
Schopflocher, Siegfried 7
Schwarz, Consul 2
Scotland 47
Seven Martyrs
of Tehran 119
of Yazd 105
Seven Year Plan 5
Sháh 'Abdu'l-A'zím, Shrine of 73
Shahíd-ibn-i-Shahíd 185, 187-8
Sháhmírzád village 86, 87
Sháh Mosque, Tehran 54
Sháh-Muḥammad-i-Amín, Trustee of Ḥuqúqu'lláh 26, 42-4
Shahrokh, Darius 56
Sháhrúd 120, 164
Shawkata'al-Mulk 170
Shawkat Pasha 143
Sháhsavan tribe 66
Shaykhí(s) 127
Shaykh Ṭabarsí, Fort 24, 76, 86, 119, 130, 185
Shemr 179
She-Serpent *see* Mír Muḥammad Ḥusayn
Shi'a 103, 113, 124, 175, 179
Shibl, Muḥammad 136-7
Shiraz 14, 66, 79-80, 103, 118, 122, 123, 142, 158-9, 185
House of the Báb in 122
Shoghi Effendi 1-3, 5-9, 15, 33, 39, 41, 48, 79, 83, 126, 139, 144, 173

God Passes By 15
Shrine(s) 16
of 'Abdu'l-Azím 87-8
of the Báb 84, 88, 109
of Bahá'u'lláh 134-5
of Imám Ḥusayn 97, 127
in Ma<u>sh</u>had 164
of <u>Sh</u>áh 'Abdu'l-Azím 73
Sidq-'Alí Darvi<u>sh</u> 143, 145
Sina 69
Síyáh-<u>Ch</u>ál (prison) 16, 115, 186
Siyyid Muḥammad 103, 104
smoking 58
Sohrab, Ahmad 46-7
Son of the Wolf *see* Najafí, <u>Sh</u>ay<u>kh</u>
Epistle to 178, 183
Sprague, Sydney 149, 159-60
Subotich, General 107-8
Sudan 123
Sulaymani, Azizu'llah vii, 3
Sulaymaniyah 17-8, 24, 120, 178
Sulaymán Quli-Turk 176
Sulṭán-i-Karbilá'í, <u>Sh</u>ay<u>kh</u> 18
Sulṭán Salím, Show of 53, 55
Sulṭánu<u>sh</u>-<u>Sh</u>uhadá (King of Martyrs) *see* Ḥasan-i-Nahrí
Supreme Tribunal 192
Surat, India 171
Syria 46, 84

Ṭabarsí, Fort 24, 76, 86, 119, 130, 185
Tabríz 25, 44, 66, 68, 70, 127, 128, 129, 135, 142, 171
Taherzadeh, Adíb 2-3, 26, 89, 152-3, 179
Ṭáhirih 9, 14-15, 120, 127-8, 136-7
Taliqán, Iran 151
Ṭalíqání *see* Ḥasan-i-Adíb
Taqí, Mullá 127
Tarbash (a Bahá'í in Beirut) 190
Tarbíyát schools 153
Tashkent 173
teaching 110
Tehran
assassination of Sháh 55, 73, 80
attempted 94
Bahá'ís in 47, 48, 49-51, 81, 87-9, 92-3, 100-01, 116, 119-20, 133, 135, 142, 151, 152, 160, 163-4, 165, 188-9, 192
Bahá'í Administrative Order in 92, 116, 135, 153
Bahá'u'lláh in 16-17
British Legation in 105
Hands of the Cause in 116, 162, 170, 189
imprisonment of Bahá'ís in 45, 73, 88-9, 91-2, 100, 110, 115, 186
martyrdoms in 36-9, 119
and Mullá Ḥusayn 14, 137
and remains of the Báb 16, 87-8
schools and colleges 49, 56, 152, 153
and Ṭáhirih 14-15
Ten Year Crusade 4
Thacher, Chester viii, 3
Thompson, Juliet 7
Thornburgh, Harriet 2
<u>Th</u>urayyá (daughter of Samandar) 134-5
Tiflís 131, 190
Tigris river 20
Trabzon, Turkey 43
Turkey 43, 46, 132, 144
Turkistan 46, 107, 189
Turkmenistan, Turkmen 58, 78, 186

Ubaydullah, <u>Sh</u>ay<u>kh</u> 43-4
U<u>dh</u>rá <u>Kh</u>ánum 186
Universal House of Justice 3, 7, 15, 48, 108, 186
Uthman, Caliph 179
Uzbekistan 102, 124

Vaḥíd 16, 66, 129
Vakílu'd-Dawlih (Muḥammad-Taqí-i-Afnán, Kabír-i-Afnán 2, 10, 103-09, 164
Varqá (Mírzá 'Alí-Muḥammad 10, 56, 66-75, 133
Varqá, Dr 'Alí-Muḥammad 75
Varqá, Válíyu'lláh 7, 72, 75

Washington DC 59
Wills, Dr C.J. 34
Windust, Albert 6
wisdom, meaning of 90

Ya'aqub, Siyyid 95-6
Yaḥyá, Mírzá (Azal) 15-17, 20-22, 44-5, 67, 97, 111, 120, 122, 130, 143, 145, 177-8
Yaḥyá-i-Dárábí, Siyyid (Vaḥíd) 16, 66, 129
Yazd, Iran 25, 41, 44, 66, 67, 69, 76, 81, 104-6, 118, 158, 164
Yazdání, Aḥmad, 191-2
Yazdí, Aḥmad 61, 170
Yazid 179
Youness Khan (Afroukhteh) 138-40
Zanján, Iran 72-3, 110, 111, 112-14, 135
Zarand, Iran 118-19
Zarandí *see* Nabíl-i-A'ẓam
Zarqán (near Shiraz) 80, 159
Zarqání, Maḥmúd 2, 116, 159
Zaynu'l-Ábidín Najafábádí (Zaynu'l-Muqarrabín) 10, 22, 34, 129, 142, 174-84
Zaynu'l-Muqarrabín (uncle of Bahá'u'lláh) 129
Ẓillu's-Sulṭán 33, 35-7, 39-40, 57, 69-70, 105, 165
Zoroastrians 56, 167

www.ingramcontent.com/pod-product-compliance
Lightning Source LLC
Chambersburg PA
CBHW041313240426
43669CB00024B/2976
9780853986829